D0929591

AMERICAN CATHOLICS

THROUGH THE

TWENTIETH CENTURY

AMERICAN CATHOLICS

THROUGH THE

TWENTIETH CENTURY

Spirituality, Lay Experience, and Public Life

CLAIRE E. WOLFTEICH

A Crossroad Book
The Crossroad Publishing Company
New York

The Crossroad Publishing Company
481 Eighth Avenue, New York, NY 10001

Printed in the United States of America

Library of Congress Cataloging-in-Publication Data
Wolfteich, Claire E.
    American Catholics through the twentieth century : spirituality, lay experience, and public life / Claire E. Wolfteich.
        p.   cm.
    Includes bibliographical references.
    ISBN 0-8245-1953-1
    1. Catholics – United States – History – 20th century. 2. Laity – Catholic Church – History – 20th century. 3. Spirituality – Catholic Church – History – 20th century. 4. Laity – United States – History – 20th century. 5. Spirituality – United States – History – 20th century. 6. Catholic Church – United States – History – 20th century. I. Title.
BX1406.3 .W65 2001
282′.73′0904 – dc21
                                                                2001002828

1   2   3   4   5   6   7   8   9   10   06   05   04   03   02   01

This book is dedicated to some very special lay Catholics:
To my parents,
Alice Helen Clegg Wolfteich and Paul Arthur Wolfteich,
for your gift of faith and love
And to my husband, John Frederick Griffin,
in our first of many years.

CONTENTS

ACKNOWLEDGMENTS

I N WRITING THIS BOOK, I benefited from conversations with numerous people. Here I thank in particular professors from the
University of Chicago Divinity School, who guided me in my
earlier studies of lay Catholics, American religious history, spirituality, and practical theology. Don S. Browning, Martin Marty, Jean
Bethke Elshtain, and Anne Carr have been insightful and support-
ive mentors. I also thank Peter Berger and Robert Neville of Boston
University for reading portions of this manuscript and providing
very helpful comments. Bryan Stone pointed me to several relevant
sermons by John Wesley. I am grateful to them and to all the faculty and staff at Boston University School of Theology for their
collegiality. Thomas Groome of Boston College contributed greatly
too with concrete suggestions and encouragement. My students at
Boston University keep me motivated and spark my thinking.

I must express my appreciation for the excellent work of two
research assistants. Georgia Maheras located article after article;
she also worked diligently tracking down citations and organizing the bibliography. Nori Henk's consistently good research for
a related grant project also informed this book. Library staff at
Boston University School of Theology and the Boston Theological Institute—particularly Dawn Piscitello, Will Bergmann, and
Dan Gioffre—provided enormous help in procuring the books and
articles I requested. Shirley Budden lent technical assistance with
computer equipment. I am grateful for all that Paul McMahon, my
editor at Crossroad, did to see this book through to publication. He
and the rest of the staff at Crossroad were unfailingly helpful; it was
a pleasure to work with them. Finally, I give thanks to my family
and friends for all their love, inspiration, and support.

INTRODUCTION

WHILE MANY CLASSIC SPIRITUAL TEACHINGS emphasize the beauty of contemplation, lay Christians must live "in the world," making practical judgments every day in private and public spheres. This is a complex vocation that requires far more guidance than the church has provided. The everyday contexts of work, family, public interaction are the spheres of meaning—or alienation—for most. And yet faith can seem far removed from the everyday. Religion then becomes a compartmentalized sphere alongside other spheres. It cannot invigorate the whole. Amid American pluralism and the ambiguities of public engagement, always there is the temptation to retreat into a privatized or compartmentalized spirituality. Yet to be Christian and public is the distinctive task of the layperson, one that should not be neglected.

There is a great need for more reflection on the life of faith as it relates to public responsibility, private commitments, and culture. This book responds to that need. I will explore the lay vocation through the eyes of American Catholics in the twentieth century. This lively group of disciples illustrates larger issues confronting religious persons today. For imbedded in the story of American lay Catholics is a deep struggle over the Spirit, the church, and the meaning of private and public life. From the Catholic Worker to the United Farm Workers, from the Christian Family Movement to the charismatics, from John F. Kennedy to Mario Cuomo, laity wrestled with the place of their faith in a changing American culture. This book delves into their stories with a theological eye and the intent to shed light on the formation of religious people today.

I argue that lay Christians in twentieth-century America were engaged—often unknowingly—in a struggle to define spirituality. While monastics have shaped much of the classic Christian spiritual traditions, laity face different questions. Their faith takes shape within the complex exigencies of daily life. They must deal with "the world" up close and personal. They need to find meaning in intimate relationships, in work, in wider public engagement. They see the world in its grittiness. They deal with screaming children, flooded basements, and broken relationships. They work in structures and institutions that are mixed moral bags and beyond their control. They act as citizens—and elected officials—in a political system that contains enormous moral ambiguities. It is difficult to be a "white knight." What does faith mean in this world? Some laity leave this question hanging painfully. Others weave theological insights and visions of the spiritual life to make sense of the world.

At the same time, Christian faith must be in some sense "otherworldly." That is, Christian faith anticipates that which it cannot see in this world; it hopes and waits and trusts that the divine is intimately close and yet ultimately transcendent. Laity must be otherworldly as well as worldly, all at the same time. We have yet to understand the tensions implicit in this lay life of faith—the necessary balance between the "worldly" and the "otherworldly" dimensions of spirituality. There remains a vacuum for laity—and a need for clear analysis about potential models of holiness.

The "worldly" part of Christian spirituality may be the most confusing. To be "in the world" means to go in and out of both public spaces and the private sphere of the home and family. Laypersons have a bridge vocation; they straddle multiple worlds, both private and public. They struggle to strike a balance between the inner, personal search and the demands of public life. If laity are to lead vibrant lives of faith, they must be able to find the religious meaning of these worldly private and public spaces. This is no easy task. The sacred can easily fall out of view amid the secularity and pluralism of the public arena or the inwardness and mundane busyness of the private. At the core of the struggle over spirituality is a wrestling with private and public meaning.

I will explore this spiritual struggle throughout this book, identifying the complex theological dilemmas that laity addressed—explicitly or implicitly—in the practice of their faith. I emphasize the importance and difficulty of the public vocation. Specifically, how can one be a faithful Christian in the particularities of the democratic, pluralistic, secular American public scene? Secularity actually heightens the importance of the lay role even as it complicates it.

For in more highly secularized societies, the public influence of the church depends more on the layperson in politics, business, labor, and other spheres. They are the ones in a position to bring the vision of their faith into their work, while the clergy may be regarded as trespassing (or at least out of their depth). This is not to minimize the importance of an authentic personal faith, nourished in solitude, particular communities, or the family. Indeed, the laity discussed here point out that the family and the interior life present their own challenges. Yet public engagement is perhaps a particularly confusing religious task. There are risks to the lay vocation, and risks particular to the American context. On the one hand, as laypersons engage the American public sphere, they risk a diffusion of religious identity. Secularity and pluralism may challenge the distinctive core of their faith. Religious people may find themselves assimilated, engaged, and a bit far away from their faith. They become distant from the sources of revelation and the community of prayer. On the other hand, laypersons may cling ferociously to their religious roots as they seek to infuse American society with the Spirit. They may avoid the complexity of public dilemmas and find themselves ineffective (or wrong-headed) in the peculiar American context. This is a public spirituality that misses the subtlety demanded of wise apostles, that skips to easy answers or meaningless platitudes.

Because the role of the layperson arises in a particularly sharp way within Catholicism, the Catholic story will show in relief the tensions present in many religious traditions. This is not intended to be a comprehensive history, but rather a sustained exploration of lay struggles over spirituality in the American context. I cast a theological eye on these stories, sorting out the issues at the root of each movement or individual dilemma. I will identify the varying theological beliefs and spiritual practices that ground public involvement—or withdrawal. I will show that imbedded in the story of American lay Catholics is a deep struggle over the Spirit and alternative visions of the lay vocation.

The Story

In chapter 1, I will explore visions of lay spirituality in the thirty years before the Second Vatican Council. Lay leaders and movements then saw spirituality as an integrative force, Christianizing an increasingly secular or faithless American society. They developed means of spiritual formation to prepare laity for this task. Some movements, such as Opus Dei, emphasized the public role of the laity. Others, such as the Grail, emphasized the private sphere as the means to accomplish social transformation. Several—such as the Catholic Worker—blended public and private in very interesting ways. The continued vibrancy of some of these models would be challenged by the new openness to pluralism and expanded avenues for social conscience in the 1960s.

The election of John F. Kennedy in 1960 marks a watershed year. In the debates over Kennedy's Catholicism, he made a pragmatic move to protect his candidacy. Kennedy argued that his faith was private and would in no way influence his political judgments as president of the United States. He won the election, but at a theological cost. He established a model of a privatized faith irrelevant to public commitments (although in practice, Kennedy was quite willing to draw upon religious support). Religious groups in fact mobilized to support Kennedy's civil rights legislation, making the church a strong political force, delving into lay fields of action. The story became more complicated as the Second Vatican Council gave new emphasis to the lay life of faith and showed new openness to pluralism and the secular world. The Council brought heightened appreciation for the lay vocation as leaven in the public world. Combined with the turbulent social context in the United States, it also brought great confusion about religious identity and distinctions between sacred and secular.

I will trace another important juxtaposition of events, this in the late 1960s, examined in chapter 3. The Catholic Charismatic Renewal took off in 1967. Laity claimed the Spirit directly, speaking in tongues and witnessing to an incredible transformation within. Pluralism influenced this movement, as Catholic charismatics learned much from the rise of neo-Pentecostalism in Protestant circles. This also was part of a wider turn to the interior life. At the same time that the charismatics claimed the Spirit in their lay experience, the controversy over birth control stirred a serious conflict over the Spirit. The experience of marriage led many laity to assert the validity of artificial birth control, even as important in sustaining a healthy marital spirituality. The 1968 papal encyclical *Humanae Vitae* quashed that claim. According to *Humanae Vitae* the Spirit spoke through the authority of the church magisterium. It worked through lay experience by enlightening the laity about the wisdom of the hierarchy. Here I see a great struggle over the meaning of family life, and indeed over the locus of the Spirit.

In the next chapter I move to the 1980s, where again an interesting coincidence of events occurs. When pressured by church hierarchy about their political stance on abortion, prominent Catholic politicians such as Mario Cuomo and Geraldine Ferraro asserted (as had Kennedy) that their faith was private. It should not influence political judgments over a pluralistic, democratic citizenry. At the same time, the American Catholic bishops were moving decisively into the public sphere with their pastoral letters on peace and economic justice. This all happened in the context of the rise of the religious right. Conservative evangelicals were insisting (as did their liberal Protestant counterparts in the 1960s civil rights movement) that religious faith must be engaged with American politics. Meanwhile, countless laity tried to make sense of their particular public spaces in work and wrestled with faithful love in their private lives.

At the heart of the lay struggle were questions about the working of the Holy Spirit. As one looks back over the twentieth century, various understandings of the Spirit emerge. Dorothy Day found the Spirit in the faces of the poor and hungry who frequent the hospitality houses of the Catholic Worker. John F. Kennedy relegated the Spirit to private life. The charismatics saw the Spirit working dramatically through their personal experience, the "baptism of the Spirit." Is the Spirit in the public square? If so, who hears the Spirit correctly? Questions about the location of the Holy Spirit carry enormous implications for our understanding of the church (and similarly understandings of the church bear on how we understand the Spirit). In other words, spirituality, theology, and ecclesiology are intricately interconnected. This story of lay Catholics illustrates those interconnections. The controversy over birth control in the late 1960s, for example, raised profound questions about both the church and the working of the Holy Spirit. The church hierarchy claimed to be the primary mediator of the Spirit. Many laypersons asserted the priority of their consciences and experience. How should the body of believers evaluate competing claims to the Spirit? Protestant and Catholic charismatic movements also raised questions about individual experience and ecclesial identity. Charismatics could be overwhelmed by the power of their experience; many blurred denominational lines and prioritized their prayer meetings over traditional liturgy. Could the church accommodate this experience? The Spirit's free, unmediated movement inevitably threatens the institutional church. How one defines the church too is critical to one's understanding of lay spirituality. Opus Dei promoted a spirituality very much tied to the hierarchical authority of the magisterium. Call to Action laity, on the other hand, proclaimed, "We are the church," a statement that captured a different orientation to the spiritual life. These interrelated concerns about spirituality, theology, and the church arise throughout this story.

In the final chapter, I will explore spiritual formation for laity, highlighting several particularly difficult theological issues raised throughout this story. I will address the fundamental issues of how to understand spirituality and the church. Moreover, I explore areas of spiritual practice important to lay Christians. One such spiritual practice is discernment. Laity must make complex judgments in their political lives, work, and private relationships. The controversies about birth control and abortion legislation illustrate this responsibility. Yet many laypersons do not see practical reason as a religious exercise in any way. I will attempt to show that the exercise of practical reason can be more integrally related to faith, although religion should not absolutize practical judgments.

Public and Private Spheres:
The Meaning of Work and Family

Imbedded in debates about the meaning of politics, work, and family are deep spiritual questions. Work and family are primary spheres of lay action and responsibility, and hence logical loci for spirituality. People often define themselves through their work and their family relationships, which become centers of meaning or alienation. And yet domestic and economic responsibilities can divert attention from religious reflection and spiritual disciplines. People become diffused in their roles and activities. They encounter others who make them question their identity, who present alternative, plausible worldviews. Political leadership seems crucial to the lay vocation and yet in the United States often results in a privatized faith. How sanctify worldly life without ignoring its power to dissipate or fragment faith?

This is a religious question. Yet the meaning of work and family also is a larger cultural issue. Religious groups today find themselves in the midst of "culture wars" about family, economics, and the public realm. What values must be safeguarded? If faith carries public implications, *how* should religion enter the public sphere, particularly in a highly pluralistic society such as the United States? Many studies have debated the public role of religion.[1] This book focuses on the implications of those debates not only for society or for religious institutions, but for the very understanding of the nature of religious faith and the spiritual life.

Even defining terms presents many thorny issues. Religious people debate how to define family and work, private and public. Those debates will form part of this story. Generally, I see paid employment as a contribution to the public sphere and family as centered in the private sphere. However, I would not characterize childrearing as a strictly private undertaking; it also has great significance for the public order. Moreover, work is not purely public. It has an essential personal dimension and for many people is primarily a means of supporting their own identities and their "private" family relationships.

The women's movement challenged the notion that the family is strictly private. The slogan "the personal is political" is a prime example of how the lines blur. And yet many authors argue that family relationships and the full development of the self require a distinct private world.[2] People also see their paid employment in different lights. While it brings us out of the home and into the public sphere, still work "can go hand in hand with an isolating preoccupation with the self."[3] Work can be seen simply as the means to material possession, the measure of one's achievement, and a source of self-esteem. When viewed as a calling or vocation, however, work is an activity with inherent meaning and value which "links a person to the larger community. . . . The calling is a crucial link between the individual and the public world. Work in the sense of the calling can never be merely private."[4] I will explore how laypersons connect spirituality to the private and the public meanings of work and family.

This leads to questions about the private and public nature of the church. At the heart of Christian spirituality are notions of the church and the relationship between church and world, sacred and secular. Is the local congregation, for example, a private sphere of religious activity, a participant in public life, or both? Scholars have identified churches as "mediating structures"[5] and as "meeting places" of public and private.[6] This study of lay spirituality clearly has ecclesial implications, as I will explore.

Sources

This book examines the lay struggle for an authentic spirituality. My particular focus will be twentieth-century lay Catholic writings, although I will look throughout for broader theological questions and insights. The major sources are religious magazines (important carriers of lay opinion), national newspapers (indicators of social and cultural context and influential interpreters of religious events), theological writings by church bodies and individual Christians, and works of historical scholarship. We will hear from prominent lay voices such as John F. Kennedy, Mario Cuomo, Dorothy Day, and David J. O'Brien. Yet we also hear from laypersons who write just one letter to the editor, who are stirred in the midst of their busy lives to add their words to a debate or contribute a theological insight. Indeed, these letters are themselves ventures into the public sphere, affirmations of the idea that faith is not purely an individual concern.

The picture I paint is by no means comprehensive, but it is intended to serve as an important lens through which to view the historical and theological dimensions of spirituality and to explore practical implications for contemporary persons seeking to find religious meaning in private and public worlds. The questions and reflections raised will resound with people outside of Catholicism. My decision to focus on American lay Catholics reflects my conviction that one cannot study spirituality in a vacuum; spirituality must be studied in historical and cultural context. Spirituality is "an experience rooted in a particular community's history."[7] A study of spirituality thus is most meaningful if it focuses on a particular group's experience and then suggests broader implications.

Who Are the Laity?

One might ask how to define a layperson, and why the experiences of laypeople deserve special attention. The term "lay" derives from the Greek word *laos,* meaning "people." Across religious traditions, the laity were those who did not have special roles of power and sacred authority. They were the people involved in ordinary life, concerned with domestic and economic responsibilities, with less time for intense spiritual training.

The role of the layperson is today an important issue within Christianity and other religious traditions. The interest in lay spirituality can be seen as an awakening, an invigorated search for authentic Christian life in the world. It is not an entirely new phenomenon, but rather a sharpened effort to invite all Christians into faith and holiness. As theologian Hans Urs von Balthasar writes:

> there seem to be moments in the history of the Church when a particular state of life becomes more conscious of its special task and function than before, and, through reflection, frees itself from its previous dormancy.... Today seems to be the time of the laity, which, having attained its majority, needs an appropriate spirituality, and one no longer governed by the standards and categories of the religious state.[8]

The time of the laity has come in other faiths as well. Buddhist scholar Rita Gross observes:

> When the women insist on practicing Buddhism as fully as do the men, and when lay Buddhists with families and careers insist that the heart of their involvement in Buddhism is meditation and study, not just donating to those who meditate and study, vast changes are required.... Traditionally, one of the reasons lay people were not expected to practice meditation very seriously is precisely because of overwhelming time

demands thought to be unavoidable in their domestic and economic lives.[9]

Catholic teaching often defined the laity negatively, as those who are not clergy or religious. The sharp distinction between laity and clergy arose in the early Middle Ages. This was not a "separate but equal" philosophy, but rather carried a presumption that the clergy and religious traveled a more perfect road. Worldly affairs—including both family life and economic activity—were implicitly debased as lower (although not evil) occupations. They were, at the very least, distracting. Hence, while the Council of Trent (1545–63) upheld the sacramentality of marriage, it also declared: "If anyone saith that the marriage state is to be placed above the state of virginity or celibacy, and that it is not better and more blessed to remain in virginity or in celibacy than to be in matrimony; let him be anathema."[10] Thus we find this commentary in a recent definition of laity:

> Laity were not only considered the lowest rung on the ladder of the Church membership, but, under the influence of philosophical movements (e.g., Neoplatonism), many in the Church began to think that anything material was bad and only the spiritual was good. Since the laity spent every day of their lives dealing with the material aspects of life—work, politics, family, sex—they were seen to be at a disadvantage for spiritual growth. The subordination of the laity in the Church continued for over eighteen hundred years.[11]

Medieval Lay Sanctity

Of course, within this broad generalization there are many nuances. In fact, the lines between laity, clergy, and religious were not always clear-cut. Medievalist Carolyn Bynum points out that clergy strongly influenced laity, and that priests were themselves recruited from lay society.[12] Jacques Fontaine notes too that the cultural and spiritual role of monasticism was irreplaceable in the early Middle Ages, and monasticism nourished the spirituality of the best laity.[13]

Certainly, monastic traditions of spirituality have contributed much to the spirituality of laypersons for centuries. This is demonstrated by the proliferation of Third Order groups, in which laypeople associate themselves with a religious order, follow a rule approved by the pope, and bring the charism of the order into their lay lives. Third Orders date as far back as the twelfth or early thirteenth century. St. Francis of Assisi founded a Franciscan Third Order (rule approved in 1221), as did others such as the Augustinians (rule approved 1400), Dominicans (rule approved 1406), and Carmelites (rule approved 1452). Tertiaries often take vows of chastity and obedience, which they fulfill in the context of their secular life.

The penitential movements that arose in the late twelfth century also reflected lay attempts to infuse everyday life with sacred meaning, drawing from monastic models but carving out a distinct lay charism. A penitential movement that flourished in the thirteenth century involved groups of laywomen who were called Beguines and laymen called Beghards. The Beguines and Beghards arose in France, Germany, the Netherlands, and Belgium. They devoted themselves to prayer, charity, and manual labor. Most lived in community, although they could live alone. While they practiced obedience and celibacy, they did not take formal religious vows and they lived autonomously from monastic orders or clerical communities. The Beguines and Beghards eventually aroused suspicion and were condemned at the Council of Vienne in 1312. Their influence persisted through, for example, the mystical writings of Hadewijch of Antwerp.[14]

Medieval lay penitential movements and lay individuals of holy reputation emphasized charity. This was a concrete way of living out one's faith in the world, often closely interactive with clerical and monastic piety but still distinct. For example, one of the few laymen canonized in the Middle Ages, the married Italian St. Omobono (d. 1197, canonized 1199), was known for his great charity and piety. He also was a fine draper-tailor; he would become the patron saint of confraternities of tailors and clothing merchants. As historian André Vauchez notes, his canonization indicated not only approval of the penitential path of holiness flourishing among the laity, but also signaled that temporal work need not hinder sanctification. Indeed, St. Louis IX, king of France (1226–70), was another rare instance of sanctified lay life. The king clearly was active "in the world." He fought wars and negotiated treaties. He undertook two crusades, meeting death near Tunis during the 1270 crusade. Influenced by the new active mendicant orders (particularly the Franciscans and Dominicans), Louis IX exemplified the virtue of charity. He built hospitals for the sick and homes for the poor, including a home for reformed prostitutes and one for blind men. He is known for his personal concern for his subjects and for justice, as the popular image of him holding court under the oak at Vincennes conveys. Louis IX also is known for his piety, for devout prayer and fasting. He was canonized in 1297.

Unfortunately, the practical understanding of sanctity characteristic of St. Omobono and St. Louis shifted with the rise of a highly contemplative mysticism: "the criteria of sanctity were to become more and more extraordinary, ... visions, revelations, exchanges of heart, anorexic crises, and other mystical and paramystical phenomena.... This evolution led inevitably to the disappearance of the modest and useful movement of lay sanctity, a victim of the dual processes of clericalization and spiritualization of religious life which characterized the final centuries of the Western Middle Ages."[15]

Still, some of those extraordinary mystics did integrate contemplation and action. Laywoman Catherine of Siena (1347–80), for example, blended contemplative mysticism with active involvement in the ecclesiastical and political problems of her day. She was canonized in 1461 and made a Doctor of the Church in 1970. While Catherine is best known for the mystical visions described in her book *The Dialogue,* she was extremely active, particularly in the last five years of her life. She even persuaded Pope Gregory XI to return the papacy from Avignon back to Rome in 1377, thus ending the church's "Babylonian Captivity." Catherine was no enclosed nun; she traveled and acted as a kind of diplomat. She entreated the Florentines, for example, to make peace with the papacy. As we read in one of her letters to the Florentines (1376), she appealed to both spiritual virtue and pragmatic consequences as she pressed for a change in policy:

> I Catherine, servant and slave of the servants of Jesus Christ, write to you in His precious Blood.... I summon you to true

humiliation of your hearts... if you wish to be received in the arms of your father.... But I complain strongly of you, if it is true what is said in these parts, that you have imposed a tax upon the clergy. If this is so, it is a very great evil for two reasons. The first is that you are wronging God by it.... Beside the evil I spoke of that comes from wronging God, I tell you that such action is ruin to your peace. For the Holy Father, if he knew it, would conceive greater indignation against you.[16]

When two popes were elected after the death of Gregory XI in 1378, the Roman Pope Urban VI recruited Catherine to try to end the Great Schism. Still, hagiographical literature and the canonization proceedings emphasize her mystical experiences and virginity, downplaying her active worldly engagement and lay status. This indicates the pressure of a particular notion of sanctity.[17]

The Reformers and a More Democratic Sanctity

Sixteenth-century reformers Martin Luther and John Calvin sharply critiqued that notion of sanctity. Luther abolished monasteries and denounced the two-tiered notions of holiness prevalent in his day. He erased the sharp distinction between clergy and religious, on the one hand, and laity on the other. Laity were in fact priests: "Now we, who have been baptized, are all uniformly priests in virtue of that very fact."[18] Luther cited 1 Peter 2:9: "But you are a chosen race, a royal priesthood, a holy nation, God's own people, in order that you may proclaim the mighty acts of him who called you out of darkness into his marvelous light." God called the whole People of God into the light. Luther resisted a distinction between religious and secular, which downplayed the holiness of the whole people: "To call popes, bishops, priests, monks, and nuns, the religious class, but princes, lords, artisans, and farm-workers the secular class, this is a specious device.... For all Christians whatsoever really and truly belong to the religious class, and there is no difference among them except in so far as they do different work.... For baptism, gospel, and faith alone make men religious."[19]

Reformers combined this interpretation of the priesthood of all believers with a strong notion of the lay vocation. Devaluing clerical life, they argued for the vocation of secular persons in their occupations and household duties. They also asserted the goodness and holiness of marriage, a divine calling, and railed against those who disparaged the institution (e.g., see Luther's *The Estate of Marriage*). On the other hand, reformers such as Luther and Calvin also rid marriage of its sacramental designation, with which the Catholic Church afforded marriage a significant spiritual status. In addition, they refused to permit ecclesiastical authority governance over marriage. Placing marriage under civil law did make it more public, but also may have contributed to the eventual secularization of marriage, an unintended consequence of desacramentalization.[20]

Another unintended consequence resulted from the reformers' notion of worldly holiness. Calvin, for example, strongly emphasized the worldly calling and the importance of ascetic discipline. Medieval notions of sanctity had gradually exalted mystical experience above charity and ascetic practices, which became the beginning points of prayer but not the height of sanctity. Calvin reasserted the importance of asceticism. Indeed, as Max Weber persuasively argued, Calvinistic notions of vocation and worldly asceticism may have unintentionally propelled the development of modern capitalism. Fearing for their salvation, the Puritans looked to economic success as marks of election. Their industry and frugal discipline produced capital. Indeed, the Reformation understanding of the religious meaning of everyday life had a downside. Integration of faith and everyday life could actually cause a loss of lay autonomy:

> The Reformation meant not the elimination of the Church's control over everyday life, but rather the substitution of a new form of control for the previous one. It meant the repudiation of a control which was very lax ... in favour of a regulation of the whole of conduct which, penetrating to all departments of private and public life, was infinitely burdensome and earnestly enforced.[21]

In the eighteenth century, John Wesley (1703–91) further modified the Protestant understanding of holiness. This Anglican reformer would become the founder of Methodism. He believed that while salvation came through faith, God works in human beings to sanctify them after justification. The Christian is called to perfection even in this life. Every person needs to progress day by day to deeper knowledge and love of God. Wesley equates perfection and holiness: "They are two names for the same thing. Thus everyone that is perfect is holy, and everyone that is holy is, in the Scripture sense, perfect."[22] Wesley's doctrine of sanctification resonates with the Catholic tradition of spirituality. The spiritual life is an ongoing process toward greater virtue, love, and understanding. Wesley also saw the importance of discipline in the spiritual life; the methodical practices of his Holy Clubs gave his following the derogative nickname "Methodists."

Wesley did not see himself as breaking from the Anglican tradition, although his followers became more and more separatist. Wesley did not want to ordain ministers within his movement as this would signal a clear break with the Anglican Church. Hence, he embraced lay preachers who could go out and speak to the common person in England and the United States. Laity played a central role in ministry. Moreover, the Wesleyan revivals and preaching promoted a democratic sanctity—open to all, all were called. The laity were called to perfection; Wesley did not distinguish here between ordained and lay.

And yet Wesley did see the Christian life as one of progress or stages, and hence some Christians were more developed than others. He cites 1 John 2:12–14 as he distinguishes between babes in Christ, young men, and fathers.[23] This notion of "maturity" (seen also in, for example, Hebrews 5:11–14) lends itself to a kind of two-tiered sanctity. In one sermon, Wesley specifically endorses this hierarchy of holiness:

> There have been from the beginning two orders of Christians. The one lived an innocent life, conforming in all things not sinful to the customs and fashions of the world, doing many good works, abstaining from gross evils, and attending the ordinances of God.... The other sort of Christians not only abstained from all appearance of evil, were zealous of good works in every kind, and attended all the ordinances of God; but likewise used all diligence to attain the whole mind that was in Christist.... They spared no pains to arrive at the sum-

mit of Christian holiness: "leaving the first principles of the doctrine of Christ, to go on to perfection."[24]

Still, Wesley did not limit the "more excellent way" to ordained clergy, monks, or nuns. Rather, perfection meant living the everyday Christian calling more intensely and devoutly, with a more intentional relationship to God. Hence, every Christian is called to work, to "apply themselves to the business of their calling."[25] Yet the more holy path demands that one work not only diligently, but piously, not thinking only of one's family but seeking also to do the will of God. Mature Christianity is not limited to those of a celibate vocation or to ordained clergy, but rather is the goal of each person in this lifetime.

Jane de Chantal and Francis de Sales

While the Protestant reformers redefined holiness, Catholic teaching maintained a two-tiered notion of perfection that generally kept laity looking up at the more elite saints. There were some efforts to encourage laity toward perfection, but these efforts must be seen against the dominant backdrop. An exploration into the spirituality of Francis de Sales (1567–1622) and Jane de Chantal (1572–1641) reveals this tension.

While she lived in the wake of the Reformation, French laywoman Jane de Chantal struggled with the dominant Catholic notion of sanctity. A widowed mother of four children with responsibilities for administering an estate, she experienced a growing desire to give herself totally to God. Given the church's understanding of sanctity, Jane believed that she could fulfill that desire only by entering a convent. Yet Jane's worldly duties would not permit that move. She had children to raise and a business to run. Jane felt a painful spiritual conflict. She corresponded with Francis de Sales, bishop of Geneva and spiritual director to numerous laypersons. Francis perceived that the Catholic teachings about holiness were part of the problem: "Almost all those who have hitherto written about devotion have been concerned with instructing persons wholly withdrawn from the world or have at least taught a kind of devotion that leads to such complete retirement."[26] As they wrestled with Jane's dilemma, they developed a broader notion of holiness.

Salesian spirituality depends on a connection between the concepts of "devotion" and "vocation." Devotion is not a rigid, prescribed program of piety, but rather an ardent love of God. Divine love manifests itself as grace; it also strengthens us to do good works, charity. Devotion is charity enflamed by the will, by "great ardor and readiness in performing charitable actions." Devotion is an outburst of charity; the two are like flame and fire. "Charity is a spiritual fire and when it bursts into flames, it is called devotion." Devotion is the "perfection of charity."[27]

The exercise of devotion must be adapted to the different circumstances in which people live, as well as to their possibilities and temperaments. Implicit in Francis's flexible discussion of devotion is an appreciation of worldly life as a possible arena for encounter with God:

> When he created things God commanded plants to bring forth their fruits, each one according to its kind, and in like manner he commands Christians, the living plants of his Church, to bring forth the fruits of devotion, each according to his position and vocation. Devotion must be exercised in different ways by the gentleman, the worker, the servant, the prince, the widow, the young girl and the married woman.[28]

Thus, all individuals can practice devotion; only its expression will vary. Francis advises individuals to exercise devotion as its suits their vocation. What is foolish is to seek a piety counter to one's state in life, for a bishop to seek a solitary life, for a married man to want to own no more property than a Capuchin, for a skilled workman to spend all day in church like a religious.

True devotion cannot run contrary to one's lawful vocation. Devotion can never harm a person, but perfects all things. Just as charity is enflamed by the ardor of devotion, so too every vocation is made more agreeable when united with devotion: "Care of one's family is rendered more peaceable, love of husband and wife more sincere, service of one's prince more faithful, and every type of employment more pleasant."[29] Francis thus maintains that devotion may be integrated into private and public life and all states in life.

He recognizes that some situations may not permit contemplative devotion, and asserts that perfection can nevertheless be reached in the secular state. Francis identifies as role models such figures as Abraham, St. Joseph, St. Monica, Constantine, and St. Louis, all of whom, he says, practiced true devotion in the world.

Jane's children take a good deal of attention, and Francis urges her to incorporate their care generously into her practice of piety. Love of neighbor is an essential part of devotion, particularly for those in the world. Moreover, full acceptance of God's will as found in one's situation precludes excessive attachment to certain means to perfection. Francis explains:

> If you really love obedience and docility, I'd like to think that when some legitimate or charitable cause takes you away from your religious exercises, this would be for you another form of obedience and that your love would make up for whatever you have to omit in your religious practice.[30]

Thus, Francis de Sales and Jane de Chantal developed a spirituality that imbued the everyday with great sanctity. Like Catherine of Siena, they counseled numerous lay and clergy. In 1610, the two founded the Visitation of Holy Mary community, a congregation for women who could not—often due to family responsibilities—join one of the more strict religious communities. The Visitation balanced prayer, intimate communal life, and work. Jane's counsel to her brother, the archbishop of Bourges and a politician in the Parliament of Burgundy and the court of Louis XIII, reveals her flexible notion of vocation: "Do not think that by this I mean for us to retire into solitude, or to flee those occupations and legitimate contacts necessary to our vocations; oh no, for I very much like each one to stay in his state of life and not throw himself into the excesses of a hermit's devotion, especially you, my dearest Lord, for whom this would be most inappropriate."[31]

This heritage of lay spirituality needs to be recovered, even as we explore contemporary models. Of course, historical figures cannot be transplanted as models for contemporary Christians without regard for the particular historical contexts in which they arose. Moreover, we must engage with past figures with a critical theological eye. One might critique, for example, the Salesian concept of divine will. Francis works with a clear conviction about the sovereignty of God. Devotion is a matter of releasing one's self-will and joyfully embracing the situation in which God has placed one. Many today question the equation of circumstance with divine will, noting the human oppression and political manipulation that can result. Identifying God's will is perhaps far more complicated than Francis assumed. Still, this wrestling with the tradition is an important practical theological task. For too long, clerical and monastic models of holiness dominated, and these lay stirrings did not make their way into the spiritual teachings of the church.

Catholic Shifts in the Twentieth Century

One can trace two major trajectories in spirituality from the eighteenth century to the twentieth century. On one side, the Protestant redefinition of laity became an assumed part of most Protestant notions of holiness. On the other side, despite the power of Protestant ideas and movements and despite the examples of medieval charity and Salesian spirituality, Catholic teaching into the twentieth century continued to assume a two-tiered sanctity that explicitly placed laity on the lower path. The celibate path was more perfect than lay life. Sanctity was focused primarily within the church rather than in the world.

Of course, there was much variation within this broad generalization. The debates about lay trusteeism in the nineteenth century, for example, show that lay and clerical roles varied among different ethnic communities. Germans, for example, were far more accustomed to lay involvement than were Irish. Immigrants—particularly those from Eastern Europe—expected to play an active role in parish governance in the nineteenth century. As historian Jay Dolan shows, at stake in this conflict were alternative visions of the church. A congregational model of the church saw laity and clergy cooperating on a local level. A clerical model of the church gave the priest and the church hierarchy far more control, relegating the layperson to the "pay, pray, and obey" role. By the twentieth century, the hierarchical model prevailed.[32]

Authority, then, would distinguish clergy and laity. The authority extended out into the public sphere. Particularly in the first five decades of the twentieth century, clergy were the public face of the church for a community still ensconced in a separate world. In an interview conducted by R. Scott Appleby, Boston area priest John Tackney described this role: "In Dorchester in the 1920s and '30s was a man named Monsignor Haviland.... No government—state, federal, or local—ever did anything without consulting him. That's how powerful he was. He was the most educated, he was the most powerful, he was the most revered. Why? Because the whole parish was made up of immigrants! And he was articulate. He spoke for them."[33] Thus, the story of this book begins with laity operating in a hierarchical model of church, within a framework of understanding that assumes a two-tiered notion of sanctity. Clergy had a substantial public role and their authority went hand in hand with an unquestioning assumption of their superior holiness.

What is important to see is that the twentieth century eventually brought the two tracks—Catholic and Protestant—more closely together. As will be shown in chapter 1, diverse lay movements energized the laity with a sense of mission. Laity claimed a public apostolate. In the process, they put pressure on the more hierarchical understandings of the lay role. They also pushed out of ghettoized Catholicism. These movements prepared the way for the Second Vatican Council, which placed a new emphasis on lay holiness and vocation in official Catholic teaching. The Council affirmed lay holiness in the secular world, as will be discussed in detail in chapter 2.

The Second Vatican Council also signaled a shift in the understanding of clerical and lay roles. While the priest in ethnic American Catholic communities had been the public face of the church to society, the Council specifically defined laity as those whose apostolate centers in the secular world. Laity do not withdraw from the world, but rather seek to bring Christ into it: "The characteristic of the lay state being a life led in the midst of the world and of secular affairs, laymen are called by God to make of their apostolate, through the vigor of their Christian spirit, a leaven in the world."[34] It is important to emphasize that laity are here defined in terms of their secular character. While priests and religious may engage in temporal affairs, this is not their primary sphere. They "are principally and expressly ordained to the sacred ministry." On the other hand: "Their secular character is proper and peculiar to the laity."[35] Implicit in these definitions of lay and clerical vocations, then, is a distinction between secular (the sphere of the laity) and sacred (the sphere of the ordained clergy).

In practice, of course, there were many variations on these roles. Active clergy and religious have always faced some of the same spiritual issues as do laypersons, especially the relation between action and contemplation. The parish priest, for example, must be "in the world," managing finances, supervising employees, engaging in community affairs. Particularly as clergy and religious left their vocations in large numbers in the late 1960s and 1970s, laity stepped in to previously "churchy" roles in schools and parishes. Ministry became a professionalized skill not restricted to celibates. Religious left their habits behind so as to work more easily in the secular world. Clergy too got directly into political causes: civil rights, Vietnam War protests. The Berrigan brothers were a prime example. Jesuit priest Robert Drinan was another. The 1970s also saw a rise in religious women who moved into "political ministry."[36] Whatever the official church teachings, distinctions between clergy, religious, and laity did not hold in practice. This was perhaps a good and healthy situation that responded to context, pushing the boundaries of church teachings. Yet it certainly resulted in vocational confusion for ordained, religious, and laity. I address this confusion in this book.

What one witnesses by the end of the twentieth century, particularly regarding the lay "vocation" in the secular world and the blurring of lines between clergy and lay, could be seen as a Protestantization of Catholicism. At the same time, official Catholic teachings and Catholic laity appropriate Protestant ideas within a Catholic theological framework. This is a complex story of how Catholics both draw on central Protestant understandings of spirituality and draw deeply from traditional Catholic wells in a changing historical context. The diverse Catholic lay spiritualities that emerge reveal the profound pastoral and theological issues at stake. In this study, then, I hope to present fresh and differently nuanced understandings of lay spirituality that also may be useful now to Protestants and other traditions struggling to clarify the position of the laity and theologies of ordination. Indeed, Protestants today also are hungering for spiritual renewal. Many seek to recover from the pre-Reformation tradition resources for contemporary spirituality. One sees, for example, the appeal of monasticism in ecumenical movements such as the Taizé community, founded by Protestant minister Roger Schutz in 1949. Established in a small village in Burgundy, France, Taizé is a Protestant form of monasticism that draws large numbers of young laity from around the world to share in prayer and ecumenical fellowships.

Lay understandings of faith have not received due attention, yet they are indispensable to convey the complexity of the spiritual life for many contemporary persons. The reflections of laypersons may guide others to deeper devotion. At the same time, lay understandings must be accessible for critical examination; they too may be misguided. This book explores twentieth-century lay experience in America, casting an eye on the struggle for an authentic spirituality.

– Chapter One –

SEIZING THE LAY VOCATION

Lay Movements before the Second Vatican Council

THE DECADES PRECEDING the Second Vatican Council are often described as an era of "pray, pay, and obey" Catholics. Laity followed the rules, going to Mass, going to Confession, fasting, following. At least, this is the stereotype—with a great deal of truth imbedded in it. What it does not capture is the development of a new sense of mission and agency among certain laity, seen particularly in the burgeoning lay movements of the 1930s, 1940s, and 1950s. These were laity who bucked the trend, who claimed a vocation of their own, who analyzed their faith and their culture in very intentional ways. In different ways, these lay movements struggled to merge social consciousness with the life of faith. They carved out their own space distinct from the local parish, directing attention outward. The Catholic Worker, *Commonweal,* Young Christian Workers, the Christian Family Movement, the Grail, *Integrity* magazine, and Opus Dei: on all sides of the ideological spectrum lay groups brought faith into the public arena. They also connected public discipleship with concern for the family; some movements even saw the family as a primary agent of social transformation. The movements show Catholics' multifaceted interactions with the dominant Protestant ethos of American culture. These lay leaders and movements assert spirituality as an integrative force, Christianizing an increasingly secular or faithless American society.

The Context

Most of the lay movements arose in the 1930s and 1940s. Democrat Franklin D. Roosevelt was president during much of this time. He

23

had resoundingly defeated Herbert Hoover in the 1932 presidential election, after the stock market crash of 1929 had plunged the
country into the Great Depression. He remained in office until his
death in 1945. The effects of industrialization and depression were
felt strongly in the largely working-class Catholic communities of
the 1930s and 1940s. Catholic responses tended to be pragmatic.
John Cort and other laymen, for example, founded the Association
of Catholic Trade Unionists (ACTU) in 1937. The ACTU promoted
union organization, garnered Catholic support for striking workers, and defended the Congress of Industrial Organizations (CIO)
against accusations of Communism.

Lay labor leaders found support in the social teachings of the
church and in the examples of advocates such as Fr. John A. Ryan.
This "Right Reverend New Dealer" directed the Social Action Department of the National Catholic Welfare Conference from 1919 to
1944.[1] He endorsed minimum wage legislation, a minimum working
age, legal guarantees of workers' right to organize, unemployment
insurance, and partnerships between labor and management. In the
papal encyclical *Quadragesimo Anno* (1931), Pope Pius XI tied just
working conditions and social reconstruction to spiritual well-being:
"The whole scheme of social and economic life is now such as to
put in the way of vast numbers of mankind most serious obstacles
which prevent them from caring for the one thing necessary; namely,
their eternal salvation."[2] The pope endorsed workers' associations
and argued for just wages, sufficient for the support of the worker
and his family.

And yet despite a growing tradition of Catholic social teaching
on economics extending at least back to *Rerum Novarum* in 1891,
there seemed still to be a large gap between faith and economic
life among Catholics. It is telling that Al Smith, running for president in 1928, said that he did not know what an encyclical was.
And Dorothy Day too relates that she had never read an encyclical
when she joined the church. This was not just American ignorance.
An Irish professor commented in 1931 that although there was
probably no country in the world where the ordinary layman is
so well grounded in Catholic social teaching as Ireland, still very
few Irish professors, politicians, or trade unionists could identify
fundamental Catholic principles on the economy.[3] Despite their ig-

norance of official teachings, Catholics generally supported labor in practice.

At the same time that Americans confronted economic problems, secular and religious groups expressed grave concerns about the family, citing divorce, falling fertility rates, increasing female employment, and a decline in male authority in the home. Papal encyclicals such as *Casti Connubi* (1930) set out a strong vision of the holiness of marriage and described evils that undermined Christian family life. Contraception was one of the most important family issues in the twentieth century for Catholics. Pope Pius XI responded to the qualified acceptance of birth control at the Anglican Lambeth Conference by firmly rejecting contraception. At the same time, church teaching elevated marriage as a central feature of lay spirituality. The outward expression of love between husband and wife

> must have as its primary purpose that man and wife help each other day by day in forming and perfecting themselves in the interior life, so that through their partnership in life they may advance ever more and more in virtue, and above all that they may grow in true love toward God and their neighbor.[4]

With these ideals in the background, Catholic leaders in the 1930s, 1940s, and 1950s expressed alarm about the condition of American family life. Their rhetoric was charged. Part of the concern stemmed from the effects of a changing American society on Catholic immigrant families. While ethnic domestic traditions remained strong for many Catholics in the twentieth century, some Catholics began to marry outside of their ethnic groups and move to the suburbs, particularly in the 1940s and 1950s. Declining rates of Catholic immigration following the Johnson-Reed Act of 1924 spurred assimilation into American culture. While suburban Catholics were freer from the economic and social problems of the city, they now faced the spiritual dangers of modern life. These dangers threatened the future of the church, as the family was a needed school of Catholic culture. Fr. Andrew Greeley warned in 1958:

> Catholics can accept much of the American way of life with little hesitation, but in certain matters—birth control, divorce,

and premarital sex experience, for example—we must part company with the average American. We simply cannot accept his ideas.... In the suburbs they [Catholics] are in the main line of the enemy's fire.[5]

A New Lay Energy

The burgeoning lay movements clearly responded to this concern about workers and the family. Yet they were not simply social outreach movements. They carried distinctive theological visions and practices that they understood to be critical for social transformation. Of course, these theological visions did not arise in a vacuum. Strong European influence can be seen in the founding stories of many of these movements—the influence of Peter Maurin for the Catholic Worker, Jacques van Ginneken for Grail, Joseph Cardijn for Young Christian Workers and the Christian Family Movement. The intellectual Catholic Revival, the development of Catholic Action, and liturgical renewal inspired European Catholicism, and these influences spread across the ocean. The burgeoning lay movements carried different visions of the spiritual life. They also shifted the power of the laity:

> It was the new family apostolates on the fringes of the parish that served as major catalysts in restructuring the relationship between the priests and the parishioners.... In the arena of family, marriage, and sexuality, the married couples quite naturally assumed an expertise and inherent authority that their pastors could not claim, and this resulted in a subtle, but significant change in the dynamic of clergy-lay relationships.[6]

Laity engaged in these movements were part of a vibrant, expanding lay apostolate which sought to connect Christian faith to everyday life, including family and work. Indeed, these laypersons were redefining Christian spirituality:

> They had caught a vision of the meaning the Gospels gave to their young lives; they had a sense of vocation to bring that vision to others, but to bring it as lay persons remaining amid the challenges and complexities of the every-day

world.... A central preoccupation of the young lay apostles was the development of a spirituality of the laity.[7]

These lay apostles found sustenance in the life of the church and traditional spiritual disciplines such as liturgy, meditation on scripture, and personal prayer. The liturgical movement and particularly the revived understanding of the church as the Mystical Body of Christ supported the outward move of laity. The liturgical renewal originated in Europe and became influential in the United States in the 1930s and 1940s. For Virgil Michel, a leader of the liturgical movement in the United States, the liturgy was "the indispensable basis of social regeneration."[8] Laying the groundwork for the liturgical reform of the Second Vatican Council, the renewal movement brought laity into fuller participation in the liturgy. It breathed a fresh spirit into the church. At the same time, the new emphasis on the church as the Mystical Body of Christ gave a dignity to the whole community of believers, who together through their diverse gifts become Christ's presence in the world. As Paul writes to the early Christian community in Corinth: "For just as the body is one and has many members, and all the members of the body, though many, are one body, so it is with Christ. For in the one Spirit we were all baptized into one body—Jews or Greeks, slaves or free—and we were all made to drink of one Spirit.... Now you are the body of Christ and individually members of it" (1 Cor. 12: 12–13, 27).

In a 1943 encyclical, Pope Pius XII endorsed the Mystical Body of Christ ecclesiology and specifically linked it to the hierarchical Roman Catholic Church. According to Pius XII, Christ governs the church through the visible head of the pope. The laity work with the hierarchy, unified but with a subordinate position within the Body. This fit the traditional notion of Catholic Action, an endorsement of the lay vocation that the papacy defined as "the participation of the laity in the work of the hierarchy." The papal interpretation of the Mystical Body ecclesiology maintained a two-tiered understanding of sanctity: "fathers and mothers of families...and in particular those members of the laity who collaborate with the ecclesiastical hierarchy in spreading the Kingdom of the Divine Redeemer occupy an honorable, if often a lowly, place in the Christian community, and

even they under the impulse of God and with His help, can reach
the heights of supreme holiness."⁹

Lay movements in the United States, however, pushed the edges
of this hierarchical interpretation of the Mystical Body and the lay
vocation. They claimed a unique space for lay action, and reveled
in a heady sense of mission. When compared to European Catholic
Action, American Catholic movements generally looked more independent. Lay spirituality was not disconnected from the spiritual
traditions of the church, nor from the official teachings of the institutional church. Indeed, church teachings such as *Divini Redemptoris*
(1937), which promoted Catholic Action as a way to combat Communism, and *Mediator Dei* (1947), which propelled the liturgical
movement, gave force and inspiration to many young lay apostles.
Yet members of the lay apostolates "gained a sense of critical distance from mainstream 'parish Catholicism' that empowered them
to dream new dreams and glean a new vision of the responsibilities
of the laity."¹⁰

Mary Irene Zotti, a leader in the Young Christian Workers movement, described a gradual shift in the spirituality of members of
YCW from the beginnings of the movement in the late 1930s into
the 1940s and 1950s, as they moved from traditional Catholic devo-
tionalism to a more public spirituality that could incorporate social
action in the workplace and in the home. Zotti wrote: "All of us
who became cell members in the late thirties were intrigued by the
idea that we should make the world more Christian, but our notion
of problems usually centered on matters of religious observance and
moral behavior."¹¹ By the late 1940s, members were redefining lay
spirituality:

> They were no longer willing to sit back as praying, paying
> church members primarily concerned with personal piety. The
> message of the so-called social encyclicals on social justice
> in the world, beginning with *Rerum Novarum*, On Capi-
> tal and Labor (1891), and continued in *Divini Redemptoris*,
> On Atheistic Communism (1937), and *Quadragesimo Anno*,
> On Social Reconstruction (1941), had clearly identified the
> need for Catholics to be concerned with the problems of
> industrialism and the resulting injustices and dehumanizing

conditions impacting on the lives of twentieth-century men and women.[12]

One former member described the YCW spirituality as a kind of Christian "osmosis," in which one's growing Christian maturity and awareness permeated all aspects of life.[13]

This was an exciting and spiritually rich time for those lay-persons caught up in these movements. One laywoman described her experience:

> I met people active with the Young Christian Workers and with *Integrity* magazine. I read *Seven Storey Mountain* and discov-ered Dorothy Day and the Catholic Worker, the Baroness de Hueck and Friendship House and I heard Frank Sheed address small groups on Sunday evenings at Columbia University....
>
> I grew up with the Baltimore Catechism and learned in the 1940s to scratch the surface for better understanding.... Born again in the 1940s! ... Church was a moving force in our lives and "Catholicism was (indeed) a total way of life...." We believed that we were the leaven and that conviction was not easily shaken. The quest for perfection—sainthood—was a real goal.[14]

The *Commonweal* "Outlook"

Begun in 1924, *Commonweal* was independent and lay-edited, designed to provide a Catholic perspective on American "public affairs, religion, literature, and the arts." Calvin Coolidge was pres-ident. The Ku Klux Klan was alive and well, targeting Catholics. Catholics were a tight-knit group, still suspect in and segregated from the larger American public. *Commonweal* was founded by Michael Williams and the Calvert Associates as an attempt to con-vey a Catholic "outlook" on life, as opposed to a Catholic "inlook," to the whole American people. The editors sought to break open what they perceived to be a stagnant, parochial American Ca-tholicism, still shaped by its long years of immigrant status, its intellectual growth stunted by the condemnations of Americanism in 1899 and Modernism in 1907.

Laity founded *Commonweal* and they would run it. The magazine was not, the editors proclaimed, "an authoritative or authorized mouthpiece of the Catholic Church. It will be the independent, personal product of its editors and contributors, who, for the most part, will be laymen."[15] One historian called *Commonweal* "perhaps the most important significant lay enterprise and achievement in the history of American Catholicism."[16]

The editors argued that Christianity—and specifically, Catholicism—had something important and distinctive to contribute to American society. Indeed, as the country fell into the Great Depression, *Commonweal* even argued that Catholic social teaching held the key to relief: "the maze of misery in which the whole world is wandering at present can never be understood; still less traversed safely, unless the statesmen and the leaders of our economic system...pay heed to the voice of the Catholic Church."[17] The magazine promoted a public faith unusual for the American lay Catholic at that time. *Commonweal* editors in the twenties, thirties, forties, and fifties were the

> voice of and the connection for those laity who laid claim to the right to be church in the world. Those were the decades in which it was not at all certain that the laity had that right. The term "*Commonweal* Catholic" was a term of opprobrium or a badge of moral bravery, depending on the point of view.[18]

Commonweal criticized lay passivity:

> While the Pope is calling on the Catholic laity for action, to apply the principles which he proclaims "with which to meet the present troubles of the age," the Catholic laity is not responding in any measure commensurate with the peril that faces the Church. There is lip service. But there is no effective action.[19]

For those laity who did assert their own vocations and began to redefine spirituality in light of their own experiences, these were daring and heady times:

> It is hard to explain to those who did not know it what life in much of the church in America was like in those days when

Commonweal was young. They were still the days of fortress America and fortress church....

We were a docile laity expected only to attend Mass, receive the sacraments, keep Advent and Lent, avoid personal sin, and support the church....

In that world the idea that Catholic laymen could publish a journal to discuss Catholic thought on politics, social trends, literature, and the arts was almost revolutionary. The "*Commonweal* Catholic" who took the responsibility for lay participation in the affairs of the commonweal, who felt that he or she could define the terms of that participation in light of his or her experience as someone lay, Catholic, and American, seemed heroic on the one hand, suspect and dangerous on the other.[20]

Due to its strong vision of the lay apostolate in American society, *Commonweal* provides an important lens through which to view the debates, struggles, and insights of laity. I will use this angle of vision throughout this book. It is a lens that zooms in with most clarity on moderate to "progressive" Catholics.

Dorothy Day and the Catholic Worker

It was almost a decade after the first issue of *Commonweal* hit the presses that Dorothy Day began passing out the new *Catholic Worker* newspaper, an alternative to the Marxist *Worker* newspaper. It was 1933, New York City in the depths of the Great Depression. Day began the Catholic Worker movement together with Peter Maurin. Day was a New York journalist with leftist leanings who had converted to Catholicism. Maurin was a French Catholic wandering philosopher. Together, they began publishing the *Catholic Worker* newspaper in 1933 and later opened houses of hospitality and farming communes for the poor, unemployed, and homeless. By 1942 Catholic Workers were running thirty-two houses of hospitality and twelve farms in the East and the Midwest.[21] Day, in particular, would capture the imagination and inspire the spirituality of laypersons throughout the twentieth century.

The Catholic Worker was to be a spiritually rooted response to the human indignities brought on by the capitalist system. While Franklin D. Roosevelt was outlining the New Deal, the Catholic Worker promoted a "gentle personalism." Day and Maurin distrusted the modern state and its ability to serve human needs. Rather than advocating political engagement, they argued that society would be reconstructed through acts of individual love and service and through renouncing violence. Social renewal would occur person by person by upholding the dignity of each and every individual. Day wrote: "Love is indeed a 'harsh and dreadful thing' to ask of us, of each one of us, but it is the only answer."[22] Social renewal and civil society depended on intentional Christian communities stretching to extend love: "We have all known the long loneliness and we have learned that the only solution is love and that love comes with community."[23]

Day and Maurin were gripped by the struggles of the working class, injustice, and the effects of modern industrialized society on the human spirit. The first issues of the *Catholic Worker* newspaper discussed, for example, African-American workers in the South, coal miner strikes, and child labor. The Worker movement supported workers with food and housing during the many labor disputes of the 1930s. John Cort, a Catholic Worker who later wrote extensively on labor issues for *Commonweal*, remarked:

> It was Dorothy who sold me on the labor movement.... Dorothy realized that to ignore the unions during the mid-thirties would have made as much sense as a radical movement ignoring the black revolution during the sixties and seventies. Labor was where the live action was.[24]

The Catholic Worker's attention to the laborer stemmed from a deep conviction about human dignity,

> the fundamental truth that men should not be treated as chattels, but as human beings, as "temples of the Holy Ghost." When Christ took on our human nature, when He became man, he dignified and ennobled human nature.... When men are striking, they are following an impulse, often blind, often uninformed, but a good impulse—one could even say an inspiration of the Holy Spirit.[25]

The Catholic Worker commitments included a firm pacifist conviction that brought it into tension with the American government, the public, and the prevailing anti-Communist, patriotic Catholic mentality. Throughout World War II, the movement maintained its pacifist stance (a move that cost the Catholic Worker public support and resulted in internal dissension and closure of many houses of hospitality). In this January 1942 letter, Day explained their spiritual convictions and even referred to the laity as "other Christs": " ... reminds us today that we are all 'called to be saints,' that we are other Christs, reminding us of the priesthood of the laity. We are still pacifists. Our manifesto is the Sermon on the Mount, which means that we will try to be peacemakers."[26] When the United States dropped the atomic bomb on Hiroshima and Nagasaki in 1945, Dorothy Day wrote this trenchant criticism of President Truman: "Mr. Truman was jubilant.... He was not a son of God, brother of Christ, brother of the Japanese, jubilating as he did.... *Jubilate Deo.* We have killed 318,000 Japanese."[27]

This was a public witness, deeply rooted in Christian spirituality, but sharply critical of the political sphere with its moral horrors and compromise. It is a model quite different from those we will see later from John F. Kennedy or Mario Cuomo. Indeed, Day refused even to pay federal income tax or to register the Catholic Worker as a tax-exempt institution. The Catholic Worker movement stood on the fringes of American society, critiquing from a radical social and spiritual perspective. Mel Piehl rightly notes that the Catholic Worker ultimately had its strongest effect not as a radical social movement but as a movement of spiritual renewal that combined a keen social conscience, intellectual power, and a contemplative impulse.[28]

Day was born in 1897, third in a family of five children. As her father was a journalist, her family lived in several different places across the United States. Her parents were not religious. While Day recounts happy experiences of childhood religion experienced through her contacts with Methodist neighbors, she drifted from her early attraction to faith and threw herself into more radical circles. Like her father, Day took up journalism. She wrote for the socialist *Call* and lived a bohemian lifestyle in Greenwich Village. She was heavily involved in socialist causes and the suffragist movement.

After living with journalist Lionel Moise, Day had an abortion that caused her such pain that she contemplated suicide.

Restless, she finally found great joy as the common-law wife of Forster Batterham: "I have always felt that it was life with him that brought me natural happiness, that brought me to God."[29] The two lived in a fisherman's shack on Staten Island, and she delighted in her love, her friends, and the beauty of the bay, the fields, and the woods. Day saw sexuality as a good, one deeply embedded in her spiritual journey:

> The very sexual act itself was used again and again in Scripture as a figure of the beatific vision. It was not because I was tired of sex, satiated, disillusioned, that I turned to God. Radical friends used to insinuate this. It was because through a whole love, both physical and spiritual, I came to know God.[30]

She conceived a child with Forster, an event which brought great joy and great grief. Forster was an ardent atheist, while she gradually had been drawn powerfully to God and to prayer. Day wrote: "I could not see that love between man and woman was incompatible with love of God. God is the Creator, and the very fact that we were begetting a child made me have a sense that we were made in the image and likeness of God, co-creators with him."[31] Her deep happiness with Forster gave way to a feeling of struggle. She wanted to have this child, Tamar, baptized, a decision she knew would mean the agonizing rending of her life with Forster. Day showed here the great value she attached to family life:

> A woman does not want to be alone at such a time. Even the most hardened, the most irreverent, is awed by the stupendous fact of creation. Becoming a Catholic would mean facing life alone and I clung to family life. . . . I had known enough of love to know that a good healthy family life was as near to heaven as one could get in this life.[32]

Yet she could not have Tamar "floundering through many years as I had done, doubting and hesitating, undisciplined and amoral."[33] Knowing the heavy cost, she eventually gathered her strength, left Forster, and joined the Catholic Church.

She loved the church, although she was disturbed by what she saw as its tacit support of an oppressive capitalist system. The church offered charity but too little justice; it supported the state and did not critique the social order that made charity necessary. Moreover, Day critiqued the church for its failure to truly embrace pluralism. As historian James Fisher shows, she gave a radical interpretation to the Mystical Body of Christ ecclesiology. Whereas prominent theological interpretations emphasized the unity of the church and its stance against the dominant culture, Day emphasized the church of compassion and inclusion. To be part of the Mystical Body of Christ meant to share in Christ's own Passion and in the suffering of any fellow human being. Day wrote:

> What does the Mystical Body include? Only Roman Catholics? That is heresy. Only one nationality, one color, one social status? Heresy. The Mystical Body is the union of the human race through His redemptive will, from Adam to the last man.... Can I have any animosity towards any Japanese, German, Italian, Negro or white? If we have prejudices we are liars in Christ. There is no nationality. The only foreigner is he who has not Jesus in him.[34]

As committed as she was to the cause of the poor, the workers, and peace, Day did not join the church because of its social teachings; one recalls that she had not read an encyclical at that time. Rather, she expressed her spirituality primarily in terms of intimacy. She joined the church because there she found Christ, and, "like all women in love, I wanted to be united to my love."[35] She drew on her experiences as a lover in her prayer life: "But more and more I see that prayer is the answer, it is the clasp of the hand, the joy and keen delight in the consciousness of that Other. Indeed, it is like falling in love."[36] Day's spirituality then was deeply shaped by her experiences as a lover and mother and by her appreciation for the meaning of family life.

Yet she insisted on the interconnections between private loves and public witness. Public witness was an integral part of being Catholic: "We reacted sharply to the accusation that when it came to private morality, the Catholics shone, but when it came to social and political morality, they were often conscienceless."[37] Her later public action would include protests against the Vietnam War, support for the civil rights movement in the 1960s, and defense of Cesar Chavez's farm workers movement in the 1970s. The Catholic Worker movement recognized the dignity of the person, but moved outward to community. Day shows a way of Christian discipleship that weaves public and private lives more seamlessly than is usual. As June O'Connor wrote:

> Day did not belabor any opposition or dichotomy between "public" and "private," "historical" and "personal," nor did she struggle to combine or integrate two aspects of life which were somehow preconceived or experienced as opposed or conflictual. As a communitarian radical by inclination and choice, Day operated out of a fundamental sense of connection between the public and the private.[38]

Her own identity was deeply shaped by her experiences as lover and mother, "yet she never seemed to cast the mother in her and the worker in her in any opposition. She took it as a given that she had a distinctive voice to speak to questions of public and social policy precisely because of her being a woman and mother."[39]

This merging of public and private roles was not without some cost, particularly in her life with her daughter, Tamar, and her separation from her longtime companion, Forster. Day was lonely, raising Tamar by herself. At times she felt a definite conflict between her public mission in the Catholic Worker movement and the satisfactions of family life:

> I was thirty-eight, wishing I were married and living the ordinary naturally happy life and had not come under the dynamic influence of Peter Maurin. . . .
>
> A woman does not feel whole without a man. And for a woman who had known the joys of marriage, yes, it was hard. It was years before I awakened without that longing for a face pressed against my breast, an arm about my shoulder. The sense of loss was there. It was a price I had paid.[40]

She also felt tensions between her obligations to her daughter and the needs of the communities in which they lived. Yet Day brought her experience as a mother and her sense of the holiness of family into her public work. She portrayed the Catholic Worker communities as her family: "I am a mother, and the mother of a very large family at that. Being a mother is fulfillment, it is surrender to others, it is Love and therefore of course it is suffering."[41] The irony was that Day spent her whole life building community and yet was, still, a victim of the long loneliness.

The Grail Movement

It is no surprise that Dorothy Day participated in a Grail workshop in 1943 and delighted in the rhythm of liturgy and work that was part of the Grail formation. The Catholic Worker and the Grail movement were both embodiments of the new Catholic Action, and both integrated prayer and apostolic work. Day reportedly said after two weeks at the Grail workshop with her daughter, Tamar: "We have learned to meditate *and* bake bread, pray *and* extract honey, sing *and* make butter, cheese, cider, wine, and sauerkraut."[42]

As can be seen from Day's comment, the Grail was a rural program that emphasized the domestic vocation. Until the 1960s, Grail leaders strongly taught that women and men had complementary natures and vocations. Women's rising employment outside the home actually endangered their true mission; indeed, the laywomen's public mission required a return to the domestic vocation. The story is complex, however, for at the same time the Grail was sending single women off to be foreign missionaries. And, in the 1960s and 1970s, the movement would do a major turnaround, embracing feminist thought and becoming an ecumenical center for women's liberation, spiritual growth, and social transformation.

The Dutch Jesuit priest Jacques van Ginneken began the Grail movement in the Netherlands in 1921. Two Dutch laywomen, Lydwine van Kersbergen and Joan Overboss, boarded a ship to carry the movement to the United States in 1940. The Grail headquartered first at Doddridge Farm outside Chicago and later at Grailville near Loveland, Ohio. It reached about fourteen thousand women by the early 1960s.[43]

The Grail formed young women apostles through a deep immersion in the liturgy, farm and domestic work, and theological discussion. Young single women traveled to Grailville for summer programs and retreats; many came from decidedly nonrural locations such as Brooklyn. The Grail encouraged active participation in the liturgy and incorporated the dialogue Mass, offertory processions, and congregational singing into its liturgies.[44] It promoted liturgical renewal and the idea of the church as the Mystical Body of Christ. Leaders emphasized the connections between the liturgy and the women's work. The quasi-monastic rhythm of life was intended to inspire women to go out and infuse secular culture with a deep Christian spirit. This was an approach very much in the spirit of the retreat. Spiritual formation happened in settings separated from the rhythm of the women's normal daily lives. It should be noted that the Grail has been called "romantic" and "otherworldly."[45]

In its early period from the founding of Grailville in 1944 to the early 1960s, Grail leaders promoted an interesting mix of progressivism and conservativism as regards women. On the one hand, the Grail trained laywomen for active apostolates, including professional service in ministry abroad. Women were called to be "apostles," "co-offerers of the Holy Sacrifice of the Mass," and "lay priests [sharing] in Christ's mission as prophet and teacher." Grail leader Janet Kalven stated that "confirmation is a kind of ordination," which represents "a real sharing in the priesthood of Christ." Kalven's thought was influenced by Fr. Martin Hellriegel's charge to Grail members not to be "pious goody-goodies," but rather to be "women with intelligence and holy impertinence ... women with vision and radical conviction ... who are determined to live on principle twenty-four hours a day."[46]

At the same time, the Grail upheld traditional notions of female virtue and taught women that their apostolate should be centered primarily in the home. Women possessed a fundamentally different nature from men, as complementary nature. As van Ginneken put it, women were meant

> to counterbalance in the world all masculine hardness, all the angles of masculine character, all cruelty, all the results of alcoholism and prostitution and capitalism, which are ultra masculine, and to Christianize that with a womanly charity.[47]

Janet Kalven concurred. Women's "real career" was as wife and mother; business and other professional work should be temporary at best. Feminism was destroying the differences between the sexes, and hence impeding the needed reconstruction of the social order. It was misguided "to think as women that we must be in the forefront of public affairs, politics, or business to influence the course of the world." Rather, as wives and mothers, women could pass on cultural and religious traditions and inspire men through their love.[48]

Confronted with a trend toward secularization, women had a special mission. According to van Kersbergen, "woman has a unique opportunity to exercise a redeeming influence. But she must first recover her own fundamental spiritual orientation. If she returns to the deep wells of the spirit, she will find again the power of surrender to draw down grace upon the world."[49] Hence, women's public role depended on a spirituality of surrender and receptivity. Van Kersbergen lifted up Mary as the model of the spiritual woman: receptive and redeeming.

Grail leaders taught that the denigration of women's true role and nature adversely affected the family. They promoted a spirituality of family life that asserted women's vocation in the home and that incorporated the family into the understanding of the church as the Mystical Body of Christ. Hence, the ecclesiology so influential in the Grail's liturgical practice was translated into the woman's vocation: "The family is a little church, the Mystical Body in miniature. Hence it should act like a cell of the Mystical Body."[50] At least for women, the home was the locus of spirituality. Here was lay church; here was women's means of social transformation. This is the domestic church, which we will see elevated years later at the Second Vatican Council.

The Second Vatican Council deeply influenced the Grail, leading to a participative style of leadership within the organization and a heightened ecumenical sensitivity. In 1969 the Grail General Assembly offered membership to Protestant women. United Methodist minister Barbara Troxell; Claire Randall, former executive secretary of the National Council of Churches; and Nancy Richardson, founder of the Women's Theological Center in Boston, became members. The Grail welcomed Jewish women in the 1970s. The feminist movement also profoundly shaped the Grail, a huge shift from the movement's earlier teachings of complementarity. The Grail would come to define itself as "an education and conference center offering programs relating to ecology, spirituality, feminism, the arts, and social justice . . . an international movement of women in 20 countries working for social transformation."[51]

The Christian Family Movement

The Christian Family Movement emerged in the Midwest in the mid-1940s, became an international movement, and claimed about fifty thousand American members by its peak in the early 1960s. It was a staunchly lay, urban and suburban, middle-class couple's movement. According to the CFM philosophy, the way to facilitate Christian family life was to sanctify the environment, to empower laity to fulfill their vocation in the world. It was a powerful effort to integrate private and public spiritual spaces through a specific method of spiritual formation. In the end, however, as the movement became more and more engaged in controversial public issues and more ecumenically oriented, it splintered and membership plummeted.

Like Young Christian Workers and Young Christian Students, the Christian Family Movement arose out of Catholic Action group meetings and followed the Cardijn observe-judge-act method (also called see-judge-act). Joseph Cardijn (1882–1967) was a Belgian priest (later made cardinal) who developed this inquiry technique in which small groups met and systematically observed and analyzed their environment, judged it in light of the gospels, and then acted in a concrete way to bring the environment more in line with the gospels. This reoriented laity; it grounded them in Scripture and taught them to think theologically about the tradition and concrete issues in their social context. The Cardijn method required empirical study, theological reflection, and concrete action.

Cardijn was appalled by the religious alienation felt by European workers. He sought to win them back to the church and to bring the church into the everyday life of the masses (not just the elite). In effect, Cardijn critiqued religious liberalism, which privatized and sanitized faith. This "apostasy" deceived Catholics into abandoning the working classes. Cardijn instead described religion as "a whole life which, like the host, should be consecrated to God." The Young Christian Worker movement, which he founded after World War I, would "Christianize the entire secular life in its individual as well as its social dimensions."[52]

Cardijn understood the work of the layperson to be an integral part of the work of the church, the Mystical Body of Christ. He saw the Mystical Body to be a profoundly unifying and transforming reality that posits no distinction between the human and the Christian. In a 1951 speech, Cardijn stated: "The lay apostolate does not create a new Church, it does not introduce new structures into the Church, it does not confide a new mission to the Church in the world. The Church and the lay apostolate are not two separate things. The apostolate of the laity is the vocation both Christian and human of the laity in the Church and in the world."[53]

Several American priests, including Donald Kanaly, Louis Putz, Jack Egan, and Reynold Hillenbrand, introduced the see-judge-act method in the United States in the late 1930s; it quickly became popular with specialized Catholic Action groups. This was a like-to-like apostolate, a kind of peer group spiritual guidance and practical theological reflection. The model would expand into lay movements of students (Young Christian Students) and families (Christian Family Movement). One former member of the YCW wrote that the Cardijn method

> cannot be equaled as a method of spiritual formation. By always observing our environment in the light of the gospels and assuming responsibility to act as Christians in that environment, we learned or acquired habits and convictions and a way of life that would not leave us.... It can form individual consciences and those individuals will affect those around them throughout their lives—families, neighbors, co-workers.[54]

Regina Weissert, a Christian Family Movement member since 1947, said that CFM formed people to be "both spiritually and socially aware." It changed their whole orientation and made them more reflective about their faith life: "Prayers did not have to be by rote. We had more of a sense of lay vocation."[55]

The Christian Family Movement evolved in the early 1940s when groups in South Bend and Chicago began applying the Cardijn method to groups of couples. Pat and Patty Crowley, together with Helene and Burnie Bauer, launched the new movement nationally in 1949. In its beginning years, CFM groups focused more directly on family concerns, yet turned to more controversial social issues in the 1950s and 1960s. CFM leaders saw this outward turn as facilitating a truly lay spirituality for families, enabling them to bear witness to Christ in their concrete social environments.

Like other lay movements of this period, CFM was influenced by the idea of the church as the Mystical Body of Christ. Hillenbrand, a guiding force for CFM as for YCW, expressed the implications of this model of the church for lay spirituality. His words became a slogan for the CFM as he called on laity to be the hands, feet, eyes, lips, and heart of Christ. Indeed, CFM leaders connected the Mystical Body of Christ ecclesiology to a social mission (as did Dorothy Day), seen here in a call for racial justice: "If charity is the bond that unites Christians, racial injustice and hatred are the greatest evils. They tear the Body of Christ apart."[56] Some criticized CFM for emphasizing the environment and social action and neglecting the interior life. Yet CFM did promote personal prayer and active participation in the liturgy, which would increase one's understanding of one's role in the Mystical Body of Christ.

A typical meeting began with opening prayer and a thirty-minute Scripture-Liturgy before proceeding to the social inquiry. The see-judge-act method was a prayerful way of analyzing the social environment, reflecting theologically, and seeking change through a small, concrete act. CFM sought to integrate traditional religious practices with the layperson's work in the world. Indeed, CFM emphasized that lay spirituality was deeply *worldly*. While prayer was important, it could not be separated from action. Actually, the lay perspective correlated with a certain view of God. Just as the layperson was active in the world, so too was God. A CFM couple wrote that to attain the "perfection of God," one must be active as "the life of God is ceaseless, infinite activity."[57]

The basic unit or cell of CFM consisted of six couples and a chaplain who met twice a month. The Christian Family Movement was fairly decentralized; each cell met separately and decided on its own actions. Yet there was an overall structure and a national newsletter, *ACT*. While the Crowleys worked closely with Monsignor Hillenbrand and other clergy, CFM remained a movement of and for the laity.

Each year, CFM took up a different issue. Leaders gradually propelled CFM more and more into serious social and international concerns. Membership declined sharply by the late 1960s. The decline resulted in part from leaders' focus on controversial public issues such as civil rights (to be discussed in the next chapter), rather than on more private concerns of family life. At the 1961 national convention, Monsignor George Kelly, family life director of the Archdiocese of New York, sharply criticized the social focus of the CFM leadership: "Some theorists have downgraded CFM as a family organization and have sought to make married couples primarily responsible for the reconstruction of society."[58] Membership in CFM also waned as it became increasingly ecumenical. The Crowleys' public opposition to *Humanae Vitae* estranged them from church hierarchy, and this too likely led to breakdown. CFM also may have lost ground due to its sponsorship of Marriage Encounter, imported by CFM from Spain in 1966. Unlike its operation in other nations, Marriage Encounter in the United States split off from CFM and captured some of CFM's support, particularly those who gravitated away from the more public focus of CFM and sought more attention to the interior dynamics of marriage and the development of greater intimacy. The Crowleys continued to insist that good dialogue within groups of couples was not enough; couples had to move beyond themselves and act on behalf of the community.[59]

Seeking Integrity

While the Christian Family Movement sought to improve the social environment and hence the family, *Integrity* magazine arose in 1946 with a far more radical, sectarian position. The lay Catholic—through the family—carried the awesome task of Christianizing a pagan society. Founders and co-editors Ed Willock and Carol Jackson insisted on the distinctiveness of the Christian life and the evil of American capitalist culture. If a Catholic looked closely enough at his work and the whole economic system, "he would come to grips with the enemy that is stalemating the apostolate. He would see all this seething activity of our daily lives as a huge tornado spinning and, at its center, the soul of man sitting in immobility."[60]

The only solution was to work toward a radically new social order that preexists in the mind of God.

Jackson was a convert to Catholicism, a Wellesley graduate inspired by Catholic Action. Willock had been a Catholic Worker in Worcester, Massachusetts, and he carried a Worker personalist philosophy to *Integrity* magazine. Society would be transformed family by family. Like other lay leaders, Jackson and Willock gravitated to the Mystical Body of Christ ecclesiology. Yet whereas Dorothy Day used this vision of the church as an inclusive metaphor, *Integrity* saw it as the new world order, a superimposition of the church on the world. Jackson anticipated that "the Mystical Body will be coterminous with the human race."[61]

Integrity perceived a divide in modern society between religion and the rest of life. It sought to forge "a new synthesis of religion and life," to restore "the integration of the natural and supernatural orders."[62] An author described laypersons' artificial separation of these two orders, "a separation of their sacramental lives from their daily lives and work," as "the true contemporary schizophrenia."[63] The editors understood integrity as wholeness, a unity of public and private. This was the holiness toward which laypersons should strive:

> Integral Catholicism is already becoming a popular expression. It does not mean piety so much as wholeness. It means that what we profess to believe is consistent with the assumed principles by which we live out our daily lives. It suggests a consistency of theory and practice; a unity of public life and private morals; a reconciliation of commercial ethics and religious dogma, of individual conscience and statutory law.... The relationship between "wholeness" and "holiness" is as direct as the derivation of the second word from the first. It becomes daily more difficult to lead holy lives in disregard of the contradictory nature of the circumstances thereof.[64]

Integrity sharply criticized contemporary American society as "an indifferent brutal age."[65] The family—a primary sphere of lay activity—would be a key force in the radical transformation of society. Like several other lay movements, *Integrity* magazine arose in the post–World War II concern for family. Willock and Jackson taught that both spiritual growth and the good of the public order depended on the holiness of the family: "Every issue of *Integrity* is a family issue. All the ideas pertaining to the reintegration of religion and life directly concern the family, for next to the salvation of souls, there is no task more important than the holiness of the family."[66] As Ed Willock explained, to improve society one had to better each individual within the family, and each family within the society.[67] Families bore a responsibility for the common good: "Any individual within the society who seeks his own good or his family's profit, apart from the common good, is an enemy of that society."[68]

Integrity sharply denounced birth control. Birth control was one of the evils of the age, an unnatural accommodation to materialist, individualistic culture. While Jackson never married, Willock and his wife raised twelve children on precarious amounts of income. In fact, they joined with several other couples to build the Marycrest community in rural New York in the 1950s. This was a wildly utopian venture, aiming at a Christian community of fertile families that adhered to voluntary poverty. The families built the homes themselves, twelve in all by the late 1950s. As historian James Fisher writes: "Fertility was the community's most conspicuous sign of contradiction. . . . Marycrest made unplanned and prodigious reproduction the most visible sign of its antirationalist convictions."[69] The community stood against materialism, modernity, and worldly wisdom. With large numbers of children to feed, house, and protect, it also encapsulated the tensions within Christian spirituality. On the one hand, family life was elevated and dignified. On the other hand, the community retained an ideal of holiness most appropriate to monastic life, or to those without dependents.

Marycrest has been described as patriarchal. This fit with the views of Willock and Jackson, who saw the perversion of holy family life through the demise of traditional sex roles as another evil of the age. *Integrity* asserted male headship of the family and the woman's vocation as mother. Authors decried the "masculinization" of women, who increasingly took up public roles and abandoned their place in the home. Moreover, fathers' roles in the family seemed to be diminishing. Willock argued that the American family was "approaching a matriarchy" and that changing gender roles led to a feminization of Catholic spirituality:

The expression of the Faith today is primarily private devotion and not public apostolicity, and it is the former that appeals most to women, and the latter which appeals most to men. Even the parochial men's groups have taken on a feminine flavor hardly relieved by an occasional "Sport Nite."[70]

Authors proposed a traditional Marian spirituality as a way to restore appropriate gender roles: "Through the practice of Mary's most neglected virtues, modesty, humility, poverty, and silence, we can stage our small revolt on the modern perversion of woman's status."[71]

Integrity author Elizabeth Sheehan illustrates the magazine's typical understanding of gender roles. Like Dorothy Day, Sheehan described the terrible loneliness that afflicted women. Yet unlike Day, who esteemed family life but also found her vocation in public mission, Sheehan saw marriage as the only vocation for women and the only relief from loneliness:

> Why is this paralyzing loneliness so widespread among women of our time? Perhaps it is because so many of us sometimes do not realize in time that while a career may demand all our strength, time, talents and endurance, only a vocation can possess the heart.
>
> And it is just this which we, as women, long above all to give. God in His Providence, while bestowing upon man and woman similar intellectual powers, did not give woman that special drive which enables man to continue putting the things of the mind in first place. This blessed shortcoming of women is what has always held Christian homes together, developed religious vocations, and brought saints into the world.
>
> For this reason, and because they find it more difficult to approach God directly, most women find the solace to their peculiar loneliness and the pathway to salvation in the vocation of marriage.[72]

New editor Dorothy Dohen liberalized *Integrity* after 1952. The magazine relaxed its emphasis on women's private domestic role, allowing for more public participation. More strikingly, the magazine softened its position on birth control. *Integrity* had a short history;

it died in 1956. It reached a readership of about ten thousand at its most popular.

Opus Dei

Like many other lay movements, the Opus Dei ("work of God") movement clearly called for laypeople to integrate their faith and their work. Opus Dei, however, did not share the negative view of capitalist society that characterized the Catholic Worker and *Integrity* magazine. Rather, the group cultivated an elite corps of lay professionals to bring faith into public life. While Opus Dei emphasized lay spirituality, it maintained a hierarchical structure and kept the laity in close cooperation with priests and religious. Opus Dei has been seen as "a convergence of two historic developments: the development of the movements of lay apostolates and the development of the movements of spirituality of the religious and the priests."[73] Its public focus was clear, its appreciation for family life more ambiguous—at least in its early days.

Opus Dei combined orthodox Catholicism with fervent advocacy of the lay vocation. The group presented a model of lay spirituality that was closely tied to hierarchical church authority and traditional Catholic piety. Its founder was a Spanish priest (later a Monsignor), Josemaría Escrivá. While Escrivá continually distinguished his group from the religious, its juridical status (a "secular institute" from 1947 to 1982 and a "personal prelature of the Catholic Church" from 1982 to the present) distinguished it from other lay apostolates. And while members clearly focused their ministry in the world, a core group of members lived together in community (which they called "family"), committed themselves to celibacy, and upheld the virtue of obedience. Opus Dei was a kind of secular institute that required "total consecration" of its members' lives to "the acquisition of perfection . . . and total and complete dedication to the apostolate."[74] While one entering a secular institute did not become a religious, still the model of perfection "clearly is very distant from the mere secular state."[75]

Critics have denounced what they see as the controlling aspects of Opus Dei. Opus Dei asserted that its members are free—freely obedient. Clearly, Escrivá encouraged obedience as a path to holiness: "Obedience, the sure way. Blind obedience to your superior, the way of sanctity. Obedience in your apostolate, the only way: for, in a work of God, the spirit must be to obey or to leave."[76] The layperson is subject to error and therefore must obey the judgment of a superior, who possesses special grace from God.[77] Escrivá insisted that laypeople cannot love God or the church if they do not revere clergy. Both in the thought of its founder and in its later modus operandi, then, Opus Dei represents a model of lay spirituality that defends the teaching authority of the church and Opus Dei's own hierarchical leadership, in contrast to some other lay movements that distanced themselves more from or directly challenged church authority.

Opus Dei in fact may well illustrate both the Protestantization of Catholicism and a resurgence of religious grounding for economic pursuits that has been lost in Protestantism. One sociologist wrote, "the fundamental parallel between 'Protestant ethic' and 'Opus ethic' is more than justified."[78] Opus Dei members are enjoined to exercise leadership in the secular world, particularly in economic, political, and intellectual life. Opus Dei joins its traditional Catholicism with a recovery of the idea of worldly vocation typical of the Protestant reformers. This is a fascinating aspect of the movement; it looks quite Protestant from certain angles, and yet it remains definitively within a traditional Roman Catholic theological and ecclesiastical framework.

Escrivá founded Opus Dei in 1928 in Spain. From its beginnings the group aimed to sanctify lay work in the world. Escrivá presented professional life as an apostolate and a means of sanctification, warned against idleness, and extolled the virtues of order, perseverance, and leadership. His book *The Way* was published in 1939, shortly after the end of the Spanish Civil War. It encouraged study, daring, professional ambition, and achievement. Yet Escrivá knew the spiritual dangers that could accompany these goals. The professional apostolate must serve Christ, not self-glorification. When done in a spirit of service, humility, and "holy shamelessness," work in the world was a means of sanctifying both others and oneself: "When you are engrossed in professional work, the life of your soul will improve." Discipleship can begin right in the midst of secular work: "What amazes you seems quite natural to me: God has sought you out right in the midst of your work. That is how he sought the first, Peter and Andrew, John and James, beside their nets, and Matthew, sitting in the custom house."[79] Work was an opportunity to meet Christ.[80]

As Opus Dei emerged, it combined a traditional Catholic piety with an emphasis on the sanctity of lay work in the world. Escrivá maintained the importance of the Eucharist, the rosary, novenas, and the daily use of holy water. While active work was important, he wrote in *The Way*: "I'll tell you that your apostolic life is worth only as much as your prayer." Members were encouraged to attend daily Mass. The apostolic life "must be the 'overflow' of your life 'within.' " The interior life directs one's work, so that it does not become a misguided reinforcement of one's own ego: "What a pity if in the end you had carried out *your* apostolate and not *his* apostolate."[81]

Opus Dei originally focused more on the integration of faith and work, with family being a peripheral concern. The group admitted only unmarried persons from 1928 to 1948. Some of Escrivá's writings relegate marriage and parenting to an inferior status. *The Way* states, for example, that marriage is "for the rank and file, not for the officers of Christ's army.... A desire to have children? Behind us we shall leave children—many children... and a lasting trail of light, if we sacrifice the selfishness of the flesh." On the other hand, Escrivá refers to the "vocation" of marriage and repeats the church's teaching that marriage is a "holy sacrament." Yet clearly *The Way* does not offer a positive view of sexuality; Escrivá calls the body "a treacherous enemy" and "an enemy of your sanctification."[82] Purity and chastity are indispensable spiritual values.

Opus Dei also has been accused of subjugating women. Some critics, including former Opus Dei members, allege that women within the organization are relegated to housekeeping roles for the men. Escrivá's own writing reveals problematic attitudes toward women. It is true that in a rare reference to women in *The Way*, he writes: "We cannot disdain the cooperation of women in the apostolate." Yet the book primarily promotes a masculine, even machismo, spirituality which may reflect Opus Dei's Spanish roots. Escrivá exhorts the reader to "Be a man!" and to "Let your prayer be manly. To be a child does not mean to be effeminate."[83]

Opus Dei expanded internationally from 1947 to 1958. It reached the United States in 1949, when Escrivá sent a priest and a young physicist to Chicago to establish the group. They opened Wood-lawn Residence, a student residence near the University of Chicago. Several Opus Dei women came to the United States in 1950 and opened another residence in Chicago. In the United States the group's apostolic works focused primarily on education and spiritual development.

Conclusion

These lay movements all strove toward a new social order pen-etrated by the spirit of the gospels, and they saw laypersons as indispensable architects of this new order. Laypersons were gaining a voice; they said that their Christian life called them into the world. They said that their mission was not merely to support the work of church hierarchy, but that they had a distinct role to play. These movements do not represent the many Catholics whose religiousness continued to find expression primarily in the prescribed disciplines of the church and parish activities, that majority of Catholics re-ferred to as "praying, paying, and obeying." Yet the lay movements prepared the way for a more vocal and active laity, and indeed for the new emphases of the Second Vatican Council.

The movements may point contemporary Christians to a new sense of public mission. Despite their many differences, these laity sensed their mission in the world. They were fired up with the pos-sibility that they could pray and work in very intentional ways, that they were the church, indeed, that their lives could be holy. This spirituality arose in a particular context, of course, and we cannot recreate that context. Nor would I want to recapture the hostile views of American society held by groups such as the *In-tegrity* staff (although a more critical and counter-cultural stance may be needed today for a thoroughly assimilated church), nor the restrictive views of women's vocation promoted by *Integrity*, the Grail, and Opus Dei. Yet it is critical to recover the sense of voca-tion and the integrative impulse expressed by the pre–Vatican II lay movements.

How can contemporary Christians be formed with this vocational sense? I would recommend that we recover the Cardijn method, an excellent model of spiritual formation and practical theological reflection. Moreover, the Mystical Body of Christ ecclesiology provides a scriptural image that gives dignity to a variety of gifts, provides a way of living unity-in-diversity (and hence responding positively to pluralism while retaining identity), and offers a concrete image of an intimate union with Christ and the incarnate mission of the People of God. I will explore these points further in the final chapter of this book.

– Chapter Two –

THE CALL OF THE PUBLIC SPHERE

Authentic Spirituality or Secular Drift?

F ROM THE GRAIL TO *Integrity,* Catholic Worker to *Common-weal,* lay movements of the pre–Vatican II era strove for a new social order penetrated by the gospels. Laity would be architects of this new order. Prayer, the liturgy, and ecclesial identity grounded the public ventures of these movements. As American Catholics moved into the 1960s, their world changed dramatically. The church itself underwent enormous transformation through the Second Vatican Council (1962–65). Rapid changes in American culture coincided. The landscape had shifted, and laity faced new questions about faith, public life, secularity, and pluralism.

John F. Kennedy's bid for president in 1960 brought to the fore questions about the role of faith in American public life. Ironically, Kennedy's election secured the place of Catholics in the American public sphere even as he relegated faith to the private sphere. Meanwhile, the Second Vatican Council did spring cleaning on the church, opening up the windows of the church to the modern world. As it confronted secularity, it gave new emphasis to the holiness of the lay vocation in the world. New openness to pluralism, influenced strongly by the American Jesuit John Courtney Murray, further made it possible for Catholics to find a public place in American democracy. In many ways, the Second Vatican Council gave the theological rationales for a public spirituality. And the public world called frighteningly, insistingly. This was a decade of enormous social upheaval—the civil rights movement, the Vietnam War, race riots, violent student protests, the assassinations of John F. Kennedy, Dr. Martin Luther King, and Robert Kennedy.

The pull of the secular world and pluralistic engagement created tremendous crises of identity for laity. Under fire in the presidential campaign, Kennedy relinquished the public claims of faith. In the late 1960s, *Commonweal* editor Daniel Callahan fought unsuccessfully to broaden the magazine's identity—and then departed for a secular career. Christian Family Movement leaders pushed members to engage in the civil rights movement, and then to become ecumenical, only to see membership drop. On the other hand, Cesar Chavez and the United Farm Workers movement seemed better able to negotiate public life while retaining a sense of religious identity. Chavez publicly integrated religious practices such as fasting, pilgrimage, and the celebration of the Mass into a political campaign. Yet even his movement encountered internal divisions about the place of religion. The confusion about the public place of faith in an increasingly secular, pluralistic America hit hard.

Kennedy's Run for the Presidency

John F. Kennedy's bid for president in 1960 sparked a heated conversation about the relationship between faith and the public sphere. Catholics had come a long way. Economically and socially, they had moved into the American mainstream. Kennedy himself came from a wealthy, politically connected family. He had not gone to Catholic schools; he had attended Harvard University. Still, it was unclear whether the country could abide a Catholic in the highest office of the land. Would his loyalty be first to Rome? Would Catholic doctrine dictate his political decisions? Even in 1960, *Time* magazine reported: "A great many Americans still see their Catholic fellow citizens as vaguely alien and as narrow-minded servants of an absolutist theology."[1]

With these questions plaguing him, and with the legacy of Alfred Smith's 1928 defeat trailing along, Kennedy swiftly moved to allay any concerns about his religious convictions. In a 1959 interview in the magazine *Look*, Kennedy asserted his support of a strict separation between church and state, which takes precedence over any religious convictions the politician might hold "in his private life."[2] In a speech before a convention of Houston ministers, he proclaimed his belief in "an America where the separation of church and state is absolute. . . . I believe in a President whose religious views are his own private affair."[3] He would make decisions on the basis of "public interest, without regard to my private religious views."[4] He did not seek to integrate his faith and his work; rather, he was, in the words of Gary Wills, "the champion compartmentalizer."[5] Kennedy implied that faith was a purely private matter. He won the election, and the first American Catholic president took the oath of office. Yet not all Christians agreed with the way he banished his faith from the public arena. His candidacy sparked a wider debate about the role of faith in public life.

Commonweal magazine saw this debate as critical. In many ways, Kennedy's position went against the central convictions of the magazine. *Commonweal* billed itself as a review of "public affairs, literature, and the arts" which sought to "express a point of view on temporal matters in conformity with [the editors'] religious principles.... In the light of their religious beliefs, the editors see the temporal order as being directly related to the spiritual, and their day-to-day judgments reflect this conviction."[6] Editors called Kennedy's strictly personal understanding of religion "unnecessarily simple." Kennedy did not address the many possible interpretations of constitutional questions; he thus equated a secularist position with the "American way." He implicitly accepted the assumption that a Catholic position on public issues would be difficult to reconcile with American political values. Moreover, Kennedy did not counter the argument that there was a single "Catholic position" on these questions. *Commonweal* asserted: "Senator Kennedy should have made the elementary point that there is no 'Catholic position' on these matters, that they are not doctrinally religious questions at all, merely points of Constitutional interpretation and practical judgment, on which Catholics are perfectly free to disagree and on which they often do disagree."[7] This distinction between doctrine and practical reason will continue to be an important issue for laity as this story unfolds.

Other Catholic editors also objected to Kennedy's strict separation of public life and faith. Some felt that he had bent over backward to appease bigots. An editorial in *America* magazine stated:

> We were somewhat taken aback, for instance, by the unvarnished statement that "whatever one's religion in his private life

...nothing takes precedence over his oath...." Mr. Kennedy doesn't really believe that. No religious man, be he Catholic, Protestant, or Jew, holds such an opinion. A man's conscience has a bearing on his public as well as his private life.[8]

Ave Maria asserted: "To relegate your conscience to your 'private life' is not only unrealistic, but dangerous as well. It is dangerous because it leads to secularism in public life."[9]

In the midst of this debate, a group of Catholic laity publicly expressed their commitment to both religious freedom and public involvement. Catholics should not be sectarian, but as individuals they have a right to bring their faith into their actions as American citizens. In a statement released a month before the 1960 election, the group asserted:

> In his public acts as they affect the whole community the Catholic is bound in conscience to promote the common good and to avoid any seeking of a merely sectarian advantage.... It is as individual citizens and office holders, not as a religious bloc, that we make the specific application of these principles in political life. Here we function not as "Catholic citizens," but as citizens who are Catholics.[10]

Clearly, Kennedy's comments raised concerns among Catholics. They also did not completely allay the fears of Protestants. The evangelical magazine *Christianity Today,* along with the Southern Baptists and the National Association of Evangelicals, continued to raise questions about "Roman Catholicism's notorious incursion into political arenas for sectarian benefit."[11] The magazine complained about a press that presented only mediating or liberal positions while denigrating the "traditional Protestant position."[12] In one respect *Christianity Today* had much in common with *America* and *Ave Maria,* for the evangelical editors also deplored the "widening public judgment that all religion is irrelevant to political attitudes and acts." *Christianity Today* did not endorse a public sphere stripped of all faith but did retain the right to evaluate the truth of any religion in the public sphere. Pluralism need not mean a tolerance devoid of normative claims: "The American mentality rapidly is losing any distinction of true versus false religion, and is dismissing this contrast as based on unbrotherliness and intolerance."[13] They criticized Protestant leaders for acquiescing in this mentality.

Despite his assertions about the private nature of faith, Kennedy's election as president actually fed a more public spirituality. Kennedy became a symbol that Catholics had made it in America. With Kennedy in the highest public office in America, Catholics could see a public vocation as a real possibility and even an ideal. Yet the question remained: Was Kennedy's approach to faith and his political career a good model for the lay Christian?

John Courtney Murray and a Shift in Catholic Thought

In the same year that Kennedy was elected the first Roman Catholic president of the United States, *Time* magazine featured an American Jesuit named John Courtney Murray on its cover. Murray had published his important book *We Hold These Truths* that same year. In many ways, Murray orchestrated an Americanization of Roman Catholic thinking on religious freedom and pluralism, a shift that would bear fruit at the Second Vatican Council's. Murray's thought arose out of his struggle to relate the American, democratic, pluralistic public sphere with traditional Catholicism. The result was a vision of the relation between faith and public life that could both preserve the integrity of the American system and ground a public Christian spirituality. Murray proposed a public model subtly different from that of Kennedy.

In 1864 Pope Pius IX had issued a sweeping condemnation of modernity and democracy. The *Syllabus of Errors* denounced religious toleration and proclaimed: "Error has no rights." A century later, the Second Vatican Council "Declaration on Religious Freedom" (*Dignitatis Humanae*) asserted that both believers and nonbelievers had a right to religious liberty. What accounts for this dramatic shift in the Catholic response to pluralism? One profound influence was the thought of John Courtney Murray (1904–67). For nearly thirty years Murray wrote extensively on the relation between church and society. His arguments for religious liberty and the separation of church and state provoked concern among church authorities. Rome and the Jesuit order silenced him in the mid-

1950s. He obeyed the order, ceasing publication on this topic for years. Eventually, though, his arguments gained favor and shaped the teachings of the Second Vatican Council.

Murray argued that limited government helps to preserve human freedom. He bases both limited government and religious liberty in the "Gelasian principle," a radical Christian distinction between sacred and secular. In 494 C.E., Pope Gelasius I wrote to the Byzantine emperor Anastasius I: "Two there are, august Emperor, by which this world is ruled on title of original and sovereign right—the consecrated authority of the priesthood and the royal power." While medieval popes may have tried to be theocrats and the emerging nation-states subsumed the church, the Christian tradition in principle rejects monism. Secular powers cannot reach into the sacred, transcendent world. Murray made an important distinction between "state" and "society." He argued emphatically that the state has no competence in matters religious. He acknowledged that the state can intervene when religious liberty infringes on the "public order." Generally, however, the state has specific tasks that are far more narrow than the goals of society as a whole. Society extends well beyond the state, which is a limited entity entrusted with the preservation of public order.

Murray's influence can be seen in this text of Vatican II:

It is of supreme importance, especially in a pluralistic society, to work out a proper vision of the relationship between the political community and the Church, and to distinguish clearly between the activities of Christians, acting individually or collectively in their own name as citizens guided by the dictates of a Christian conscience, and their activity along with their pastors in the name of the Church.

The Church, by reason of her role and competence, is not identified with any political community nor bound by ties to any political system. It is at once the sign and the safeguard of the transcendental dimension of the human person.

The political community and the Church are autonomous and independent of each other in their own fields.[14]

Murray's arguments for religious liberty depended on his distinctions between church and state and between sacred and secular. The government simply does not have competence in matters religious. Similarly, "the Church has no secular arm."[15] This is a striking comment with enormous implications for the place of religion in public life. Murray was walking a fine line which risks pushing religious institutions into contained private spaces. Yet he did not intend to privatize religion, nor to secularize public life.

As a political right, religious liberty provides immunity from government coercion in religious affairs. Persons have the freedom to believe and the freedom to act, including action in the public sphere. While Murray keeps the state out of religious matters, he retains a broader sense of public space in which religion may thrive. So too did the Second Vatican Council. The "Declaration on Religious Freedom," for example, asserts: "Also included in the right to religious freedom is the right of religious groups not to be prevented from freely demonstrating the special value of their teaching for the organization of society and the inspiration of all human activity."[16]

Indeed, Murray carved out a vision of the lay vocation that encouraged public, democratic engagement. He allowed for religious liberty and the separation of church and state without privatizing faith. Murray himself saw this connection as early as the 1940s: "But if the Church has definitively retired from politics, she has not bowed to the command of the liberals to retire to the sacristy. Her task of furthering the common good of mankind remains a necessary, if secondary, part of her saving mission.... The answer was an appeal and a command to the laity."[17] Murray affirmed the priesthood of all believers, with distinct tasks for ordained and lay. The "lay priesthood is to mediate the Christian spirit to the institutions of civil society."[18] Murray presented an alternative to Kennedy, a more nuanced vision of how religious faith can coexist with genuine engagement in a pluralistic public arena.

The Secular World: Spiritual Call or Threat?

Liberal Protestant theologian Harvey Cox called Kennedy the prototype of the urban-secular man, the ultimate pragmatist.[19] This was not meant as an insult. Cox set out a Christian vision of secularization in his popular book *The Secular City: Secularization and Urbanization in Theological Perspective,* published in 1965 as the

Second Vatican Council concluded its work. Cox argued that Christians should turn to this world and its problems, just as God does in the gift of Jesus Christ. He conceded that secularization can threaten traditional religion, divorcing religion from the public sphere and thus producing an overly privatized faith. Yet secularization also liberated people from religious domination and otherworldliness. Cox saw it as a process that promotes true Christianity and that can claim roots in the biblical faith. Cox approvingly called pluralism and tolerance "the children of secularization."[20]

Cox was not alone in his concern with secularization, although many interpreted the process less optimistically. Secularization clearly demanded theological evaluation. It was a spiritual issue. Would secularization mean the demise of faith—or the emergence of a freer, more authentic Christianity? If laity heeded the call of the Second Vatican Council to bring Christ to the world, what would sustain their faith there? Rev. William Clancy wrote:

> I fear that the average man in the latter part of the twentieth century will simply be bored with religion.... He will feel no interest in or need for it in his new, totally secular world. Can we so live and act and speak in such a world that our neighbor will see, and feel, the need for the Gospel? None of us knows the answer to this; but it is the question we must ask all the days of our lives.[21]

Conservative Catholics were dismayed to see clergy and religious embracing secularization. James Hitchcock writes: "The fact that priests and religious are, ironically, often more secularized than their lay counterparts reflects the very intensity with which religious elites confronted the changed ecclesiastical circumstances of the Vatican II era." Some lamented the decline in traditional Catholic piety in the wake of Vatican II. In fact, clergy, religious, and laity all were redefining the locus of spirituality, shifting from a "vertical" spirituality to a more "horizontal" faith: "The professionalization and specialization of ministries in the Catholic Church that occurred in the wake of the Council reinforced in those priests and sisters the momentum away from a vertical faith and toward a corresponding interest in public issues."[22]

Even more liberal Catholics conceded that a public focus could cause—or mask—deep spiritual problems. *Commonweal* associate editor Daniel Callahan saw underneath the call for relevance a deep hunger for greater personal connection to faith. Many laypersons really wanted the church to be more relevant to them in some very personal way, but expressed this desire as a social or political need: "Many people are, I am convinced, having deep personal problems about the nature of the Church, about their faith. There is a tendency to project these problems to the less unsettling level of social problems."[23] This was a time of confusion about the personal and social dimensions of faith. It was natural to seek connections between Christian belief and the urgent social problems of the day. Yet people of faith came out on different sides of, for example, the Vietnam War and desegregation. How define the authoritative social implications of Christianity? Was it faithful to assert a separation between church and world?

Spiritual gurus such as Thomas Merton encouraged a Christian public role in the secular arena:

> To choose the world is not then merely a pious admission that the world is acceptable because it comes from the hand of God. It is first of all an acceptance of a task and a vocation in the world, in history and in time. To choose the world is to choose to do the work I am capable of doing, in collaboration with my brother, to make the world better, more free, more just, more livable, more human.[24]

Merton asserted the unity of the personal and the social, the sacred and the secular, Christ and the world: "The world cannot be a problem to anyone who sees that ultimately Christ, the world, his brother and his own inmost ground are made one and the same in grace and redemptive love."[25] And yet the world was indeed a problem to Christian laity, as we will see.

Church Teachings Reevaluate Secular Life

The Second Vatican Council opened up the windows of the church to the modern world, particularly the questions of secularity and pluralism. The Council framed this task as a process of discernment: "At all times the Church carries the responsibility of reading the signs of the time and of interpreting them in the light of the Gospel, if it is to carry out its task."[26] Another passage states: "The people of God believes that it is led by the Spirit of the Lord who fills the whole world. Moved by that faith it tries to discern in the events, the needs, and the longings which it shares with other men of our time, what may be genuine signs of the presence or of the purpose of God."[27] Reading the signs of the times and interpreting them in light of the gospel is essential to the mission of the whole church. That larger task of discernment depends on another kind of discernment, one entrusted primarily to the teaching magisterium. For while the Holy Spirit gives various gifts to the People of God: "Those who have charge over the Church should judge the genuineness and proper use of these gifts, through their office not indeed to extinguish the Spirit, but to test all things and hold fast to what is good (cf. Th. 5:12 and 19–21)."[28]

Given the gifts of the Holy Spirit and guided by the church hierarchy, then, the laity were sent out to be church in the world. Indeed, the mission of the church in the secular world depended on the laity. The Council emphasized a more inclusive ecclesiology; the church was "the people of God." All were called to holiness. Laypersons did not lead a spiritually inferior life: "It is therefore quite clear that all Christians in any state or walk of life are called to the fullness of Christian life and to the perfection of love, and by this holiness a more human manner of life is fostered also in earthly society."[29] The laity by definition lived their faith in the midst of secular affairs. They were to be like yeast, dissolved into the whole society, invisibly yet powerfully causing it to rise: "The characteristic of the lay state being a life led in the midst of the world and of secular affairs, laymen are called by God to make of their apostolate, through the vigor of their Christian spirit, a leaven in the world."[30]

The Second Vatican Council asserted that the lay apostolate in the world needed to be nourished by active participation in the liturgy, "for it is the primary and indispensable source from which the faithful are to derive the true Christian spirit."[31] The Council replaced the Latin Mass with the vernacular Mass, for example, to encourage laypeople to participate more directly. Hearing the Mass in a language they could understand, it was thought, would deepen laypersons' spirituality.

The liturgy would send out the laity to the world, which was their sphere of mission. The Second Vatican Council strongly affirmed the worldly mission of the laity, both in public spaces and in the domestic church. Laypersons could transform the world and help usher in the kingdom of God:

> Hence the laity, dedicated as they are to Christ and anointed by the Holy Spirit, are marvellously called and prepared so that even richer fruits of the Spirit may be produced in them. For all their works, prayers, and apostolic undertakings, family and married life, daily work, relaxation of mind and body, if they are accomplished in the Spirit... all these become spiritual sacrifices acceptable to God through Jesus Christ (cf. 1 Pet. 2:5).[32]

Papal writings in the early 1960s also emphasized the importance of public roles. Pope John XXIII reminded the laity of their duty to take an active part in public life. He affirmed women's increasing roles in the public sphere as consonant with natural dignity and human rights.[33] Work was a religious endeavor, necessary to help ensure that economic, social, cultural, and political institutions facilitate, rather than impede, human perfection both in the natural and the supernatural order. While faith and good will are important, the pragmatic pontiff noted that technical skill also is essential: "no one can insinuate himself into public life unless he be scientifically competent, technically capable, and skilled in the practice of his own profession."[34] This was an important church affirmation of the value of specific lay competencies.

Moreover, these worldly competencies were integrally related with spiritual values. For society itself is a spiritual reality, not a distraction from the religious:

> We must think of human society as being primarily a spiritual reality. By its means enlightened men can share their knowledge of the truth, can claim their rights and fulfill their duties, receive encouragement in their aspirations for the goods of the spirit, share their enjoyment of all the wholesome pleasures of the world, and strive continually to pass on to others all that is best in themselves and to make their own the spiri-

tual riches of others. It is these spiritual values which exert a guiding influence on culture, economics, social institutions, political movements and forms, laws, and all the other components which go to make up the external community of men and its continual development.[35]

Work in the world, then, is a spiritual endeavor aiming to shape society toward its ideal. Work also can perfect the individual. It is a means of spiritual formation: "That a man should develop and perfect himself through his daily work—which in most cases is of a temporal character—is perfectly in keeping with the plan of divine Providence."[36]

Secular Work, Teilhard de Chardin, and Harvey Cox

However, Harvey Cox offered a cautionary word. While the Second Vatican Council spoke of the sanctity of secular work, Cox warned that people too easily idolize our jobs. He critiqued the devotion to the job in the capitalist system and envisioned a secular liberation: "Our confusion of human work with a job produced by a market economy proves that our attitudes about work have not yet been liberated from religious or metaphysical meanings, often held below the level of consciousness." Cox believed that a "spirituality of work" in fact could perpetuate economic injustice, whereas the secularization of work freed people from economic bondage. He wrote: "Rather than fighting and opposing secularization, we would do better to discern in it the action of the same One who called an earlier people out of endless toil, in a land where the taskmasters were cruel, and into a land flowing with milk and honey."[37] Clearly, Cox's theory contrasted with Weber's assertions that work has been stripped of its former religious meanings and that this secularized form of capitalism is our "iron cage."[38]

While Cox called for the secularization of work, Catholics actually were seeking to infuse more religious meaning into work. Philip Scharper complained that we have come into the twentieth century "without even an inchoate theology of work."[39] John Cogley described the frustration of a group of businessmen about the clergy's inability to offer relevant ethical guidance on professional matters. These men "hunger for guidance on how to integrate religion and life."[40] The Vatican's decree in 1959 ending the French worker-priest movement, predicated on the assumption that manual labor of any sort is "incompatible with the priestly life and duties," added to the feeling that the hierarchical church devalued temporal work.[41]

Yet many men took work as a given in their life, the primary basis of their identity. The centrality of work in the public sphere caused some anguish, even despair. A priest wrote:

> The root of all masculine despair and dejection, consequently, seems to be buried in a doubt, not about one's family and private life, but about the meaning of the eight crucial hours—or whatever it might be—of work that a man must accomplish every day to create the world as we see it and thereby to establish his dignity as man by helping in this common effort. In other words, we have here a doubt about the world itself and its tasks. It is not a question of whether men are going to perform these tasks; they will do this in some fashion. Rather it is whether these tasks have cosmic meaning while at the same time being daily, often routine enterprises in the world.[42]

The routinization of work resulted partly from increasing levels of diversification, division of labor, and automation. It seemed that the modern workplace emphasized individual efficiency at the expense of community and human dignity: "Every Sunday we espouse Christianity, but on Monday brotherhood flies out the window, particularly in the work shop. There, it is each man for himself and devil take the hindmost. It is efficiency that counts, not humanity."[43]

Of course, the dehumanization of the worker was not a new problem; it was addressed, for example, in Catholic social teaching beginning with *Rerum Novarum* in 1891. However, lay authors in the 1960s pressed for a more developed theology and spirituality of work. Former Catholic Worker and *Commonweal* editor John Cort described the anxiety of men in their forties, when

> the disillusionment with the possibilities of temporal success hits a man more sharply between the eyes than at any other time of life. For perhaps the first time it really begins to come

home that the likelihood of creating heaven on earth, either for one or for all, is at best a remote and distant dream.[44]

This disillusionment posed a threat to faith, for some men—having based their identities on their work—concluded that if their temporal effort was largely fruitless, then they equally would appear as failures in God's eyes.

The writing of theologians such as the Jesuit Pierre Teilhard de Chardin offered grounding to laity seeking meaning in secular work. Teilhard, after all, spoke of the "divinization of activity." He wrote in his influential 1960 work *The Divine Milieu:*

> We may, perhaps, imagine that the creation was finished long ago. But that would be quite wrong.... And we serve to complete it, even by the humblest work of our hands. That is, ultimately, the meaning and value of our acts. Owing to the interrelation between matter, soul and Christ, we bring part of the being which he desires back to God *in whatever we do.* With each one of our works, we labour—in individual separation, but no less really—to build the Pleroma; that is to say, we bring to Christ a little fulfillment.[45]

Of course, this may have sounded very romantic to the factory worker or the cashier. Teilhard recognized that work can be tedious and merely a means of earning a living. Yet in resigning themselves to the difficulties of whatever work they pursue, Christians endure a continual mortification which helps to complete the passion of Christ. Through their labors Christ's members—whether they be scientist, poet, or manual worker—conquer a portion of reality for Christ, and when the incarnational mission of Christ is brought to perfection, Christ will be all in all through this labor.[46]

Teilhard lamented the fact that most Christians saw their work as a spiritual encumbrance which—though necessary—kept them from living the "higher" life of prayer and contemplation: "Under the sway of this feeling, large numbers of Catholics lead a double or crippled life in practice: they have to step out of their human dress so as to have faith in themselves as Christians—and inferior Christians at that."[47] He echoed here the sentiment of some lay Catholics dissatisfied with the monastic spirituality offered to them in books and church teachings. John Cogley, for example, called this monastic spirituality "so remote from everyday concerns like raising a family, running a business, earning a living, or participating in political life." Perhaps worse, some laypersons fed "on a diet of spiritual books directed primarily to monks and nuns" and convinced themselves that life in the world was distracting. They were led to disengage from, to devalue, the very areas of life most central to the layperson.[48]

Writers such as Teilhard encouraged Christians to see prayer—both individual and communal—as one aspect of their spirituality, rather than the totality, and to integrate it with the rest of their lives. Teilhard wrote that prayer and the sacraments may be "moments of more efficient or explicit commerce with God" but that once our perception of the divine omnipresence is clear, "there is no need to fear that the most trivial or the most absorbing of occupations should force us to depart from him. To repeat: by virtue of the Creation and, still more, of the Incarnation, *nothing* here below *is profane* for those who know how to see."[49]

Cesar Chavez and the United Farm Workers

Certainly, the struggle to improve migrant laborers' working conditions was not profane for Cesar Chavez. This Mexican-American organized farm workers across the country, fighting great odds to achieve legislative change. A devout Catholic, Chavez infused La Causa with religious symbols and practices even as the movement adopted astute political strategies. Indeed, public religious acts such as prayer, the celebration of Mass, fasting, and pilgrimage *were* political acts.

Cesar Chavez was born in 1927 near Yuma, Arizona. At the age of ten his family became migrant workers in California; Chavez worked in the fields full-time after completing the eighth grade. His family was devout. Growing up in the Southwest with few priests and no local church, Chavez had his early piety formed at home. Chavez's grandmother drilled the catechism into him, and his mother influenced him with her love of charity and devotion to the saints. He married Helen Fabela in 1948, around the same time that he began reading the social teachings of the church and biographies of St. Francis of Assisi and Gandhi. These would shape his religious vision and draw him to service and nonviolence. In 1952, Chavez was working in an apricot orchard near San Jose, California, when he met community organizer Fred Ross. Ross persuaded him to work with the Community Service Organization (CSO). It was in the CSO that Chavez met another Mexican-American organizer, Dolores Huerta, who later would become his partner in founding the United Farm Workers. Chavez, Huerta, and Ross organized CSO chapters across California during the 1950s, fighting to gain political power for poor Latinos.

It was 1962 when Chavez left CSO, moved to Delano with his wife, Helen, and their eight children, and began organizing farm workers full-time with Huerta. Jack Kennedy was president. The Second Vatican Council was in its first session. Resigning from CSO to organize migrant workers was a gamble, but Chavez followed his vision. Three years later, his National Farm Workers Association (NFWA) joined with Filipino American workers in a strike against grape growers around Delano, California. On the day of the strike vote, September 16, 1965, Mexican Independence Day, thousands of workers jammed into Our Lady of Guadalupe Church in Delano.

It is important to understand the centrality of the Virgin of Guadalupe in Mexican and Mexican-American Catholicism. Tradition has it that she appeared to a poor Indian named Juan Diego in 1531 near Tepeyac, Mexico. The lady was brown-skinned and spoke in his native language, commanding Juan Diego to go to the bishop and tell him to build a temple at Tepeyac. When Juan went to the bishop, roses fell out of his coat and the image of the Virgin appeared on his clothing. For the Mexican people, this was a religious event of extraordinary significance, giving them hope and dignity at the time of the Spanish conquest and for centuries thereafter. Mary, the mother of Jesus, had appeared to one of them, showing her love and solidarity. She became a symbol of liberation and Mexican dignity. Thus it was particularly significant that the farm workers gathered in Our Lady of Guadalupe Church on September 16 and voted to join the Filipino strike. The strike would last for five years and would develop into an international grape boycott.

About 70 percent of migrant workers were Catholic.[50] Thus, there was a shared religious base from which to work. Still, not all workers or union supporters endorsed the religious element. Some supporters, for example, were nonbelievers or Jewish. Thus, Chavez faced the difficult task of retaining the spiritual identity of the movement while appealing to a broader pluralistic public. As Chavez explained in a 1977 interview:

> I think what has really happened—if we go back and analyze it—is that the more trouble we get, the more religious we get.... And so what we need to do is find a way we can express our beliefs, to deal with our spiritual life in a way that is lasting.... Some of those in the union don't want any part of this religious aspect and, of course, we respect that. But there are also those who want even more than what we are giving them, so we must strike a balance.[51]

For Chavez, it was important to keep a sense of the union as a spiritual community: "If we establish a community, a stronger, closer community, there will be even more religion present. If we don't it's going to become like most other groups."[52]

At the same time that the movement focused energy around Catholic practices, it claimed ecumenical and interfaith support. Church women had organized a migrant ministry in New Jersey as early as 1920. Sustained by ecumenical women's groups, the ministry spread to thirty-eight states, reaching California in the late 1920s. Church Women United, an ecumenical movement of Protestant, Roman Catholic, and Orthodox women founded in 1941, continued the historic support that religious women gave to the migrant farm workers. Both CWU and the California Migrant Ministry strongly supported the grape strike begun in 1965. Despite conflict within churches about the issue, the Council of Churches climbed on board, as did individuals of all faiths who came to California to join the migrant workers. National denominational boards—both Protestant and Catholic—also lent support.

Chavez insisted on a nonviolent movement. His faith shaped the strategic political acts of the movement. In 1966, a year after Martin Luther King Jr. marched with four thousand civil rights demonstrators from Selma to Montgomery, Alabama, Chavez led a 340-mile *peregrinación* (pilgrimage) from Delano to the state capital, Sacramento, to stir up support for the Delano grape strike. The march began on March 17 and reached its goal on Easter Sunday. Certainly, the march was intended to bring media coverage and boost morale. Chavez also saw an explicit spiritual purpose. It was the season of Lent, and penitence was an important theme of the march. This was a public religious display: "public penance for the sins of the strikers, their own personal sins as well as their yielding perhaps to the feelings of hatred and revenge in the strike itself."[53] The pilgrimage would strengthen the workers spiritually and keep nonviolence in the forefront. Catholic symbols were highly visible in the march; farm workers carried crosses and pictures of Our Lady of Guadalupe side by side the NFWA banners.

In 1967, the National Farm Workers Association was locked in a battle with the DiGiorgio Corporation, a huge grower. DiGiorgio was pressuring strikebreakers to sign on with the Teamsters union, and the company won an injunction that restricted pickets around its ranch in Delano. The striking farm workers had been stymied. Yet they found a way to make a public presence through religion. If they were not allowed to picket, they would pray. Chavez and several women organized a prayer meeting near the entrance to the ranch. Chavez had an altar built on the back of his station wagon, and they publicized heavily. The prayer meeting became a political success:

> The idea of praying for DiGiorgio's workers was a smashing success as well as an ingenious organizing technique. For months, Mexican farmworkers flooded into Delano by the hundreds to pray at the shrine in the station wagon. The handcrafted mobile altar, adorned nightly with flickering candles, flowers, and images of the Virgin of Guadalupe, was such an attraction that some migrant strikebreakers braved supervisors and came out from the DiGiorgio camps to look at it.[54]

The station wagon shrine to the Virgin became a fixture at strikes, along with the celebration of Mass. Some supporters objected to this religiosity, or saw it purely as a utilitarian tool to achieve political victory. Jerry Kirchner, for example, said that when the farm workers won contracts with the growers, "we won't need Our Lady."[55]

By 1968, as the boycott dragged on, some within the move-

ment wanted to resort to more violent means. Chavez decided to
make a radical move. He declared a fast to rededicate the movement to nonviolence. Chavez recalled: "There was demoralization
in the ranks, people becoming desperate, more and more talk about
violence....I thought I had to bring the Movement to a halt, do
something that would force them and me to deal with the whole
question of violence and ourselves....So I stopped eating."[56] He
fasted for twenty-five days. The fast strengthened support for the
grape boycott and quelled internal debate about using violence. Yet
it was a pragmatic risk. Many were concerned that Chavez would
die and leave the movement in disarray. Certainly, his wife, Helen,
feared for their eight children. Some saw him as playing martyr.
The fast surfaced existing tensions within the movement about its
religious dimensions:

> Some of the union's other leaders refused to talk to Cesar be-
> cause they thought the fast was an absurd waste of time. Tony
> Orendain, who thought the fast was religious folly, sat with
> his back toward Chavez when they discussed union business.
> Other volunteers found the mystical and Catholic character
> of the fast so offensive that they also quit, complaining that
> Chavez was developing a messiah complex.[57]

Indeed, Chavez's approach raises an important question: as a movement diversifies, how retain a strong religious identity while also
respecting those who resist the dominance of religious symbol-
ism? Pluralism was not just "out there"; it was part of religious
movements themselves.

Dolores Huerta described the meaning of the fast in this way: "I
know it's hard for people who are not Mexican to understand, but
this is part of the Mexican culture—the penance, the whole idea of
suffering for something, of self-inflicted punishment....Cesar has
often mentioned in speeches that we will not win through violence,
we will win through fasting and prayer." Chavez saw no dichotomy
between his spiritual practices and his public work: "I said to myself,
if I'm going to save my soul, it's going to be through the struggle
for social justice."[58]

The fast did rally enormous support. Farm workers came from all
directions to support Chavez, pray for him, and commit themselves

to the cause. Weak, on his bed, Chavez became a focal point for union organizing and religious fervor:

> Some built shrines to the Virgin of Guadalupe at the union headquarters. Priests wore vestments cut from union flags and offered mass with union wine. People slept in tents they pitched in the yard and at night had festive prayer rallies with singing and hot chocolate. "The irony of the fast was that it turned out to be the greatest organizing tool in the history of the labor movement—at least in this country," says Leroy Chatfield.[59]

Robert Kennedy sat next to Chavez when he took Communion to break the fast at a Mass with eight thousand farm workers and supporters. Kennedy called him "one of the heroic figures of our time." It was a poignant time—Kennedy and Martin Luther King Jr. were both assassinated that year.

By 1970, the farm workers union had signed contracts with most California table grape growers. Yet when these contracts came up for renewal in 1973, growers (including Gallo, the largest company) signed contracts instead with the Teamsters. It was a long summer as grape workers went on strike. Thousands were arrested and many beaten when they defied injunctions against picketing. Two workers—Naji Daifullah and Juan de la Cruz—were killed. One of the supporters jailed was Dorothy Day, whom Chavez had long admired and first met in 1965. She was seventy-six years old as she sat in the Fresno County jail with numerous nuns, Jesuits, and other religious supporters. Day recounts the religious fervor that powered the farm worker movement as she describes her time in jail: "During crucial meetings between Cesar Chavez and the Teamsters the Sisters all signed up for a night of prayer, taking two-hour shifts all through the night, while the Mexican women all knelt along the tables in the center and prayed the rosary together. Barracks A, B, and D were alive with prayer." Day herself urged people to say a prayer she had composed: "Dear Pope John—please, yourself a *campesino,* watch over the United Farm Workers. Raise up more and more leader-servants throughout the country to stand with Cesar Chavez in this nonviolent struggle with Mammon."[60]

Political success and religious support finally came together. In 1970, 78 percent of *U.S. Catholic* readers surveyed called the grape boycott justified, and 72 percent said that they would not buy grapes until the grower-worker controversy was settled.[61] In 1972, organizer Jessie De La Cruz spoke at the Democratic Convention. The following year, the National Conference of Catholic Bishops endorsed the grape and lettuce boycotts sponsored by the United Farm Workers: "Legislation must assure the farm workers the right to elections by secret ballot of a union of their own choice. We therefore accept as a pastoral necessity that we be actively concerned in the solution of an evil that has gone on far too long."[62] The United Farm Workers (AFL-CIO) was established in the early 1970s. In 1974, Pope Paul VI met with Cesar Chavez and the Vatican issued a statement supporting Chavez's efforts, an example of "the effort that is required to put the gospel into practice."[63] In 1975, the California Catholic Conference applauded the passage of the Agricultural Labor Relations Act with its "recognition and protection of the individual dignity and rights of the state's farm workers."[64] Other churches also gave their affirmation; the United Methodist Annual Conference, for example, applauded this "major legislative breakthrough" and committed themselves to continued legislative and pastoral efforts in other states.[65] Showing the strong ecumenical backing won by the United Farm Workers, the World Council of Churches also lent support.

Daniel Callahan: Questioning Catholic Identity

Chavez was fairly unique in being able to blend spirituality so seamlessly with his work. Many laity faced a sharper disjunction between their faith and their work and a kind of disorientation as they plunged into the social issues of the 1960s. The problem was, if laypeople were to carry the lay apostolate into every aspect of temporal life, what happened to the distinction between sacred and secular? If secular life and work had meaning, then what was distinctively religious or spiritual? For some, the meaning of the faith they had sought to make relevant to the world began to erode. *Commonweal* editor Daniel Callahan described Catholics who "discovered that the work of the world seems to carry its own intrinsic justification, requiring neither religious motives nor religious goals." He clearly wrestled with the meaning of secularity. How does a Christian in the secular world build a coherent human life?

> As long as he feels that life for him necessarily entails walking some delicate tight-rope between the sacred and the secular, the natural and the supernatural, the redeemed and the un-redeemed, he will always be dizzy. He won't and can't go off into the desert; but then he will always worry whether he can be as totally committed to man's life on earth as the most ardent atheist.[66]

Daniel Callahan was born in the Washington, D.C., area to a Catholic family that had made it into the American mainstream—even the elite stratum. He did not grow up in an immigrant family. He did not go to Catholic schools. In fact, Callahan pursued most of his higher education at secular research universities, a fact that both reflected and guided his orientation to the world outside of Catholicism. He went to Yale University, graduating in 1952. While at Yale, Callahan studied under visiting professor John Courtney Murray. With strong theological interests, Callahan wanted to do further studies in theology. His options as a layperson, however, were quite limited, and so Callahan opted to study philosophy instead. After completing a master's degree at Georgetown (his major Catholic educational experience), he went on for a doctorate at Harvard. While searching for a teaching job, he stumbled upon an editorial position at *Commonweal* magazine. He served as associate editor from 1961 to 1967 and executive editor in 1967–68, a time of tremendous change in the church and the country.[67]

Social and ecclesiastical changes also led to turmoil at the magazine. *Commonweal* faced a critical juncture in the late 1960s, when Callahan disagreed with editor James O'Gara and publisher Edward Skillin about the future of the magazine. Callahan's struggles at *Commonweal* mirror the struggles of many laity as they sought to make sense of their faith in secular, pluralistic America. As Callahan grew increasingly aware of the secular context, he pushed for *Commonweal* to shed its Catholic identity. Callahan argued that the context had changed, and so should the magazine. The rise of the ecumenical movement and the challenge of secularity called for a new identity and a new public mission:

The major problems before Christianity transcend the internal squabbles of the churches. The question today is not "Why Catholicism?" (or Protestantism), but "Why Christianity?" The blurring of the lines between cleric and layman, another feature of the past decade, has made exclusively lay- or cleric-edited publications marginal.[68]

O'Gara and Skillin believed that its Catholic and lay identity still had meaning. Indeed, those were defining marks of the magazine since its origins. The Catholic identity prevailed. Callahan, then executive editor, resigned from *Commonweal* in 1968.

The next year, with psychoanalyst Willard Gaylin he founded the Hastings Center, a center for the study of biomedical ethics. It would have no religious identity; the Center today claims to be "the oldest independent, nonpartisan, interdisciplinary research institute of its kind in the world." It would be concerned with broad ethical and social questions, and would help those who work in the public arena to reflect on meaning: "The Center's collaborations with policymakers, in the private as well as the public sphere, assist them in analyzing the ethical dimensions of their work."[69] Callahan would serve as president of the Center until 1996. He authored numerous books on medical ethics, including *Setting Limits: Medical Goals in an Aging Society* (1987) and *Abortion: Law, Choice, and Morality* (1970).

In the midst of this reappraisal of the secular world, some Catholics—like Callahan—turned their energies outward, away from Catholic institutions such as the Catholic press and university. This provoked anxiety in Catholic intellectual circles, especially among publishers and college officials. Yet it was in many ways consistent with the Second Vatican Council. Callahan's fellow editor at *Commonweal* could have been writing about Callahan when he remarked in 1965: "He [the layperson] is alive to the dignity of the secular career and is anxious to work out salvation in a secular atmosphere."[70] For some, however, this meant redefining salvation. The sacred seemed to be slipping out of view, eclipsed by immersion in the secular world and its problems, the pressing social issues of poverty, race, gender inequality, international development, violence, and Vietnam.

The Public, Ecumenical Church
and the Civil Rights Movement

The civil rights struggle surely was one of those pressing problems of the secular world. The struggle surfaced tensions within the Catholic community about lay and clerical roles, about the relationship between spirituality and social engagement, about pluralism. The new openness to pluralism displayed by Murray and the Second Vatican Council coincided with and spurred public ecumenical action by Catholics as the civil rights movement developed in the United States. Although Catholic clergy, religious, and laity were long accustomed to staying separately in their Catholic circles, the moral demands of racial injustice brought them into coordinated public work with Protestants and Jews. The 1963 National Conference on Religion and Race marked a turning point. More than six hundred representatives of sixty-seven national religious organizations met in Chicago in January to discuss civil rights. Jesuit civil rights activist John LaFarge noted the NCRR's "astonishingly open spirit," which "reflected to a notable degree the Council's attitude." In the same year, Pope John XXIII endorsed efforts to fight racial discrimination, a powerful statement to support the religious move outward on this public issue: "All men are equal in natural dignity; and so, on the doctrinal and theoretical level, at least, no form of approval is being given to racial discrimination. All this is of supreme significance for the formation of a human society animated by the principles We have mentioned above."[71] Pope Paul VI affirmed the civil rights movement when he met personally with Martin Luther King Jr. and Ralph Abernathy in 1964. Ecumenism seemed to be flourishing. In 1963, the National Council of Churches opened their policy-making bodies for the first time to Roman Catholic and Jewish representatives. And on August 28, 1963, Catholic priests, nuns, and laypersons joined with thousands of other religious demonstrators in the March on Washington. This was a political event as well as a religious gathering marked by the celebration of the Mass and the singing of traditional hymns. It also reflected a change in the Catholic center of gravity: "Increasingly, the Catholic reference point on civil rights matters was less the parish community than the interfaith group of religious activists located in each metropolitan area."[72] The civil rights movement gave many a new experience of joint worship and effective ecumenical social action, inspired by deep and public religious commitment.

This was a time of blurred boundaries, changing worlds. Clergy and religious took the lead in the civil rights movement, delving into lay fields of action. As the need for a public faith called louder and louder, those traditionally responsible for the "sacred ministry" redefined the boundaries of their own vocations—or left them. This resulted in some confusion about the definition of clergy and church. James Hamilton, a leader in the National Council of Churches' Commission on Religion and Race, commented on the churches' efforts to garner support for the Civil Rights Act of 1964: "[This] wasn't the church operating as a church, it was the church operating in lay fields, involving the business community, reaching into the power structure."[73]

Not all thought this was a good development. For here the secular and the sacred blurred. While there were still embarrassing lapses in church involvement, by 1963 Catholic leaders took a more active stance. Church leaders preached racial justice from the pulpit. Priests escorted African-Americans into homes in white neighborhoods. Nuns in full habit marched down the streets of Harlem in solidarity with the Selma marchers. In Chicago five nuns and seven priests were arrested as they protested school segregation. Was this their place? Was this the church?

The American Catholic bishops insisted that ecumenical action for civil rights was the work of the church. Two statements a decade apart reveal their guiding theological beliefs. In 1958, the National Catholic Welfare Conference stated: "The heart of the race question is moral and religious." Human dignity and human rights were at stake. Moreover, "Our Christian faith is of its nature universal."[74] Ten years later, the bishops acknowledged the church's own practice of discrimination and pledged itself to continued ecumenical work for civil rights: "Here we pledge our continued cooperation with the National Council of Churches, the Synagogue Council of America, and with other religious groups. Effective action is demanded of us all in the midst of this crisis in American life."[75]

Clearly, the civil rights movement united people of different faiths in a common cause. Yet the movement also caused serious division and threatened stability. Civil rights supporters saw joint religious action as a move of unity to counter racial division and segregation. Detractors saw a splintering within religious groups, as (for example) Catholic police officers were forced to arrest clergy and Catholic leaders stood against heavily Catholic white neighborhoods. Some laity saw the clergy's public role as divisive. One can sense the fragility of religious identity during this time of political upheaval and ecclesiastical change: "this show of nuns and priests marching for this and that.... We can accept the changes in the liturgy or theology, but these peacemakers stirring up trouble because of their conscience, God forbid. I have all I can do to keep my faith in God the way things are going in this world. What has happened to the beautiful Catholic Church's unity, togetherness, same belief?"[76] The issue was complicated, as clergy and religious often took the lead on civil rights while many laity resisted integration.

One Protestant clergyman justified his public silence during civil rights demonstrations as a sign of respect for the laity:

> Each of us has some fine, noble laymen who love the Lord, neighbor, and church, and who feel keenly that "kneel-ins" are no part of Christianity. To talk and pray and plead with deacons in trying to arrive at the will of the Lord with reference to a specific matter is a procedure many of us have followed. But to go over their head, and to disregard their counsel, is to fly into the face of all that we believe in the priesthood of believers, the competency of the individual, and the right of private interpretation.[77]

Thus, the priesthood of all believers became an affirmation of private religion; each individual could interpret the faith for himself or herself.

Tensions within the Christian Family Movement

The Christian Family Movement found itself in the midst of tensions about race and pluralism in the mid- to late 1960s. Within five years, the movement experienced serious internal dissension and a decline in membership. The decline cannot be attributed to a single cause. Multiple factors came into play, including expanded opportunities for laity following Vatican II and controversy over birth control (in which the Crowleys played a leading dissenting role, as will be seen in the next chapter). Yet the leaders' attempt to push CFM to more public engagement on civil rights, and to embrace ecumenism, certainly played a role. Whereas the national CFM claimed more than forty thousand couples at its peak in the early 1960s, by 1971 it had only nine thousand couples.[78] (In 2001, it claimed only about two thousand members nationwide.)[79]

In 1963, CFM for the first time took an official position on a social issue, breaking its policy of leaving such determinations to local groups. It endorsed Martin Luther King Jr.'s March on Washington and pledged that CFM would join with all people of good will to support civil rights.[80] The official CFM newsletter *ACT* then called on members to write their state representatives in support of the 1964 Civil Rights Legislation.[81] Some members protested; the dissension only grew with the unveiling of the next year's program. In 1964 the annual program of the Christian Family Movement focused on race. The inquiry book, *Encounter in Politics and Race*, was quite forceful. CFM leaders made it clear that no Christian could abstain from the civil rights movement: "Every member of CFM...must take an active part in the organized movement for equal civil rights for all....If CFM members should not become involved in politics or should not become actively involved in civil rights, they would not only deny the goals of CFM, they would deny their Christian witness."[82] The inquiry book directed members to personally encounter an African-American (usually through home visitation), to join an organization devoted to interracial justice, and to counter prejudice through education in schools, parishes, and local communities. Woven into the inquiry book were quotations from Scripture, John XXIII, Martin Luther King Jr., the American Catholic bishops, the Jesuit Robert Drinan, and James Baldwin.

Race was a controversial topic, leading to dissension within CFM and a loss in membership. Half of CFM groups did not do the personal encounter with African-Americans. Only one-fourth encountered a civil rights organization. Some chapters did show great commitment. Milwaukee CFM families, for example, fought for school segregation by joining an NAACP suit against the public school district.[83] Yet many CFM groups resisted the annual program. According to longtime member Regina Weissert, the inquiry on race was "the biggest turning point" for the movement. Many people were "scared off by it."[84] The focus on civil rights ignited a long-standing tension between those who wanted to emphasize the family and those who wanted to bring family concerns into a more outward-looking focus.

As the civil rights movement challenged the identity of the Christian Family Movement, so too did ecumenism, although in a milder way. The Christian Family Movement was from its origins a distinctly Catholic organization, fueled by lay visions of the church and the guidance of priest chaplains. However, it had generally displayed a spirit of openness, as the name (Christian, not Catholic, Family Movement) specifically implies. CFM had always allowed for Protestant spouses. In the 1950s, CFM ecumenical involvement centered primarily on joint actions in the community. The 1955–56 inquiry book included an inquiry on "Our Non-Catholic Neighbors." By the early 1960s, CFM leadership was working with Episcopal clergy and laity to develop a separate Episcopal CFM in Chicago. According to Patty Crowley, CFM did very well in working with interfaith couples; this was the movement's most successful ecumenical effort.[85] The rise of ecumenical sensibility in the 1960s, however, fueled a far more assertive ecumenical shift. CFM was profoundly influenced by the Second Vatican Council, which reinforced its sense of lay vocation and encouraged openness to people of diverse faiths.

In 1967 CFM couple Jodie and Joe Adler from Joliet, Illinois, argued to the CFM Executive Committee that the movement should become interfaith. Their rationale rested primarily on social effectiveness:

> Realistic and effective study and evaluation of and solutions to community problems must come from all the people in the community, not just from the Catholics present. To suppose that a group entirely, or even primarily, composed of Catholic members can bring about effective change is a continuation of the ghetto mentality we have been working to eradicate. . . . [It] unrealistically and unjustifiably puts up barriers to positive attitudes that are imperative to any really meaningful civic progress.[86]

In 1968, the CFM Executive Committee officially declared CFM to be an interfaith movement. Annual inquiry books were revised for use by couples of all faiths.

This changed the spirit of CFM. A member since 1947, Regina Weissert recalled that going ecumenical meant changing the language used in the groups. They would not refer, for example, to the Mystical Body, so central to the early ecclesial vision of CFM. The eucharistic liturgy would not be celebrated as much within a mixed group.[87] From the origin of CFM, the Mass was a central means of spiritual formation and sustenance for social action. Indeed, the Mass reinforced the ecclesiology; Christians were the Body of Christ in the world. When CFM officially went ecumenical, the inquiries focused on the liturgy were replaced with reflections on Scripture and contemporary writings. This shift away from the liturgy—the primary and indispensable source of the true Christian spirit, according to the Second Vatican Council—represented a significant revision of spirituality. The CFM leadership had a pattern of pushing the movement in directions not entirely embraced by the membership. This certainly was the case with the civil rights issue; it also occurred with ecumenism. The decline in CFM membership spurred a shift in the 1970s away from ecumenism and social activism, back toward a Catholic family orientation.

Conclusion

John F. Kennedy won for Catholics public visibility and place. Yet I would argue that he did so at an unacceptable theological cost. When so many laity yearned to integrate their lives, to overcome fragmentation, Kennedy argued for a compartmentalized faith. By emphasizing the private nature of his beliefs, Kennedy abdicated the public sphere to secularity. He also dampened public pluralism. Rather than bringing his interpretation of Catholicism into dialogue with differing religious positions, he stated that religious voices should not be part of the political conversation. In reality, that meant that the dominant American civil religion would continue to dominate. In my view, public life must have space for a reflective interchange of ideas—whether religious or not.

John Courtney Murray perhaps laid the groundwork for Kennedy's position. Yet Murray emphasized that the public sphere is wider than the government. Religious people have a responsibility to work for the public good, despite the fact that the church should be distinguished from the state. Murray thus kept an opening for religious engagement in American public life. Moreover, Murray offered a religious rationale for the separation of church and state. Kennedy simply said that his beliefs in no way affected his constitutional interpretation. Murray's faith engaged the political question, even as it justified the American system. Kennedy refused to engage. Murray is a better model.

This story shows that prophets have an easier time with integrity than do politicians. Politicians, after all, must work within the logic of the system. Prophets can stand outside to bring critique. Both take risks, but the politician's beliefs may be particularly difficult to connect with her or his public role. Cesar Chavez, as a prophet, offers a helpful model of integrity. His faith and his work and his politics blend rather seamlessly. They flow from his person; they ring authentic. Most strikingly, Chavez is able to draw upon American pluralism in support of his movement through (not in spite of) his own particular religious practice and clear sense of mission. Pluralism need not require concealment of faith and religious practice. However, Chavez's story raises its own questions. How does one balance religious identity with pluralism internal to a movement? Moreover, when does a "public" spirituality become utilitarian or manipulative? Spiritual practices have a place in the public arena. Yet social aims should not co-opt religion. In my view, Chavez managed to walk this fine line.

It is a difficult line, as the civil rights struggle indicates. Racial injustice called for strong action. How could the church be the church and not resist this injustice? Yet when it finally plunged into the fight, deep questions arose not only about race but also about clergy and lay roles and the border between sacred and secular. From the presidential campaign trail to the civil rights fight, from the editorial desk of *Commonweal* magazine to the group meetings of the Christian Family Movement, lay Catholics struggled to define spirituality and their church.

Chapter Three

TURNING INWARD

The Spirit and the Private Self

B Y THE END OF THE 1960s, the emerging public spirituality had to compete with a move inward—away from the complexity of public life. Many lay Christians turned to the private sphere as the center of spiritual life. Affective, emotionally intense prayer held great appeal, seen particularly in the rise of both Protestant and Catholic neo-Pentecostal movements. Catholic Charismatic Renewal brought fresh life, but in its American manifestations promoted a spirituality that was rather unengaged with social issues. Secular concerns and pluralism continued to challenge religious identity. The struggle over the Spirit manifested itself also in debates about birth control and the meaning of the family. Pope Paul VI's controversial encyclical *Humanae Vitae* challenged the authority of lay experience and reasserted the spiritual power of the teaching authority of the church. The official position also posed new challenges for laity defining their relationship to wider American society and, indeed, defining the church itself. The turn to interior experience and the quest for meaning in the private sphere were natural reactions to the turbulent 1960s, but also a loss. Spirituality as inner power did not lead to public power when grappling with complex social questions.

Going Inward

In the wake of the intensely public strivings of the 1960s, the spiritual quest traveled inward. Disillusionment with politics and with institutional authority led people to look for more secure and unambiguous truth. Many craved immediate religious experience. As

Carlo Weber wrote: "The faith now demanded of the man in transition means precisely the discovery of God within himself. . . . He is to be found most radically and essentially in ourselves."[1] The growing inwardness held both spiritual dangers and possibilities. It lacked the political optimism of the 1960s; indeed, former *Commonweal* editor Peter Steinfels called it "the child of recent political defeats." He explained: "If there is any pattern which qualifies as a law of history, it is that the defeat of political and social hopes leads to a search inward. If the Kingdom cannot be established on earth, it will be found within." Steinfels saw the new interiorism as a reasonable response to the political climate, but he also cautioned against complete withdrawal from social engagement and romantic nostalgia for preconciliar Catholicism.[2]

Rev. Peter J. Henriot claimed that the credibility of faith demanded the integration of religious experience and social action. An "integral faith" will not mean "a substitution of action for prayer, but neither will it allow for a spirituality which avoids commitment to justice."[3] Faith will attend not only to personal renewal but also to social structures.

Rev. Henri Nouwen saw the inner journey as essential to spirituality and to true Christian leadership:

The inward man is faced with a new and often dramatic task to come to terms with the inner tremendum. Since the God out-there or up-there is more or less dissolved in the many secular structures in which we can feel relatively at ease, the God within asks an attention as never before.[4]

Yet inwardness had its dangers. Nouwen cautioned that the inward generation was "fatherless," suspicious of all authority, lacking guidance.

Another author pointed out that publicness allows for critique and accountability:

Dominant trends in traditional piety, such as the Christian's quest for perfection defined in terms of individual holiness, have led us to stress God's love so much that we have submerged the fact of his power. . . . Ironically, power has been relegated to the realm of the "unspiritual" at the same time that the actual church politicians have protected themselves from the checks and public criticisms that curb the worst secular politicians by wrapping themselves in the cultural taboos that traditionally cloak religious figures.[5]

One commentator lamented the "spiritual narcissism" imbedded in the widespread turn to interiority. This "group grope" helps people to overcome modern feelings of alienation, but at the cost of social withdrawal: "It is as though the Social Gospel of earlier years has lost its influence, and the social activists in the pulpits of the sixties have now been repudiated."[6]

Contemplation and Action

At the same time, however, clergy and religious were leaving their vocations in order to move outward, out of the cloister and the rectory into the world. In the decade following the Second Vatican Council, thousands of priests resigned from the ministry; an even greater percentage of nuns left their orders. One nun describes her decision to leave her cloistered community:

> I no longer believe that we must withdraw from the world to save and sanctify it. I have come down from the mountain— its austerity and its security—leaving behind those moments when God seemed so real, so easy to contact. Now I am in the busy world where it is often difficult to find God whose voice is no longer played back to me, but must be discerned in the pent-up frustrations and conflicts of needy, exploited, suffering, despairing man.[7]

The "new interiorism," then, competed with a more activist, socially engaged piety. With the rise of liberation theologies meeting the "new inwardness," there was bound to be conflict. As John C. Meagher queried: "Is there any point in trying to be faithful to a Christianity that is both shaky in its public credit and removed from where the action is?"[8] Here was the classic spiritual question about how contemplation relates to action.

Rev. James Schall criticized the overpoliticization of spirituality and called for a return to contemplation:

Modern social and political movements—be they anti-war, ecological, or Third World development—have so identified religion and spirituality with their this-worldly programs that they are in grave danger of losing their religious foundation and justification which is the transcendence and mystery of God.... We need to realize further that prayer is the first and most radical political act because it establishes who we are in the course of cosmic history, while it limits politics to this world.... The contemplative life as it was historically called is, then, our greatest and most immediate political and intellectual need.[9]

Others warned that prayer can be corrupted by unjust institutions. Fr. Lawrence Lucas, one of the leaders of the black Catholic movement that emerged in the 1970s, pronounced: "The Roman Catholic Church in America looks white, thinks white, and feels white. It prays white, worships white and in relation to black people, believes preeminently white.... It is legitimate to call it a white racist institution."[10] Black Catholics rejected a dichotomy between prayer and social justice. Organizations such as the National Black Catholic Clergy Caucus and the National Black Sisters' Conference, founded in 1968, and the National Black Catholic Lay Caucus and the National Office for Black Catholics, founded in 1970, sought to bring African-American culture and a commitment to equality to Catholic spirituality.[11]

Emotions and Prayer: Unleashing the Spirit?

In 1967, a group of about twenty-five students and several faculty on a weekend retreat at Duquesne University in Pittsburgh experienced a profound and life-changing movement of the Spirit. It was a turbulent year. Lyndon B. Johnson held office. The country divided over the Vietnam War. Students rioted that summer. Yet in a small chapel at Duquesne University, a group of college students found unimaginable peace. Retreatant Patty Mansfield described her experience:

I found myself prostrate, flat on my face, but flooded with a tremendous sense of the incredibly merciful love of God,

the foolishness of God's love....I felt as if I wanted to die
and be with God....As much as I wanted to stay in his
presence, I knew that if I who am no one special could experience the love and the mercy of God in that way, anyone
could!...Within about an hour God sovereignly drew many
of the young people into the chapel. Some were laughing.
Others were weeping. Some were praying with hands out-
stretched. Others were praying in tongues. Others like me felt
a warmth—a power—flowing through our hands.[12]

Influenced by contact with Protestant Pentecostals, she and other
Catholics described this encounter as "baptism in the Spirit."

From this retreat rose the Catholic Charismatic Renewal. The
CCR shared much in common with the neo-Pentecostalism taking
hold among many mainline Protestants in the 1950s and 1960s.
It was part of a broad phenomenon that captured the attention
even of secular national magazines such as *Time*.[13] CCR took root
first on college campuses—the University of Notre Dame, Michigan
State, Iowa State, the University of Michigan at Ann Arbor. Powered by enthusiasts such as Ralph Martin, a leader in the Cursillo
movement; Rev. Francis MacNutt, a healer; and author Dorothy
Ranaghan, CCR spread rapidly. Church hierarchy gave its approval
in 1969. By 1973, approximately fifty thousand Catholics in the
United States and Canada were involved in the charismatic movement, which quickly became international.[14] Charismatics met in
prayer meetings and attested to the power of the Holy Spirit through
gifts that included speaking in tongues and healing. Lay leadership
was strong. While clergy were involved, and Cardinal Léon Suenens
helped to give the movement credibility, the Catholic Charismatic
Renewal was "lay in the modalities of its expression, in its proce-
dures, in its immediacy with which it approaches religious reality,
in the lack of nuance of its religious expression."[15] Indeed, a commentator wrote: "This movement has galvanized the laity as no
movement has since the Middle Ages."[16]

For charismatics, the movement was simply a response to the
extraordinary work of the Holy Spirit. One also can see it as reflecting dissatisfaction with the intense political climate in America
and a hunger for direct, personal religious experience and for com-

munity. Charismatic literature shows that the movement attempted to counter secular culture: "There has been a remarkable failure on the part of institutional Christianity, Catholic and Protestant alike, to speak a relevant word of salvation to modern man.... We believe the baptism in the Holy Spirit with these dynamic gifts and fruits speaks radically to the secular man."[17] At the same time, the charismatic tendency to emphasize the private sphere worked with, not against, secularizing forces. In the judgment of sociologist Danièle Hervieu-Lèger, a balance was struck. Charismatic renewal was a thoroughly modern phenomenon in its movement toward individual fulfillment and personal authenticity. At the same time, it moderated this potentially secularizing subjectivity within the institution of the church.[18]

The charismatic movement critiqued what it saw as a drift away from the fundamentals of faith toward an overly secularized and politicized religion in the wake of the Second Vatican Council. Ralph Martin wrote in 1971:

Six years now of a renewal effort that has presupposed the basic foundation and has concentrated on what are in many cases very important, but in the final analysis, secondary concerns, has produced many areas of seriously deficient Christianity. There are many in positions of leadership in the Church today who... live what is basically a variety of secular humanism with what on close inspection are simply Christian trappings.[19]

Martin criticized a reliance on social scientific "wisdom" to solve social ills: "the source of man's problems is spiritual at its core and can't be dealt with except in a spiritual way.... The Word that God speaks to us about the solution is one of complete healing, complete restoration, personal and social, even the end of death, through the sacrifice of his son Jesus for us."[20]

Of course, direct claims to the Spirit were not unproblematic. The religious expression of the charismatics, particularly speaking in tongues, was unfamiliar to many Catholics. As Cardinal Suenens noted, the charismatics posed "for all those in positions of leadership in the Church a delicate problem of discernment." Following the Second Vatican Council's discussion of the charism of discernment entrusted to church leadership, Suenens noted the bishops' task to judge the Catholic charismatic movement. He stated that the "charism of discernment relies basically on prudence." However, Suenens distinguishes between human and supernatural prudence. Prayer opens the mind to God, enabling it to receive God's action even when it runs counter to human wisdom. Moreover, Suenens argued that direct experience is needed to make a balanced judgment of the charismatic movement.[21] He thus essentially counters criticism by those outside the movement. What unaided human reason might dismiss, grace-filled and prayerful supernatural prudence can judge more soundly. Experience becomes a key component of true discernment. (Incidentally, opponents of *Humanae Vitae* made a similar argument about the importance of experience. Suenens's turn to the charismatic movement in the early 1970s was in some ways a retreat from his public conflict with Pope Paul VI over birth control, a retreat welcomed by the pope.)

Charismatics often were criticized as uninterested in social justice; this was not entirely fair. The keynote speaker of the 1972 "pray-in" at Notre Dame, attended by some twenty thousand people, for example, urged concern with "every human need, every human problem," including war, abortion, racial injustice, unemployment, and migrant workers.[22] Still, the movement tended to be middle class and undeveloped politically, as this British commentator expresses:

> But it will certainly be necessary for the renewal to work out much more fully and consciously its own political role, both within the church and in society. Any genuine return to the roots of Christianity in the New Testament must at the same time be a return to a situation in which Christians have to confront "the world": and this means confronting imperialist oppression, economic domination, military might, religious conformism, state bureaucracy.[23]

Weak social engagement, then, was not just a problem in the United States. Latin American Archbishop Alfonso López Trujillo, coadjutor archbishop of Medellín and secretary general of the Conference of Latin American Bishops (CELAM), stated in 1977:

One of the most widespread criticisms of the charismatic movement is the limited interest which is shown for social commitment. This phenomenon seems to pervade all Latin America. Perhaps it is explainable if we take into account the polarization of so many people in the social and political sphere, even changing the social and political sphere into a privileged place for Christian "praxis." This can lead to a strong impulse, namely, for the sake of the transcendent to break away from the horizontal, from immanence.[24]

López Trujillo did not see this break as inevitable, or even as intended by charismatic leaders. He expressed hope that the charismatic movement could actually synthesize the transcendent and the immanent in the heart of the church.

Another observer listed dangers of the charismatic movement: "excessive emotionalism, a tendency to schism, unsubstantiated Biblical exegesis, the development of a self-identified spiritual elite, and preoccupation with personal spiritual growth at the expense of Christian service."[25] Some charismatics, however, saw their movement as socially transformative and as *the* force capable of renewing the Catholic Church. As one *U.S. Catholic* reader commented: "I think lay people can handle the Pentecostal movement and get it working in the right direction. Social involvement through the Holy Spirit!"[26]

Cardinal Suenens responded to concerns about social commitment in a 1979 published dialogue with Brazilian archbishop Dom Helder Camara. Suenens exhorted charismatics to integrate their piety with social action. Christians "have to enter the Upper Room, then come out into the public square and bear witness.... The Christian needs the Spirit and his gifts, his charisms, not only for his personal spiritual life, but so that he may contribute to the healing of society's ills."[27]

In addition to critiquing the social apathy of the charismatics, some accused them of leaving behind denominational loyalty and concern with church structures. This was a problem among both Protestants and Catholics. In 1976, the United Methodist Church in the United States saw fit to publish guidelines for interpreting the charismatic movement. The guidelines encouraged charismatic laity to integrate their experience with the Wesleyan theological tradition and the life of the congregation. The guidelines cautioned laypersons against spiritual elitism, detachment from the church, and overemphasis on experience as opposed to the other three pillars of the Wesleyan quadrilateral: Scripture, reason, and tradition. The United Methodists here faced a difficult tension. On the one hand, they had to affirm the links between the Wesleyan doctrine of sanctification, the nineteenth-century holiness movement, and the twentieth-century charismatic movements. On the other hand, the church sought to emphasize Wesley's understanding of sanctification as a gradual process rather than the singular "baptism in the Spirit" characteristic of Pentecostals.[28]

Like the United Methodists, other mainline Protestant churches responded to the yearning for the Holy Spirit with conferences, praise groups, and pastoral statements. They also strove to infuse the charismatic movement with more of an ecclesial identity. Denver's Episcopal bishop William Frey called on fellow charismatics to serve the world from within the institutional church. The church is not "a voluntary association of people with a pious frame of reference.... The church may be in trouble, it may be weak, blind, and sinful, but it is still God's church, it is still the body of Christ."[29] A Presbyterian layperson attending the Fourth Annual International Presbyterian Conference on the Holy Spirit in North Carolina in 1975, sponsored by the Presbyterian Charismatic Communion, reflected: "We didn't talk with our pastor first.... When we became involved in the charismatic renewal we jumped in and started a prayer meeting.... We've learned that we should submit to the authority of our pastor and remain faithful to our tradition."[30]

The relation between charismatics, their tradition, and the institutional church was a significant issue for both Protestants and Catholics. Catholics had particular problems. After all, Catholic charismatics claimed direct experience of the Spirit, yet belonged to a tradition that emphasized the wisdom of the magisterium. Although they tended to doctrinal orthodoxy, authority within their own covenanted communities usually resided in laymen. Catholic charismatics easily joined hands with Protestants for prayer meetings and huge rallies; was this a step forward for ecumenism or a lapse in identity? Would Catholics convert to classical Pentecostalism? Dr. William Storey, an early leader of the movement, came to critique it; he claimed that the charismatic prayer meeting often took the place of the Mass and traditional sacramental spirituality. And even as they praised the movement, the United States Catholic bishops cautioned charismatics in 1975: "Continual or exclusive participation in ecumenical groups runs the risk of diluting the sense of Catholic identity."[31]

The Spiritual Struggle over Birth Control

Three months after the Duquesne retreat, the report of the Papal Birth Control Commission was leaked to a liberal American newspaper, the *National Catholic Reporter.* The commission was an international group of physicians, social scientists, theologians, pastors, and three lay couples (including Christian Family Movement founders Pat and Patty Crowley) appointed by the popes to study the issue of birth control. Cardinal Suenens had persuaded Pope John XXIII to establish the commission in 1963. Prompted in part by the birth control pill, which had raised the hopes of many looking for acceptable means of family planning, the commission met to study the issue of artificial birth control over a period of four years. The United States Food and Drug Administration had approved the pill for contraceptive use in 1960, and large numbers of married women had begun using it immediately. When the Papal Birth Control Commission's long-awaited report was leaked to the American press, Catholics breathed a sigh of relief. The commission had overwhelmingly voted to recommend that the church permit the use of artificial birth control within marriage. Its majority report made the theological arguments.

Laity need reliable means of birth control in order to "cultivate all the essential values of marriage," stated the report. Couples need not intend a child with each and every sexual act: "For it is natural to man to use his skill in order to put under human control what is given by physical nature."[32] A more personal testimony by Patty Crowley to the commission made the case too. After submitting letters on the topic from numerous Christian Family Movement couples, Crowley had argued:

We think it is time that this Commission recommended that the sacredness of conjugal love not be violated by thermometers and calendars.... We do not need the impetus of legislation to procreate. It is the very instinct of life, love, and sexuality. It is in fact largely our very love for children as persons and our desire for their full development as committed Christians that leads us to realize that numbers alone and the large size of a family is by no means a Christian ideal unless parents can truly be concerned about and capable of nurturing a high quality of Christian life.... We realize that some may be scandalized: those who have no awareness of the meaning of renewal, those who disagree with the conciliar emphasis on personhood and those who do not understand that the Church is the living People of God guided by the Holy Spirit.[33]

Crowley grounded her support of birth control, then, in a particular ecclesiology and pneumatology. The church was more than the hierarchy, and the Spirit guided the whole community of believers.

This understanding would be challenged a year later, when Pope Paul VI stunned the American Catholic community with his papal encyclical *Humanae Vitae*. The encyclical rejected the majority report of his own Papal Birth Control Commission and continued the church's opposition to all forms of artificial birth control. *Humanae Vitae* claimed the Holy Spirit in a special way for the clergy: "The pastors of the Church enjoy a special light of the Holy Spirit in teaching the truth. And this, rather than the arguments they put forward, is why you are bound to such obedience."[34] *Humanae Vitae* acknowledged that the Holy Spirit worked in the lives of the laity too, but in such a way as to urge them to conform their experience to the teachings of church authority. The Holy Spirit "illumines from within the hearts of the faithful and invites their assent" to the teachings of the magisterium.[35]

In an era when Catholics had moved decisively into the American mainstream, *Humanae Vitae* drew a sharp distinction. Americans were trained in democracy, yet American Catholics must obey the magisterium despite their own moral instincts. Almost all Protestant groups permitted birth control; Catholics would not officially join them. Of course, Protestants also had denounced birth control before about 1930, when the Anglican Lambeth Conference approved birth control. The Federal Council of Churches in Christ and most Protestant churches—including the conservative Lutheran Missouri Synod—followed suit over the next two decades. Here lay the line, then. Protestants mirrored societal attitudes on birth control; Catholic teaching told Catholics to stand apart. The situation was quite complicated by the time *Humanae Vitae* appeared. It was, after all, a Catholic doctor who had invented the progesterone pill and Catholic doctors had prescribed it for years for "irregularity." Large numbers of Catholic laity had crossed the dividing line in practice. In a Gallup poll, 62 percent of Protestants opposed the ban on birth control, while 54 percent of Catholics opposed *Humanae Vitae*.[36]

Deep theological beliefs and different visions of spirituality were at stake in the debates about birth control. One sees the theological issues sharply when one compares *Humanae Vitae* to an evangelical statement on the issue. Just one month after Paul VI promulgated *Humanae Vitae,* a symposium of evangelical scholars met and produced "A Protestant Affirmation on the Control of Human Reproduction." The document asserts that contraception is not sinful "providing the reasons for it are in harmony with the total revelation of God for the individual life." The crux of the matter, then, is the nature of revelation. We see here a different vision of the religious life, one that perhaps had tempted American Catholics living within a Protestant land. The evangelicals write: "Each man is ultimately responsible before God for his own actions, and he cannot relinquish this responsibility to others no matter how qualified they may appear to be." Like the pope, the evangelicals affirm that human experience alone does not reveal ultimate values. Both caution that sin limits our ability to discern God's will, and therefore we must rely on external guidance. However, the evangelicals rely on Scripture for that guidance, whereas *Humanae Vitae* gives that role to the pope (whose authority, presumably, Scripture and the Spirit sanction).[37]

How did American Catholics respond to the pope's position? Overall, they rejected it. *Commonweal* editors called the publication of *Humanae Vitae* "a bitter disappointment."[38] While *Commonweal* editors had opposed birth control in the early years of the magazine, by the 1960s they supported a change in the teaching: "We hope that eventually the magisterium will declare in favor of the right of couples to employ whatever methods of family limitation they find to be spiritually, psychologically and scientifically most effective."[39] Inevitably, the pope's argument from authority clashed with American Catholics socialized to believe that democracy was a moral good, even divinely blessed. Here was a tension for American lay Catholic spirituality and a critical issue for the church. As journalist Louis Cassels wrote in 1969: "Pope Paul VI must decide soon whether he will permit a little more democracy in the Roman Catholic Church or try to crush a rising demand,... forcefully reasserting papal authority. If he chooses the latter course, as seems likely, the Church may be torn by the greatest schism since the Protestant Reformation."[40]

Lay Reactions

The birth control issue was inextricably tied to questions about the meaning of family. What did the marriage commitment necessarily entail? Did birth control support or impede a faithful Christian marriage? How should laity discern the Holy Spirit in their experience of marriage? Laity struggled mightily over these questions. Many sought to give their experience of married reality more weight in the theological process. It was hard to believe that a celibate clergy knew more about sex and marriage than did laypersons. One couple stated: "The sex act is the God-given human means of communicating love." To withdraw that gift from one another "can tear a marriage apart, ruin love, cause mental breakdown or loss of Faith....If the end is right, why can't we use the means appropriate to the human reason God gave us?"[41] For Michael Novak, the decision about whether or not to use artificial birth control was not just a clash between self-indulgence and self-denial (as some church teaching implied). Discernment was complicated; the laypersons' "dilemma is that many moral demands, of seemingly equal weight, are made on him at once."[42] Daniel O'Neill asserted that *Humanae Vitae* offended the ideals of free will and individual conscience, which he considered to be "spiritual qualities" that give the person human dignity.[43] Clergy too struggled with the teaching, particularly as they tried to give pastoral care to their frustrated flock while also toeing the official line. Rev. Daniel Maguire asserted that the Holy Spirit does not have to "go through channels"; rather, its presence must be discerned by the entire living church in human processes. Maguire concluded: "Dissent to this limiting theology of discerning the Spirit is a religious necessity."[44]

Yet some laypersons and clergy defended the pope's vision. Clement Frank, O.S.B., wrote that "the Bishops, the majority of priests and laity, accept the teaching of the Holy Father because they believe that Christ and the Holy Spirit are with him and speak through him."[45] From Montana, Mrs. John Hurlbut defended papal authority against what she saw as a destructive clamor for individualistic freedom:

> Be advised that there are many of us who rejoice in the truth and beauty of the words of *Humanae Vitae*.... God is still a Provident God—it is self-sufficient man, now demanding more freedom—more self-rights, who has not yet learned to share these gifts, to really care, to love.[46]

One woman argued: "We need to face the fact anew that contraception is a crude form of self-defense against one's own acts of love."[47]

The conflict over birth control surfaced the continuing struggle about the private or public emphasis of spirituality. As early as 1964, James O'Gara had written:

> the Church has tended to put its emphasis on the wrong things, so that what people know as being Catholic involves having eight children rather than four, or in general being strict on sex, rather than being good on the race question, or being detached from the material things. In short, I am saying that the Church in this country has very often put its emphasis in the wrong places.[48]

Disgust with *Humanae Vitae* further propelled some laity to redefine the locus of their spiritual life—outward, back into the political world. Mrs. Ruth Moynihan, a mother of seven children, wrote:

The Pope's encyclical is a failure precisely because it does not challenge us enough, and in the right directions. It concentrates on biology, not on love. The only satisfactory response of Christians today is not to get bogged down any further on sex (Pope Paul and Cardinal O'Boyle notwithstanding), but to get on with the real issues of service and love for others, which brought Christ—and will bring us—to both crucifixion and eternal life.[49]

Another layperson asserted that the teaching of *Humanae Vitae* about the sacredness of human origins should lead the pope to defend life in the public sphere:

Unfortunately, public morality always lags behind individual morality. It is easier to "sit by the marriage bed" so to speak and demand heroic sacrifices of individuals than to enter into the councils of government and demand the sacrifice of super weapons which would seem to be "immoral devices" for killing even in a so-called "just" war.[50]

Marriage as Spiritual Path?

Imbedded in the debates about birth control were larger questions about the spiritual value of marriage, a sore topic in a tradition that had long seen celibacy as a more perfect way of life. As one man wrote in 1962, the church was

finally beginning to realize that marriage is the means through which most men gain their salvation, and even now progress in this area often seems slow and halting. What I am trying to stress is that laymen have not received the kind of theological and moral guidance on these important questions that they need to sanctify themselves, their families and the world, and—more to the point here—they have not been insistent enough in asking for that guidance.[51]

In a long overdue corrective, the Second Vatican Council had affirmed the value of marriage and family as a "lofty calling" from God.[52] Marriage was "an intimate partnership of life and love," a sacrament which brings spouses to encounter with Christ. The family was in fact the very core of the church; the Council affirmed the "domestic Church" that lit the fire of faith in children.[53] Indeed, "Family cares should not be foreign to their [lay] spirituality, nor any other temporal interest."[54]

Still, the legacy lingered and spiritual confusion persisted. According to Michael Novak, laypersons had been strangely silent on marriage and sexuality, "what they know best." They seemed intimidated by the difference between the daily reality of married love and the images presented by priests. Novak urged: "If every Christian state has its own proper charisma, then it is laymen who should be writing the authentic and prophetic books on the sacrament of marriage as it is lived."[55] He also offered his own view of marriage:

> Thus marriage provides for Catholic life a symbol of the Incarnation. (Who that is sensible would seek the Messiah in Nazareth, or "fulfillment" in marriage?) It is involvement in "useless" things: in smells and rashes, steak dinners and libidinous touches, yellow-smelly diapers and the insistent noise of children, temper tantrums and bitter irritations. Marriage is Catholic earthiness.[56]

Novak upheld both the value of celibacy as a "sacramental presence" and the value of marriage as a "symbol of the Incarnation." The two complement and enrich one another, reminding us of both the eternal center of our lives and the importance of the everyday.

John Garvey also praised the spiritual potential of marriage:

> Within marriage there is the possibility of a knowing and a being known which is so archetypical of the soul's relationship to God that it is a recurrent theme in mystical literature (and of course, just as in the life of prayer, the knowing and being known involved in marriage can be humiliating and uncomfortable).... In marriage the natural and the supernatural meet wonderfully.[57]

Indeed, a new appreciation for marriage was one factor leading priests out of their collars in the late 1960s and 1970s. Adrian Hastings, a British priest who announced in *Commonweal* that he considered himself free to marry, wrote:

There is simply no way apart from a married priesthood whereby a clerically controlled church can credibly demonstrate that it does not still regard the sacrament of marriage as at least one stage removed from the way of perfection....

The moral issue here relates to the whole height and depth of Christian spirituality. The point is a very simple one: for Christians one is not less wholly at the service of God because one is at the loving service of another human being, but only if one is not serving but dominating. The essence of the religion of Christ...is so to love neighbor—wife, husband, workmates, lepers, the oppressed—that one is indeed loving God and finding God.[58]

Feminist theologian Rosemary Radford Ruether argued that celibacy was not a special and higher gift of the Holy Spirit. Rather, antisexuality lay at the heart of the celibate ethic, which presumes that Christian spirituality in its highest form requires renunciation of the body.[59] She rejected that renunciation as counter to the biblical view of the goodness of creation. (It also certainly clashed with the sexual revolution underway in Western culture.) Moreover, Ruether criticized the notions that the celibate was more available to love universally or more prophetic than the married person: "The very meaning of an ethic of risk means that one has real loves and ties which are risked.... The total security system represented by clerical or monastic life is no more and probably less conducive to such a disruption of the routine and securities of daily life than marriage."[60]

The argument about celibacy was to some degree about the compatibility of public spirituality and private, committed relationships. Could one witness to Christ in a radical way in the world and still be faithful to family? Several authors, clerical and lay, objected to Ruether's article. One lay correspondent criticized "Ms. Ruether's anti-spiritual bias and her downgrading of ascetic spirituality."[61] He stated that the Holy Spirit must have been present in the church as the tradition affirmed the value of the special grace of celibacy.

Singles entered into this discussion, both by challenging the primacy of marriage as the lay vocation and also by questioning whether celibacy need be the only other faithful option for unmarried Christians. Census data showed the number of singles rising steadily in the 1970s. This trend raised questions about faith, sexuality, vocation, and the ministry of the church. Several authors pointed out that lay singles also faced the challenge of celibacy, but received little spiritual support in their lifestyles. One woman asked: "Are these people then 'incomplete' and unfit to further the building of the Kingdom? Who is to provide support for these people in their loneliness? . . . The real answer lies in stressing chastity, or balanced sexuality."[62] Mary Jo Weaver agreed. She wrote that the church and wider society should take seriously the needs and resources of single people (whether celibate or sexually active):

> Single people are treated as people with the "problem" by the churches that are, for the most part, highly oriented to families. If the family is in some trouble in the larger society, it is not in trouble in the church, the last great stronghold of family idolatry. . . . This is odd since I think it could be argued from the New Testament that singleness is the first normal state for every Christian and that there is no Christian imperative to get married or to prefer marriage.[63]

There was no question that this was a time of great confusion and a growing gap between the cultural sexual revolution and the teachings of the church. Eugene Fontinell wrote in 1972: "There is emerging a review of marriage and human sexuality on the part of some Catholics which, whatever the outcome, cannot but shake the Catholic community to its very foundations."[64] Fontinell urged the church to reconsider its traditional understandings of marriage and sexuality, even to the point of entertaining the value of multiple sexual partners within marriage. The Vatican clearly was in no mood to take up Fontinell's suggestions. It responded to changing understandings of sexuality with its 1976 "Declaration on Certain Questions Concerning Sexual Ethics," in which it proclaimed the objective immorality of all masturbation, homosexual sex, and premarital sex.

Divorce

With the liberalization of American divorce laws in 1969 (introduction of no-fault divorce), rising divorce rates also challenged

traditional norms about marriage, sexuality, and spirituality. The
rise in divorce posed urgent questions to the church. Should it
revise its laws forbidding divorce and remarriage? How could it provide spiritual guidance, support, and welcome to divorced Catholics
while at the same time upholding an ideal of the indissolubility of
marriage? The 1970s saw a proliferation of books and articles on
the subject.[65] In addition, numerous groups for divorced Catholics
emerged. One way in which the church tried to respond to couples whose marriages had broken down was to grant annulments,
which enabled Catholics to remarry in the church. In 1967, American Catholic marriage tribunals issued seven hundred annulments.
In 1978, they granted twenty-five thousand.[66]

At the National Divorced Catholics Conference in 1974, four
hundred clergy and laypeople recommended that the church alter
its interpretation of the meaning of Christian marriage and permit
divorce and remarriage in the church. They also described the suffering and spiritual need of divorced persons and emphasized the
importance of membership in the Catholic communion for divorced
and remarried Catholics. One speaker called divorce a crucible
through which some men and women arrive at a deeper spiritual
life.[67] Many Catholics seemed to agree that divorced-and-remarried
people should be fully welcomed in the life of the church. Sixty-eight
percent of *U.S. Catholic* readers surveyed stated that divorced-and-
remarried Catholics should be allowed to receive the sacraments.
In fact, 61 percent did not agree that the sacrament of matrimony
should be received only once in a person's life. On the other hand, 42
percent thought the sacrament of matrimony would be cheapened
if the church allowed divorce.[68]

One layperson excluded divorced-and-remarried people from the
church on the basis of Mark 10:11–12: "The man who divorces
his wife and marries another is guilty of adultery against her."[69]
Michael Zeik cautioned that real Christianity does not preclude suffering: "Monagamy demands painful renunciation while it bestows
the gift of rock-bottom human trust. Did Christ promise roses?"[70]

Others pleaded for compassion: "If Jesus could share the Eucharist with Judas who had already made plans to betray him,
I cannot see that Catholics who have divorced and remarried
should be excluded from the Eucharist."[71] One woman described

the painful alienation felt by many divorced Catholics, "the pain of people who not only suffer the personal tragedy of a wrecked marriage but also absolute rejection of their Church and (usually) their parish."[72] Rev. Francis X. Murphy asserted that remaining in bad marriages has "destroyed the spiritual life of millions upon millions of Catholics."[73] Abigail McCarthy, whose husband, the former presidential candidate Eugene McCarthy, left her in 1969, wrote also about the plight of the displaced homemaker. She noted that the vast majority of Catholic divorced women never remarry; their problems were not just emotional suffering but also economic survival. The law gave her and her children little financial security; it was "not only unjust, but unbelievably humiliating to the spirit."[74]

Conclusion

The late 1960s were an intense period of spiritual searching, seen in the rise of the charismatic renewal movement and debates about birth control. This was a wrenching time in American society, a natural time for religious upheaval and a hunger for certainty. As political optimism declined in the 1970s, many Christians retreated into a more private, inward spirituality. This tension between private and public spirituality surfaced in debates about the meaning of work and the meaning of family life. That tender search for meaning in family life is extremely important. Lay reflections about family— stripped of romanticism yet infused with hard-won insight—are essential to the development of an authentic spirituality. Unfortunately, however, many Catholics found it impossible to also find religious meaning in the social demands and debates of the day; rather, they sought out a more protected sphere of the spirit. One can see this as a healthy move to reconnect and regain religious identity after immersion in an increasingly secular society. Yet one also can see the dangers: the irrelevance of religion to work and politics, an overly spiritualized faith.

One needs to take very seriously the experiences of the Catholic charismatics and the hunger for a direct, powerful experience of the Spirit seen in so many laity. Dispersed in the world, Christians need prayer. They need to be touched by the Spirit, to feel the connection in an intimate, personal way. They need the sense of transcendence felt by those who are overwhelmed and overcome by something larger than our world. At the same time, the birth control controversy shows the inevitable difficulty of claims to the Spirit. Laity in a hierarchical church must be able to claim experience, but the community also needs ways to evaluate competing claims to the Spirit. *Humanae Vitae* made this argument and grounded its claims in the authority of the papal office. Laity divided among themselves—as did clergy. Some appealed to church authority; others grounded their arguments in conscience or practical reason. This raises the issue of discernment. In the final chapter, I will explore this issue in more detail, looking particularly at the relation between faith and practical judgment.

Chapter Four

THE POLITICIANS AND THE BISHOPS

Debates about Public and Private Faithfulness

M ARIO CUOMO AND GERALDINE FERRARO were serious Catholics. They also were high-level American politicians, one a governor and one a vice presidential candidate. As these two moved through Catholic schools in the 1950s, saw Kennedy elected in 1960, and heard the sending forth of Vatican II, they perhaps never could have envisioned how deeply their Catholicism would later clash with their public vocations. It all came to a head in the 1980s.

The clash between the politicians and the bishops revolved around abortion. Also important, however, were questions about lay autonomy, the church, privacy, and the public dimension of faith. Democrats Cuomo and Ferraro took pro-choice positions. When pressed by the bishops to bring their Catholic beliefs into their political action, both Cuomo and Ferraro echoed Kennedy: their faith was private. Ironically, as these prominent laypersons told the church to get out of politics, the bishops entered American public life decisively with the 1983 pastoral letter *The Challenge of Peace* and the 1986 statement *Economic Justice for All*. The debate between the bishops and the politicians occurred in a context of wider conversation about the boundaries of the church, the proper spheres of laity and clergy, and the meaning of work and personal commitments.

The Integrative Impulse

In the 1980s and 1990s, many laypersons expressed a desire for integration, for some way to pull together their disparate roles and spheres of action. One law professor and mother, for example, wrote: "I try not to live in two worlds: a world of work and a world of home; a world of prayer and faith and a 'real' or 'modern' world. I try to make one world."[1] This yearning for wholeness and integration was in part a reaction to both the overly political and overly otherworldly swings of the previous decades. Laity sought to find meaning in the world without collapsing faith into a social program or dissolving it into secularity. They still struggled against otherworldly models of sanctity:

> But when distorted spiritualities hold up to us a model of other-worldliness which is neither realizable nor desirable, we are likely to do either of two things: either we will live alienated, ineffectual, and more or less marginalized lives on the fringes of secular society (the sort of people who peddle flowers in airports and hand out religious tracts in bus stations); or else, turning our backs on the conspicuously unacceptable ideal which has been proposed to us, we will plunge headlong into the world, uncritically appropriating not just secularity but secularism as our value system.[2]

Laity sought a model of spirituality that would take their everyday responsibilities seriously:

> Even the model of spirituality now offered us by the new leadership...is essentially a clerical one....By our very choice we live in the world and we must, particularly in these hard economic times, immediately concern ourselves with the very business of survival. Most of us have not only ourselves to worry about but have others who depend on us and for whom we are responsible....Our identity crises are usually associated with the most mundane of our routinized daily lives; our serious doubts about the very value and purpose of life occur at those moments that do not readily yield the satisfaction that what we do is either worthwhile or important....
>
> What we of the laity so desperately need is to develop a spirituality that is authentically and uniquely our own....This must be one that takes into account the necessity of our diverse commitments.[3]

As in previous decades, questions emerged about discernment— about experience and authority. Laity appealed to their own experiences as a source of revelation. They continued to call on church leaders to listen "to the Spirit's presence in the lives of the believing faithful. The faithful need to 'hear' the Good News speak to their experiences."[4] At the same time, lay faith emerged in conversation with the teachings of the magisterium, most strikingly illustrated by conservative movements such as Opus Dei:

> *Opus Dei* is a universal apostolate inserted into the local dioceses and has a specific mission to foster among lay Catholics of every walk of life the pursuit of holiness and of carrying out a Christian apostolate in and through their ordinary work in the world. This includes fostering unity with the local bishop and charity with all... according to a spiritual obedience proper to the laity—that is, one that leaves them free in all temporal affairs.[5]

Indeed, Pope John Paul II called Opus Dei, which claimed eighty thousand members worldwide, an "instrument of energetic orthodoxy."[6]

Lay Styles of Prayer

Lay reflections on prayer reveal both a respect for contemplative life and an attempt to see prayer in the midst of "worldly" activity. In 1985, 60 percent of *U.S. Catholic* readers surveyed said that they set aside a specific period of time every day to pray, although a full 80 percent agreed that laypersons usually suspect that their prayer lives are not as good as the prayer lives of priests or religious. Laypersons did not reject traditional teaching or modes of prayer; 82 percent considered contemplative prayer an option for laypersons. However, by a considerable margin they also stated that their prayer lives were formed most strongly by their own experience, as opposed to parents, clergy, religious, or books about prayer.[7]

Recalling the scriptural instruction to pray constantly, *Commonweal* published several reflections by laypersons on how they pray in the course of their busy lives. Daniel Mulhollan, employed by the Library of Congress Congressional Research Service in Washington, D.C., relied on the Jesus Prayer: "Lord Jesus Christ have mercy on me." He wrote:

There appears to be something very helpful in placing oneself in a poise of always seeking mercy, to be constantly reminded that out there is one beyond my limits who is without limits. The Jesus Prayer certainly helps to remind me that anxiety is attempting to will that which cannot be willed, especially when I have a carload of kids and beach gear, and the storm clouds appear on the horizon as I park.[8]

An author reflected on prayer and her mothering love: "Believing in their goodness, I pray for the happiness of my children; I also pray, as all mothers do, to bear their pain, but, on the evidence, God wants them to bear their own pain, more's the pity."[9]

Marian Burkhart, an English teacher and book reviewer, wrote:

At praying I am inept.... If I cannot be saved but through the grace of God, that grace can act only through me and that place I am to fill in his eternal plan would without me be forever empty. I am enabled, then, to flesh out my feeble praying by offering him what I do well—reading, thinking, conversing, cooking—even bed-making, if we are really considering the quotidian.[10]

For Frank Macchiarola, business professor and former chancellor of the New York City public school system, praying for help was a natural part of thinking through an activity. He wove prayer and activity together: "The things I do have become a part of prayer, and I think that I do many of these things better as a result."[11]

Laity were, then, finding everyday life "in the world" fertile ground for prayer. Still, many continued to find monastic models vital:

I can't see why prayer style needs any sort of limitation. Monastic forms, if they suit lay Catholics, have as much efficacy as any others. In fact, is that not why we have retreats and parish missions—to create for ourselves something like monastic isolation and concentration? Not everyone will find barreling down the highway, an evening with congenial couples, or a moment before returning to the assembly line the right context for satisfactory prayer.[12]

Some criticized a preoccupation with spiritual techniques and encouraged instead a simple attentiveness. John Garvey, long-time *Commonweal* columnist who converted from Catholicism to Orthodoxy, wrote: "I do think, still, that paying attention has everything to do with spirituality.... It isn't a skill I master, but more like the effort to stay awake when the temptation to fall asleep is pressing and constant."[13] Garvey saw prayer as a kind of honest, vulnerable presence to God:

> I have such wonderful resolves, lots of good intentions. My mistake is that they form so large a part of my conscious life that I could wind up thinking that they offer a serious clue to my being, rather than a clue to what I want to be.... But it is this vague bundle of desire, dissatisfaction, emptiness, and desire pulling in all directions which constitutes whatever it is that I can truly call myself, and it is this cloud which stands before the unknowable God in prayer and is revealed in all its neediness.[14]

Connecting spirituality to everyday life was an important concern for diverse spiritual seekers, as the phenomenal success of Thomas Moore's book *Care of the Soul: A Guide for Cultivating Depth and Sacredness in Everyday Life* (1992) demonstrates. Such highly therapeutic forms of spirituality tumbled forth. This phenomenon brought attention to the interaction of psychological well-being, life stages, crisis, and spiritual growth. Yet this author rightly feared the substitution of pop psychology for authentic spirituality: "We need to know what remains of the religious after the incursion of the psychological. We need to see the difference between spiritual journeys and therapeutic paths."[15]

The charismatic movement garnered far less attention in the 1980s and 1990s than it had in the 1970s. Some continued to criticize the movement for an overemphasis on private devotion, the individual self, and family. One scholar called the Catholic Charismatic Movement the "celebration and enhancement of the privatization of religion."[16] Pope John Paul II—long a supporter of charismatic renewal—told charismatics that he wished to strengthen their "ecclesial identity."[17] Others saw charismatic renewal as a place for active lay ministry, a force moving the church toward egalitarianism.[18]

The Bishops and the Politicians

While laity expressed this hunger for integration and prayer in the midst of everyday life, several prominent lay politicians modeled a more compartmentalized faith. In the 1980s, Mario Cuomo and Geraldine Ferraro faced pressure from church hierarchs about their positions on abortion legislation. Both took pro-choice stances, although they also said that they personally opposed abortion. Both insisted that faith could not dictate their work in the public sphere. Their responses show the complexity of the lay vocation in a secular, pluralistic American democracy. They also provide an interesting comparison to John F. Kennedy. While Kennedy had to respond to non-Catholics who feared the incursion of the Catholic Church in things political, Cuomo and Ferraro had to respond to political pressure by their own church authorities. This occurred at a time when the American Catholic bishops themselves were taking quite public roles on military and economic policy questions. At the heart of the controversy were questions about the vocation and autonomy of the laity and the public character of spirituality.

Interestingly, at the same time that the bishops decisively entered American public life, the Vatican was cracking down on priests and religious who took public office. The Second Vatican Council and earlier movements such as the Sister Formation Conference had given impetus to this move outward into the secular sphere. The Jesuit Robert Drinan won a seat representing Massachusetts in the United States House of Representatives in 1970. He served five terms, establishing himself as an important figure in Congress. He participated in the impeachment proceedings against Richard Nixon in 1974. He opposed the war in Vietnam and the military draft. He worked to improve human rights abroad. Yet in 1980 the Vatican ordered him not to seek reelection. With regret, he complied with the order, ceasing the public career in which he saw himself as a "moral architect" and highly "influential as a priest."[19] The Vatican also ordered Sister Agnes Mary Mansour to resign as director of the Michigan Department of Social Services in 1983. Mansour responded that she could not obey this order, which she felt violated her faithfulness to the church, to the people of Michigan, and to her religious community. She also felt it represented church intrusion into state affairs.[20] Mansour left the Sisters of Mercy and retained her public position. The 1983 Code of Canon Law made it official: priests and religious were forbidden to hold public office (canons 285 and 672). Bishops could make exceptions to this rule, but the canon law further solidified a clear distinction in church teaching between the sphere of the clergy and religious, on the one hand, and the sphere of the laity, on the other.

At the same time, religion and politics were inextricably tangled together in the United States. In the 1980s conservative evangelicals wedded the two, as compared to the liberal Protestants who had spearheaded white church support for the civil rights movement in the 1960s. It was an ironic twist, as the conservatives learned from the tactics of the earlier liberal movement and used the tactics for quite different agendas. The New Christian Right emerged in 1979, led by Jerry Falwell. Born-again Christian Ronald Reagan, elected first in 1980, used the religious right as a key base of support. When Falwell gave the benediction at the Republican National Convention in 1984, he called Reagan and his vice presidential choice George Bush "God's instruments for rebuilding America."[21] The New Christian Right took up the fight for anti-abortion legislation and school prayer. Televangelists such as Pat Robertson (*700 Club*) and Jim Bakker (*PTL* [Praise the Lord] *Club*) made the faith very public— and some ultimately damaged its public credibility—at the same time. It is within this context that the Catholic story must be seen.

Mario Cuomo and Political Judgment

Mario Cuomo was born in 1932 to Italian immigrants and grew up in Queens, New York. His father ran a grocery store. Cuomo made his way through Catholic schools—St. John's University and its law school, eventually entering politics. Cuomo said that the Second Vatican Council influenced his decision to enter public life, as it encouraged Catholics to engage "the concerns of this world, rather than feeling that you had failed because you had not gone into a monastery to weave baskets to fill the uncomfortable interval between birth and eternity."[22] By all accounts, he took his Catholicism seriously. Cuomo was elected governor of the State of New York and served from 1983 to 1995. He asserted in the early years of his term: "I am a governor, I am a Democrat, but I am a Catholic first—my soul is more important to me than my body."[23]

That claim was put to the test in a controversy between Cuomo and church hierarchy over abortion. While Cuomo was an outspoken opponent of capital punishment, this Italian Catholic said that his religious beliefs about abortion could not influence his political response. He would uphold the right to abortion. Cuomo insisted that he had the right and the responsibility to arrive at his own conclusions with regard to the political response to abortion, even as he affirmed the church's teachings about the sanctity of fetal life. In 1984, the newly installed archbishop of New York, John J. O'Connor, publicly criticized Cuomo. Their public disagreements about abortion continued for years. The furor first erupted when O'Connor made a political judgment: he questioned whether Catholics in good conscience could vote for a candidate who explicitly supports abortions. Cuomo objected to what he saw as a religious incursion on the political sphere. He agreed that the hierarchy should teach moral principles, but claimed that they may not dictate how Catholics vote.

Cuomo was quite dismayed by the cardinal's criticism. He defended his position in a 1984 speech at the University of Notre Dame, a speech the *New York Times* called "one of the most anticipated exercises in theology ever presented by a member of the laity."[24] Cuomo explained the complexities of being a Catholic politician in a pluralistic democracy and emphasized his commitment to the constitutional right of religious freedom. He affirmed his personal opposition to abortion and his acceptance of the church's teaching authority. However, he drew a sharp distinction between his discernment in private life and the prudential decision-making required of him as a politician. "As a Catholic I have accepted certain answers as the right ones for myself and my family and because I have, they have influenced me in special ways, as Matilda's husband, as a father of five children, as a son who stood next to his own father's deathbed trying to decide if the tubes and needles no longer served a purpose."

Although Cuomo did not explicitly discuss the Holy Spirit, one may sift out his theological perspective. Cuomo implied that in these private moments, the Holy Spirit worked through both the church teaching authority and his own conscience to guide his decisions. Yet when it came to the implementation of moral ideals in the public arena, Cuomo seemed to distinguish between spirituality and practical reason: "The question whether to engage the political system in a struggle to have it adopt certain articles of our belief as part of public morality is not a matter of doctrine: It is a matter of prudential political judgment." Cuomo noted that no church encyclical or catechism dictates a political strategy to achieve legislative goals. Political strategy, apparently, was not an area for the Holy Spirit but rather for careful pragmatic judgments among less than perfect alternatives. Cuomo notes too that a number of Protestant and Jewish groups supported legal abortion. These were, ironically, "the very people who have worked with Catholics to realize the goals of social justice set out in papal encyclicals." He listed them: the American Lutheran Church, the Presbyterian Church in the United States, the Women of the Episcopal Church, the Central Conference of American Rabbis. If the Spirit were speaking clearly on abortion policy, then Catholics seemed to have better hearing.[25]

Cuomo's speech echoed Kennedy's move to privatize faith, although his comments were far more nuanced than Kennedy's. Interestingly, Kennedy was defending himself largely against non-Catholics, while Cuomo defended himself to the Catholic authorities while easily gaining support from the liberal media and non-Catholic sources. The *Christian Science Monitor,* for example, applauded his position as entirely American: "His larger brief was for the politician's right to distinguish between private faith and public responsibility. This is a position American politicians have taken since the nation's early days, and one we fully support today."[26] However, then Archbishop O'Connor and other Catholic hierarchs did not agree. The head of the United States Catholic Conference, Bishop James Malone of Youngstown, Ohio, declared that a dichotomy between personal morality and public policy was "simply not logically tenable."[27] In 1986, Bishop Joseph T. O'Keefe of the Archdiocese of New York instructed parish priests not to invite as speakers any individual whose public position opposed the teaching of the church. Governor Cuomo saw himself in these instructions and swiftly denounced the order: "We lay people have a right to be heard."[28] The debate escalated in 1990, when then Cardinal O'Connor warned that Catholic politicians who supported the right to abortion risked excommunication. That same year, the cardinal defended the staunch anti-abortion bishop Austin Vaughan, who, while in prison for trespassing at an abortion clinic, said that Cuomo was in "serious risk of going to hell" for his support of abortion rights. Indeed, these hierarchs stated that faith could not be so easily divorced from political responsibility; spiritual penalties would result from public wrongs.

Geraldine Ferraro and the Measure of a Faithful Christian

Geraldine Ferraro, another New York Catholic, also found herself denounced by several bishops due to her position on abortion. Born in 1935 to Italian immigrants, this graduate of Marymount College and Fordham Law School ran unsuccessfully on the Democratic ticket for vice president in 1984. She took a strong pro-choice position, although she—like Cuomo—claimed to oppose abortion herself. Her position drew fire all along the campaign trail. She faced vociferous anti-abortion demonstrators at speaking engagements, fueled in part by the national Republican organization. At one speech in the Midwest, an abortion protestor held up a sign picturing three tombstones for Ferraro's own children. At a press conference, a protestor held a sign that read: "Ferraro, what kind of Catholic are you?" Particularly traumatic for Ferraro was the sharp criticism coming from church hierarchy.

Ferraro knew that her position veered from the official Catholic teaching on abortion. Yet she was stunned by what she saw as partisan attacks by church leaders. Bishop James Timlin of Scranton, Pennsylvania, held a press conference to denounce Ferraro's pro-choice position as "absurd" and "not a rational position."[29] John Cardinal Krol threatened to pull all Catholic children out of the Philadelphia Columbus Day parade if Ferraro (who had been invited by Mayor Wilson Goode) marched. (Krol also had prayed the invocation at the Republican Convention the night that Reagan was renominated.) And the fiercest heat came from Archbishop O'Connor, who appeared on television in June 1984 and stated: "I do not see how a Catholic in good conscience can vote for an individual expressing himself or herself as favoring abortion."[30] A few months later he specifically named Ferraro when he told the press that she had misrepresented the views of the Catholic Church on abortion. To Ferraro, this move violated a long-standing policy of the National Conference of Catholic Bishops against direct political involvement.

O'Connor argued that Ferraro erred when in a 1982 letter she stated that Catholic positions on abortion were not monolithic. He insisted that they were. At the heart of this debate was their definition of the church. She spoke of the whole community, including lay dissenting groups such as Catholics for a Free Choice. He spoke of the magisterium, the teaching authority of the church given special authority by the Holy Spirit. Ferraro also criticized what she described as the "single-issue" focus of O'Connor, who made abortion opposition the litmus test of faithful Christianity. Ferraro pointed to her voting record on education, poverty relief, and housing as marks of her faith. When O'Connor argued publicly that no social need is more pressing than the protection of the rights of the unborn, Ferraro responded: "That was not my Church. That was not what I learned in the beatitudes. The very real suffering of the living was every bit as pressing to me and to many others as the possible suffering of a child not yet born."[31]

Ferraro objected to the "crossing of politics and piety," to how O'Connor would "step out of his spiritual pulpit into the partisan political ring." The result in the public eye was this, she thought: "Whom did it look like I was really running against? The Archbishop of New York, who, in turn, was standing in for George Bush. A vote for Reagan-Bush was a vote for the Archbishop, for the Church."[32]

Like Cuomo, Ferraro took her Catholicism seriously; she had even considered entering the convent when she was sixteen. She went to Mass every week. Yet in the flurry of the presidential campaign, she insisted: "My religion is very, very private." She compared herself to Kennedy, who had also insisted that he would not impose his Catholic views.[33] In her autobiography, Ferraro argued that her position showed respect for American pluralism: "I felt very strongly that I had been blessed with the gift of faith, but that as an elected official I had no right to impose it upon others.... When I take my oath of office, I accept the charge of serving all the people of every faith, not just some of the people of my own faith."[34] She wrote that as a Catholic, she had always accepted the idea that the fertilized ovum is a life, a baby. Yet people of other faiths disagreed. She saw no reason why her Catholic belief should "override" other beliefs. Ferraro stated bluntly: "Personal religious convictions have no place in political campaigns or in dictating public policy."[35]

Some criticized a liberal hypocrisy. Why was religious involvement in politics advocated around issues such as nuclear arms and economic policy, but denounced when the issue is abortion? Conservative Catholic Congressman Henry J. Hyde of Illinois (author of the 1976 Hyde Amendment, which prohibited federal funding for abortions) wrote at the time:

> Had the Archbishop of New York quizzed a conservative Catholic President about his commitment to nuclear arms control, would there have been impassioned hand-wringing at the *New York Times* editorial board about "mixing politics and religion"? Yet this is precisely what happened when the Archbishop of New York questioned a liberal Democratic candidate for Vice President about her approach to public policy of abortion. Why is it that Archbishop O'Connor threatens the separation of church and state when he tries to clarify Catholic teaching about abortion, and the Rev. Jesse Jackson doesn't when he organizes a partisan political campaign through the agency of dozens of churches?[36]

At the same time, Catholics certainly were not the only politicians quizzed about their religious convictions. With the strong presence of the religious right, Protestants too faced "litmus tests." Presidential candidate Walter F. Mondale, running against the Religious Right favorite Ronald Reagan in 1984, met with criticism from conservative Protestants. At a speech in Tupelo, Mississippi, a heckler asked how Mondale could call himself a "good Christian" and support the "pro-abortion, pro-gay rights and antireligion" Democratic platform. Mondale responded by affirming the American separation of church and state, which he said accounted for the fact that Americans were the most religious people on earth. Moreover, Mondale asserted that a private faith is a "pure faith": "that's why they called themselves Puritans. They wanted a pure faith and so do I. . . . From the beginning we told the government and the politicians keep your nose out of my own private religion and let me practice my faith."[37]

The Bishops' Public Stand

Interestingly, at the same moment that high-profile Catholic politicians sought to keep their faith out of political life, the American Catholic bishops moved quite vocally into the public sphere. In 1983, the United States Catholic Conference published *The Challenge of Peace*, a detailed analysis of American foreign policy and the ethics of nuclear arms. In 1986, the bishops released *Economic Justice for All*, a major statement on the American economy. Some saw these two pastoral letters as "the definitive entry of Catholicism into the center of American public life."[38]

I will focus here on *Economic Justice for All* as an illustration of a theological approach relevant to lay spirituality. I will not focus on the bishops' conclusions about the economy, but rather on their approach. The pastoral letter was the product of several years of consultations with experts from the social sciences and theology, a process that gave new respect to lay competencies. The result was not without controversy. Many disputed the political and economic policies that the bishops recommended to realize this moral vision.[39] Some Christian business executives called the pastoral "naive" and "socialistic."[40] *Commonweal* editors, on the other hand, applauded the bishops' recognition of economic rights alongside political and civil rights and their attention to the moral and spiritual dimensions of the economy.[41] The bishops themselves acknowledged the difficulty in moving from principle to policy (a difficulty Cuomo was emphasizing in his own controversy). The bishops wrote: "We are aware that the movement from principle to policy is complex and difficult and that although moral values are essential in determining public policies, they do not dictate specific solutions."[42] *Economic Justice for All* illustrates the tensions within American Catholicism about spirituality, the lay vocation, and public life in a pluralistic democracy.

The bishops addressed their letter both to Catholics and to the wider American public. Hence, they had to find a way to engage those who do not share the guiding theological principles of the Catholic faith. The Catholic tradition enabled this move, as it affirms the compatibility of reason and revelation. When the bishops asserted the dignity of the individual human being and its need for community, they relied on Scriptures (Gen. 1:27), on a tradition of philosophical and theological reflection, and on reasoned analysis of human experience. The bishops wrote as pastors, not as politicians; hence, their position was different from that of a Cuomo or a Kennedy although they too confronted public issues with a pluralistic citizenry. Yet they clearly conveyed their identity as not only Catholic clergy, but also as American citizens: "We bring to this task a dual heritage of Catholic social teaching and traditional American values."[43]

In addressing economic questions, the bishops spoke to the vocation of the laity. The laity often experienced fragmentation, a divide between their faith and their everyday lives. While some prominent lay politicians promoted this divide, the bishops saw holiness in another path: "A renewal of economic life depends on the conscious choices and commitments of individual believers who practice their faith in the world. The road to holiness for most of us lies in our secular vocations. We need a spirituality that calls forth and supports lay initiative and witness not just in our churches but also in business, in the labor movement, in the professions, in education, and in public life."[44] Indeed, while the bishops spoke specifically here about economics, one cannot help but think about the implications for abortion policy: "We cannot separate what we believe from how we act in the marketplace and the broader community, for this is where we make our primary contribution to the pursuit of economic justice."[45]

Lay Debates

How did laity react to the concurrent movements of the lay politicians and the bishops? Abigail McCarthy affirmed both the lay vocation and respect for lay judgments about their own spheres of work. She wrote:

> If being a "Commonweal Catholic" means anything it means that one sees a lay person's work in the world, his or her "lay vocation," to use an old term, as an integral part of the mission of the church to serve and save the world in the history of here and now. It also means that one sees the lay person's work as his or her responsibility—as that for which he or she has competence by reason of training and experience.[46]

Catholic historian David J. O'Brien emphasized the lay role in the secular world rather than in ecclesiastical life:

> But of course public life is religiously significant, and there can be no escape from public Catholicism.... The emphasis must fall on the Catholic member of the school board, the Catholic professional, executive, teacher, labor leader, or social worker, rather than the Catholic Worker or the lay director of religious education, important as such persons may be to the life of the church.[47]

While affirming the need for connections between spirituality, politics, and morality, John Garvey cautioned:

> The radical change of heart which Jesus called for, the turning around which repentance is, had to do with something much more profound than the question of who was right or wrong, politically....
>
> Our major problems have so much to do with our hearts— not ours collectively, but yours, and mine—that political questions can be a luxury and distraction for us. The world's deepest problems can't be answered politically, but in a sense only monastically.[48]

Frank Macchiarola described his attempts to fully integrate public responsibilities, private life, and faith:

> The influence of prayer into what I do is basically the same for me as both a public figure and private citizen. I decided many years ago—when I became an adult—that public and private

life were one, and that virtues I sought to practice would be the same for me whether I was alone, with my family, or with the larger community.[49]

In 1995, 57 percent of *U.S. Catholic* readers surveyed said that they did not expect Catholic politicians to toe the church's line on all social policy questions. Yet they did think that faith had a role in public life. A full 98 percent said that they were proud to publicly acknowledge their faith, and half believed that "privatization of faith is a sin." Eighty-four percent disagreed that "mixing religion with politics is un-American," and 76 percent agreed that "nothing the church teaches conflicts with what is good citizenship."[50] A decade after the initial confrontations between Cuomo, Ferraro, and O'Connor and the release of the bishops' pastoral letters, a *U.S. Catholic* reader commented: "In today's political and social climate, even to admit being a Christian, one is immediately suspect. For any Catholic, we need to be proud of that fact. We need not flaunt it, but we shouldn't put it in the attic like a crazy aunt, either."[51]

A Synod on the Laity

Part of the debate about Cuomo and Ferraro revolved around lay competence. Did the church hierarchy understand the complexities of the structures within which laypeople worked? Did they respect the professional competencies of the laity? The consultative processes for the bishops' pastoral letters on peace and the economy indicated that respect. The Cuomo and Ferraro affairs raised questions. Clearly, some laypersons were dissatisfied with the place of laity. Russell Barta, founding member of the Chicago-based National Center for the Laity, criticized the church for failing to implement the ideals of the Second Vatican Council.[52] Some laity looked to the 1987 Synod of Bishops on the mission of the laity for "the beginning of the end of clericalism and the affirmation of the lay vocation."[53] This international gathering of bishops in Rome was preceded by extensive consultations with laity, including some two hundred thousand laity in the United States.

The synod resulted in an official statement, "The Lay Members of Christ's Faithful People" (*Christifideles Laici*). The statement affirmed the interconnections between lay vocations in the private sphere and lay vocations in the public sphere. Family life should not become a privatized spirituality, for it is actually a foundational part of lay responsibility for the public good: "The lay faithful's duty to society primarily begins in marriage and in the family." The family is the basic cell of society and the primary place of humanization. The pope resisted any privatized notion of faith: "In order to achieve their task directed to the Christian animation of the temporal order . . . the lay faithful are never to relinquish their participation in 'public life,' that is, in the many different economic, social, legislative, administrative and cultural areas which are intended to promote organically and institutionally the common good." While echoing the Second Vatican Council's recognition that laity must "respect the autonomy of earthly realities," the pope emphasized the urgent need for lay public witnesses. Political life was not an absolute moral danger, he said, and all of its temptations (e.g., careerism, idolatry of power, corruption) did not justify withdrawal from public responsibility.[54]

The statement defined holiness in terms of charity, the particular virtue of the lay vocation: "Charity toward one's neighbor, through contemporary forms of the traditional spiritual and corporal works of mercy, represents the most immediate, ordinary, and habitual ways that lead to the Christian animation of the temporal order, the specific duty of the lay faithful." Indeed, holiness was the perfection of charity. Thus, laity could reach perfection through the normal paths of family, work, and public engagement. How, though, is love made manifest in the public sphere, particularly when one moves beyond works of mercy to the complex policy decisions that faced Cuomo and Ferraro? The pope's basic response was to connect love and justice: "A charity that loves and serves the person is never able to be separated from justice." Each in its own way, love and justice supported the dignity of the individual human person. While the statement was not terribly specific in its definition of justice, it did point in certain directions: participation, liberty, the common good, preferential love for the poor.[55]

Christifideles Laici affirmed (as did Luther) that laity share in Christ's priestly mission: "The lay faithful participate in the priestly, prophetic, and kingly mission of Christ." Yet the pope refused to identify the lay vocation with the ordained vocation. He distinguished between the "common priesthood" and the "ministerial priesthood." He was responding here to the increased lay involvement in ecclesiastical spheres after Vatican II. Whereas the lay sphere of action was traditionally the secular world, lay leadership and ministry within the church increased in the wake of the Second Vatican Council as clergy left their posts and the church became more democratic. Ministry became more professionalized and laity stepped into positions that had been off limits. To affirm this lay work, parishes began to designate "eucharistic ministers," "ministers of care," and "ministers of music." Ushers became "ministers of hospitality." The pope cautioned about "a too-indiscriminate use of the word 'ministry,' the confusion and the equating of the common priesthood and the ministerial priesthood, . . . the tendency towards a 'clericalization' of the lay faithful." He insisted that the ordained priesthood "is different, not simply in degree but in essence" from the lay priesthood.[56]

Commonweal editors panned *Christifideles Laici*, seeing in it only evasive responses to the many questions posed by the laity during the consultation process:

> With this document in hand, we still have no adequate theological framework for understanding the work of lay people in either church or world. . . . When the ordinary layperson "in the world" encounters this sort of thing from business or government, she has a term for it—bureaucratic claptrap.[57]

They lamented that the complex questions raised by laity had not been engaged and that the lengthy document was a "sea of torpid prose." *Commonweal*'s criticism focused too on the ecclesiology of the text, which gave the pope and other Vatican offices a primary role in lay spiritual formation. One sees again that ecclesiology is a fundamental issue in the development of lay theology and spirituality:

> And that is the heart of the matter: Until we develop and learn to live by an ecclesiology congruent with Vatican II and until the Vatican is able to set aside the overweening defensiveness of its own authority—only a portion of which is authentically

Petrine—the laity along with the rest of the church will be in the intolerable position of having their own concerns and queries shunted aside while being given answers to questions they did not ask.[58]

Dolores Leckey, head of the bishops' Secretariat on Laity and Family Life, gave *Christifideles Laici* a more favorable review. In her view, the text affirmed the laity's mission in the workplace and clerical consultation with laity. Despite the text's reliance on theories of complementarity and its continued rejection of women's ordination, Leckey also saw it as a step toward women's equality.[59]

"We Are the Church": A Call to Action

To put this discussion of the synod in context, it is important to note a debate about the church and the laity that began with the Call to Action conference in Detroit in 1976. The conference was the final stage in an unprecedented three-year consultation process in which the American bishops and laypersons studied and sought to correct injustices in the church and society. The process aimed to celebrate the Bicentennial with movement toward greater liberty and justice for all. Among many other topics, Call to Action participants drew up recommendations for the National Conference of Catholic Bishops. They asked the bishops to reexamine *Humanae Vitae* and to extend welcome and reconciliation to separated, divorced, and remarried Catholics. They called for the church to establish equal employment practices in its own institutions. The Detroit meeting demonstrated "a new assertiveness among lay Catholics in attempting to form church policies."[60]

The bishops did not all smile on this new assertiveness. On the one hand, they responded positively to lay desires for more influence in church structures by establishing a secretariat for the laity in 1977. They appointed laywoman Dolores Leckey as its director. On the other hand, some bishops distanced themselves or actively opposed Call to Action as it developed into an autonomous organization after the Detroit conference. In Chicago, the group publicly critiqued policies of the autocratic Cardinal John Cody. In 1981 they hosted the controversial liberal theologian Hans Küng. The Call to

Action motto "We are the Church" reflected a democratic ecclesiology. Its focus on church reform (though by no means its only
concern) gave the impression that the lay vocation was to change
the institution of the church.

In 1990, the group became a national organization and published
its platform in the *New York Times* on Ash Wednesday. The letter
(from 4,505 Catholics, with additional later signers) stated that although the laity had an important social mission, the church failed
to provide wisdom because it was "crippled by its failure to address
fundamental justice issues within its own institutional structures."[61]
Thus, the church hindered the lay vocation in the world; it could not
speak to critical social concerns. The platform asserted that internal church issues could not be divorced from the public role of the
church. Signers called for the ordination of women and the abolition
of mandatory priestly celibacy. Countering the logic of *Humanae
Vitae,* but appealing to the more recent American bishops' work,
Call to Action demanded a process of consultation and lay participation in the development of church teaching: "We call for extensive
consultation with the Catholic people in developing church teaching
on human sexuality, just as the U.S. Bishops invited participation in
developing their teaching on social justice for the pastoral letters on
peace and economic justice."[62] They also claimed that laity should
participate in the selection of local bishops. The theology of Call to
Action was clear: "The Spirit of God is at work in the whole church,
not just in its appointed leaders."[63]

Clearly, this understanding of spirituality and the lay mission
threatened church hierarchs with a more authoritarian streak. The
very conservative bishop of Lincoln, Nebraska, Fabian Bruskewitz,
banned Call to Action from the diocese in 1996 and threatened
to excommunicate its members. He cited his duty "to guard sheep
from polluted water or poisonous pastures and rather lead them to
refreshing waters of truth and the pastures of righteousness."[64] Jim
McSchane, a Call to Action member, called the bishop's warning
"an effort to invoke spiritual capital punishment."[65]

Yet other "progressive" laity also criticized Call to Action for
over-attention to internal ecclesiastical issues, neglecting the concerns of laity in their occupations. In 1977 a group of influential
lay leaders, including Ed Marciniak, former editor of the Catholic

labor journal *Work,* and CFM co-founder Patty Crowley, signed "A Chicago Declaration of Christian Concern." The statement criticized the Detroit "Call to Action" conference for overemphasizing internal church issues and cautioned that the widening involvement of lay people in traditional church ministries could lead to a devaluation of the unique secular ministries of lay people. Such trends "distract the laity from the apostolic potential that lies at the core of their professional and occupational lives."[66] *Commonweal* editors too remarked:

> Training laity for paraprofessional status appears to claim virtually all the diocesan budgets devoted to "lay" programs. Social and political transformation is equated with church lobbying, episcopal pronouncements or dramatic "witness," but not with the workaday efforts of trade unionists, business executives, professionals, government officials, educators, and parents.[67]

The "Chicago Declaration" asserted that laity should work primarily within their professional and occupational milieus to advance social justice; social action was not primarily the domain of clergy and others outside these structures. The "Declaration" favored a clear separation between lay and clerical roles:

> The Church is as present to the world in the ordinary roles of lay Christians as it is in the ecclesiastical roles of bishops and priest, though the styles of each differ. . . . The Church is present to the world in the striving of the laity to transform the world of political, economic, and social institutions. The clergy minister so that the laity will exercise their family, neighborly, and occupational roles mindful of their Christian responsibility.[68]

Ed Marciniak echoed Rev. John Coleman's statements. He wrote that a theology of social justice must be grounded

> in the lay Christian experience with the world. Faith will become justice in the world as we *laicize* our moral theology and Christian spirituality. The secular Christian is the man in the middle. As long as his/her life, which connects faith to justice,

is constantly snubbed, theologians will keep producing [naive] generalizations.[69]

Many priests also supported this affirmation of a distinct lay sphere of action. Coleman, for example, lamented a rise in religious professionalism and a decline in appreciation for the secular call:

> This depreciation of a sense of an autonomous world voca-
> tion is doubly sad since it comes at a time when for most in
> America the world-calling, by degenerating into a treadmill on
> careers which lack inner meaning, involves being trapped in
> what Weber called "an iron cage." Only religious resources
> could retrieve a new sense of worldly vocation for a genuine
> renewal of church in service of society.[70]

Catholics were raising questions here about the locus of lay spirituality. To what degree should laypersons focus their energy on ecclesiastical structures as distinct from the secular world? Does their work in the church divert attention from the "real" lay apostolate? This was in effect a debate about how to find the sacred and how to define holiness.

Finding Vocation in Secular Work?

Laity continued to call on the hierarchical church to affirm their work in the secular world. At the same time, church support for labor seemed pale. At a labor rally in Washington, D.C., that drew anywhere from 250,000 to 500,000 people, an observer noted "the relatively small representation of the religious community. The National Council of Churches had a banner flying, as did the Catholic Network, the Labor Guild of Boston, and a few others, but the marchers were few."[71] Rev. Philip J. Murnion, director of the National Pastoral Life Center, also lamented declining church support for labor and even active opposition to unions in Catholic health-care and educational institutions. Murnion noted the demise of some Catholic professional associations (e.g., the Catholic Sociological Society) and of liturgical supports for workers such as the Holy

Name Society and "communion breakfasts" for police, firefighters, and other civil servants.[72]

Some saw a crucial link between a meaningful lay spirituality of work and the power of the church in the public arena:

> Post-conciliar renewal has often come to mean a deeper and fuller involvement of the laity *in* the church rather than a greater involvement in all the institutions of our country, where the success of the laity has sometimes been seen as problematic. In their working lives, the laity find themselves less beyond or outside the church than simply detached from it. This detachment results no more from their ignoring the church than from the church ignoring them. Until church leaders learn—or care to learn—to affirm the secular lives of the laity . . . the church will not assist the political culture to face matters of war, abortion, and injustice, nor contribute anything more to the nation than resounding "no's."[73]

Indeed, it was important to stress that laypersons also had *vocations,* God-given callings, spaces of holiness in the secular world. As David Carlin Jr. wrote:

> it no longer makes sense to say that God calls some people to be priests while not calling others to be butchers, bakers, and candlestick makers. If there are such things as vocations at all, then there must be vocations to secular as well as to clerical careers.[74]

However, the privatization of religion impeded the development of a rich spirituality of work: "In this world of religious privatization and linguistic secularization, it is difficult to see how worldly occupations can even be discussed as religious vocations, let alone exist as such in actual fact."[75]

Robert Dylak contended that holiness rested in the person that worked, rather than in the type of work one performed. Workers have innate dignity, and their faith and concern for others can actualize Christianity no matter how mundane their job.[76] Another correspondent, however, lambasted the elevation of work as a space of meaning, and argued that work more often undermines our humanity: "Cutting through the gop, is the underpaid teenager bagging burgers realizing his humanity, the bored bank teller, the black-lunged coal miner hacking at the coal face, the red-eyed nit-picker on the assembly line, the licensed usurer, the prison executioner?"[77]

One author warned black Catholics that they must be active agents for economic change:

> This is not the time for black Americans or black Catholics to be passive. This is not the time to stand with open hands waiting for the nation to provide employment and economic justice, or waiting for the Catholic church to prove its catholicity. This is the time for black Catholics to be active, aggressive, and informed. This is a time for black Catholics who are trained in business, economics, law, and public policy to illuminate their knowledge with the light of the Catholic faith and come forward as responsible agents of economic development.[78]

For most laypersons, work was their primary activity in the public sphere. Despite Vatican II's increased emphasis on the priesthood of all believers and the importance of the secular world, laity still struggled to discern religious meaning in their work. Work was a mix of satisfaction and frustration, with God seeming at various times present and comforting, or irrelevant and absent. Laity faced the persistent question: How find the sacred in the midst of the secular?

An urban architect made sense of this conundrum through the sacramental heritage of Catholicism,

> which values the world in light of its being created by God and redeemed through the means of an incarnate God.
>
> That says to me that the world is an arena where it's worthwhile to pursue activities. The world is God's creation, but we are in some sense his co-conspirators. We're getting it ready. God is present in the work we do; our work is a foreshadowing of God's coming.[79]

Paul Wilkes, a Catholic writer and filmmaker, also gravitated toward a sacramental view of the world. He found spiritual sustenance and guidance for his life's work in daily Mass:

And, within the Mass, there are a couple of moments for me that always have special meaning. One is a line from the Our Father which I'm sure was written especially for the free-lance writers of the world. "Give us this day our daily bread." When money is not coming in and is not even a prospect and I am keeping our anemic checkbook balance a secret from my wife, it is a moment for ardent prayer.... I am indeed asking him for my daily bread—as well as a mortgage payment, car insurance, new roof, kids' clothes, and something to put on that bread.... The most important, most powerful, most loving Being ever comes to me in that tiny piece of unleavened bread.... I am ready to live that day and do my work.[80]

A civil attorney drew from his work an image to ground his work in the world. Faced with jammed courtrooms and bureaucratic agencies, pressured to depersonalize clients, Timothy Reuland wrote:

I know my practice of law has affected my faith and the way I see my relationship to God. In professional situations I act for others; I become their means of expression or presence in a situation. I view my role as a Christian in much the same way. I can be God's agent in all the situations that arise in my life—professional and otherwise. Just as I must make a client's viewpoint and interests felt, so too I must make the Lord's interests present in my life situations: as a lawyer, yes, but also as husband, father, citizen, friend, businessperson... I have asked myself what is this God like, who chooses, or, perhaps needs, to work through agents. Certainly God trusts us.[81]

The Family and Public Life

Reuland's comments show that while laity sought meaning in their work, so too did they seek to relate faith to their family commitments. Indeed, just as the politicians debated how to be faithful in public choices, so fidelity and discernment surfaced as important issues in private life. Actually, the very definition of the private sphere was up for grabs. Did the family need to be protected against the incursion of public life? Did marriage and parenting need to be seen as more publicly oriented ventures? These were debates about both the religious and the civic meanings of family commitments, and how to protect this meaning.

Public work and the family in fact influenced one another. The structure of the work world and cultural values that emphasized success at work exerted great stress on families. The mass media reflected these economic and cultural realities. A culture critic noted that television shows were increasingly portraying broken private lives and centering drama around the work environment rather than the home: "Suddenly, we find that our jobs matter as much, or more than, our homelife."[82] David O'Brien argued that relationships and marriage were devalued on college campuses, while professional competence was exalted.[83] On the other hand, some looked to the family as a spiritual refuge from the impersonality of work, as Christopher Lasch argued in his 1977 book *Haven in a Heartless World.*[84]

Recognizing the tensions that exist between work and family life, *Commonweal* supported a national provision for parental leave. The editors expected such legislation to further women's equality and reduce the feminization of poverty; it also "would acknowledge the central place of families in our society and restore the notion that families deserve priority in social programs."[85] Congress passed the Family and Medical Leave Act in 1993; the law guaranteed twelve weeks of unpaid leave. In 1995, 63 percent of *U.S. Catholic* readers surveyed called the policy inadequate, and 76 percent said it reflected the higher priority the United States put on work rather than family life. Eighty percent agreed that it is just as important for fathers as for mothers to get time off to spend with their young children. Readers called on Catholic organizations to blaze the trail for more generous parental-leave policies.[86] However, authors did not see public policy as the complete solution. One columnist, for example, urged the church to direct more attention in its marriage preparation programs to the tensions between family and work that couples inevitably face.[87]

The church tried to respond to changing family forms through diocesan programs. In the 1980s, numerous dioceses established Family Life Offices dedicated to developing like-to-like ministry in areas such as parenting, step-parenting, interfaith marriage, family spirituality, unwed motherhood, and divorced and separated

Catholics. The Family Life Offices resulted in part from the 1976 Call to Action conference, and they expanded the pre-1980s concentration on marriage preparation and opposition to abortion. While the American Catholic family was in flux, most laity continued to support traditional ideals of marriage. In one *U.S. Catholic* survey, for example, 93 percent of respondents stated that the church should continue to emphasize the permanency of marriage. A huge majority recommended that the church continue its practice of mandatory marriage preparation for couples marrying in the church, but 60 percent also faulted the church for inadequate support of married couples after the wedding.[88] In another survey, most respondents disapproved of cohabitation and three-fourths agreed that the "sacrament of marriage gives couples the spiritual grace that live-in couples will never have."[89] At the same time, some feared that rigid adherence to a disappearing "ideal" family form would only exclude and alienate many Catholics from faith.[90]

Changes in the family brought heightened concern about children's well-being. Amid this concern about children, one sees different approaches to the question of rights and responsibility. Some laity countered a liberal emphasis on rights; they perhaps spoke out of the Catholic tradition of subsidiarity, protecting the family from public intrusion and promoting responsibility for the common good. While Hillary Rodham Clinton advocated children's rights, for example, *Commonweal* editor Margaret O'Brien Steinfels cautioned against this strategy. Steinfels was skeptical about the promotion of children's rights. She feared the further incursion of public institutions into the lives of children, and she reasserted the importance of parental responsibility: "Lawyers can't heal families. Rights talk doesn't promote responsibility-taking."[91] John Garvey also argued that the idea of individual rights diminishes our sense of responsibility in family roles.[92]

One couple lamented the eclipse of the spiritual and social meanings of parenting:

> Today's culture is highly secular. It doesn't grant a spiritual dimension to parenthood. Thus, parenthood isn't valued as a significant calling. Its civic rationale has also lapsed. Parenthood is defined as a wholly private role, detached from any

conception of the public good. Raising children is now viewed as a lifestyle choice, just one of a whole pastry tray of equally valuable, or equally worthless, lifestyle choices. Some people choose to raise flowers. Some people choose to raise tropical fish. Some people choose to raise children. *De gustibus.*[93]

For similar reasons, laywoman Jo McGowan asserted the importance of the institution of marriage as opposed to cohabitation arrangements. McGowan saw the trend toward living together as a natural result of American individualism and privacy. A public commitment to marriage, on the other hand, asserted the meaningfulness of community; marriage was more than a private affair between the couple. As a contribution to human community, marriage was a step toward "building the kingdom of God here on earth."[94]

Yet what happens when human sin and frailty interrupt the building process? President Bill Clinton's highly publicized admissions of marital infidelity during the 1992 campaign and again in the late 1990s raised particularly complex questions about the public nature of a marriage commitment. How does a "private" commitment or betrayal affect the community? What is the relationship between private virtue and public competence? Clinton's problems showcased what is a more muted question for most. The situation was made more complicated by Clinton's public plea for forgiveness at a prayer breakfast following revelations about the Monica Lewinsky affair in 1998. Clearly, such religious overtures played a political role. Clinton's formation of an accountability circle with two evangelical ministers and one Methodist pastor also blurred the line between public faith and public relations. One of those ministers, Rev. Tony Campolo, acknowledged that spirituality and pragmatism blurred here, but he asserted: "In a sense sin was not only committed against Monica Lewinsky and against his family, but it was a sin that left the whole nation disappointed and you need to make confession to all those that you have hurt."[95]

Marriage as a "Crazy" Commitment

In the midst of these cultural debates and political embarrassments, individuals inevitably had to sort out their own values regarding personal commitments. They had to make choices about whether to marry, whether to stay married, whether to have children. They had to negotiate cultural changes in the family, religious teachings, and their own experience. Indeed, just as the politicians debated how to be faithful in public choices, so fidelity and discernment— two fundamental spiritual practices—surfaced as important issues in private life.

John Garvey distinguished the radical commitment of marriage from the individualism and subjectivity prevalent in Western culture:

> The individualism of our culture, the assumption that happiness lies in the satisfaction of desire, the unwillingness to question desire itself, all stand in the way of an appreciation of the sacramental nature of marriage....It could be that in time marriage seen as a sacrament, and lived as if it were a mystery of grace, will become nearly as radical a choice as monasticism, a counter-cultural thing.[96]

The choice for marriage, then, demanded faith. As Michael Garvey (John Garvey's brother) wrote, marriage reflected a trust in the beyond. It was a choice that required more than prudence. It demanded faith in the sacrament, in Christ's real presence in the marriage. In a society where one of two marriages ended in divorce: "The marriage vow—and I don't see how there can be a more demanding one—bears witness to any onlooker in the universe of a couple's shared belief that the birth, death, and Resurrection of Jesus are more potent and revealing than the much overrated virtue of prudence, which would regard their commitment as crazy." Garvey argued that the "scary fidelity of Jesus" is the "unique and dangerous ingredient in a Christian marriage."[97]

Marriage might have been a crazy commitment, but Catholics still held high ideals for it. Several described marriage as a path to holiness, even as a kind of priesthood and a redemptive vocation. One man who had left the active priesthood to marry wrote:

> Marriage has not fulfilled all my needs and desires but I never expected it could. Augustine was right when he said, "You have made us for yourself, O God, and our hearts are restless until they rest in you." There is loneliness and disappointment and

frustration in marriage but there is also intimacy and sharing and support. Just as I am sure that, for some, celibacy is the way to live as peaceful priests because it is their calling from God, so I am equally sure that for others, marriage is the way to live as peaceful priests because it is their calling from God.[98]

Civil attorney Timothy Reuland described his marriage as redemptive:

> This sense of being God's agent has informed my understanding of being a husband. In my marriage to my wife Kate I am one of God's means to continue to create her, to make love incarnate in her life, and to redeem any aspect of her life that may need it. She is the same for me.[99]

At the same time, his experience of marriage shaped his theology and understanding of spirituality:

> Just as faith in God has helped me understand my role in marriage, my marriage has affected my understanding of God. ...As I have learned more over the years about loving and being loved, I have seen the counterpoints of initiation and acceptance that loving involves....
>
> These experiences have appreciably softened my view of the Lord. If "God is love" to us, I imagine he has some of my same experiences. God initiates some things, accepts others. Like Kate and me, God is open, vulnerable, and at risk for all the communication, joys, and pains that a fleshy, in-depth relationship with a human being entails.[100]

Parenting and Faith: A "Ferocious" Struggle for the Domestic Church

Just as laity described marriage as both extraordinarily demanding and redemptive, so they painted a similar picture of parenting. It seemed critical to wipe out the overly romanticized visions of family woven through church teachings, the Holy Family pictures that few families mirrored. In lay writings, the family emerged as a "battleground," a "wilderness," and a "terrible gift," as well as "magical," "sacramental," and even "church."

What was clear was that family life was no easy vocation. Commitment and conflict flourished side by side in family love: "The mechanics of family life are the daily battleground for Christian principles."[101] One mother wrote: "Everything from washing dishes to making love became beautiful under God. Of course, it wasn't all sweetness and light. There were days when I could have put three of the darlings in the washer and two in the dryer. But never for a minute did I wish one of them unborn."[102] One senses that for laity, the true meaning of family could emerge only in and through a debunking of more sanitized, sanctimonious pictures. Mary Studer Shea tried to break through sentimentalized talk about motherhood; she painted a raw picture of motherhood as Christian life:

> Giving life is a terrible, terrible gift.... We have made pregnancy and motherhood a sacred cow, a false idol. We have simplified and glorified the mothering role with beautiful, meaningless clichés. The reality is much more magnificent and simultaneously much less wonderful.[103]

Another mother graphically described the physical side of parenting:

> When my son was born, I was surprised to discover how much of my love for him was purely physical. Somehow I had expected the maternal experience to be on a higher, spiritual plane—but there I was gliding his hand across my cheek.... It is not just wonderful moments that make up parenthood, however. Romanticism and sentimentality seem pretty foolish when one confronts the day's pile of dirty diapers.... Newborn babies poop more often and more alarmingly than one would believe possible, and we continue to adore them.[104]

Parenting also brought terrible challenges to faith. One mother whose eighteen-year-old son was killed by a drunk driver wrote: "I felt isolated and abandoned by God. That excruciatingly painful event initiated what I have come to call my 'wilderness experience,' a crisis situation that produced challenge, temptation, and a redefinition of my identity in relation to God and others."[105] Dolores Curran also pointed to violence against women and children, and criticized the church for its failure to counter such violence in hom-

ilies and through programs of diocesan family life offices.[106] John
Garvey confronted God's silence in the face of family violence:

> Then I pick up the newspaper and read about...a child be-
> ing starved to death by his parents.... There are, day after
> day, stories about the abuse or murder of children by their
> mothers' boyfriends. God's presence is there, too. Nothing
> happens.... How can a good God be present where children
> are tormented, and remain silent?[107]

At the same time, taking nothing away from the reality of these
wilderness experiences, parents described enormous meaning and
even revelation in their work. Jo McGowan described giving life
as a sacramental experience: "Just being pregnant and giving birth
were such magical, earth-shattering events I can hardly believe they
are in fact ordinary and common, the stuff of everyday life. They
are, for me, treasured memories, almost sacramental in their significance."[108] One pregnant woman described the awesome sense of
responsibility and humility in being a "co-creator" with God.[109]

Parenting could be a source of revelation. One mother wrote: "I
am convinced that children are mystics until they are about 6. My
children have shown me that again and again. We're sacrificing a
great deal by not spending a lot more time listening to what they
have to say about faith."[110] Kathy Coffey also described children as
spiritual teachers. Children refuse the adult addiction to schedules,
to a hectic pace of life. In their sometimes frustrating attentiveness
to the detail of the present moment, they share much in common
with the classic teachers of contemplation: "Our divided selves keep
a frantic pace, but our children call us to the gracious givenness of
now.... Through simple presence to the moment, children help us
realign our priorities."[111] In learning to let go of her children, Coffey
felt kinship with God:

> I know intimately the God who longs desperately for her
> children, misses their humor, likes their noise, and aches
> for the sight of them.... In this mixture of good-byes and
> hellos, I have seen God lifting the divine hands from cre-
> ation. Poised in the air for a terrible moment, those hands
> grant us freedom.... Participating in this paradox, I learn

how God's constant care can be intertwined with the gift of independence.[112]

Timothy Reuland too found theological insight as he learned to nurture his children's independence; his experience as a father "has enriched my sense of God, who, like me, has helped bring into the world persons who are destined to grow, change, decide. God must have the same sense of having to step back, stand by, and watch as a developing human being learns life's skills.... What respect and love this takes!"[113]

The family, then, was this combination of wisdom and wilderness, beauty and battleground. Its meaning was ambiguous, and perhaps in this ambiguity lay its sacramentality. The everyday, with all its physicality, conflict, and question, was the space for the sacred. In this sense, laity affirmed the ideal of the family as "domestic church." The domestic church was not a "pure" space set apart. It was holy ground because it was the human ground where one struggled to love, to be faithful, to let go, to understand. To take the idea of the "domestic church" seriously pushes the borders of the church in general, blurs the distinctions between sacred and secular. As one author wrote, referring to the Hispanic custom of the home altar:

> My family had never been very clear about the boundary where worship (or service) begins or ends. Much less, my family had never identified the church building itself as defining that sacred space. Our family's home altar...embodied this resistance to defining sacred space.... The home altar is not so much making worship private but a sign of bold faith amidst ferocious struggle, a struggle for the domestic church.[114]

Conclusion

The struggle for the domestic church symbolized a larger struggle to find meaning in everyday, ambiguous spheres of action. This larger issue arose in debates about work and vocation. It also showed itself in painful complexity as lay politicians debated with church authorities. Underlying all these struggles were questions about the church, authority, spirituality, and the boundary between private and public.

John Garvey asked the hard question: How can a good God be present and remain silent? The silence of God often confronts Christians in times of crisis. Yet they also may find divine silence in the ordinary experiences of family life and work, in corporate and governmental structures, and in the church. These spaces may feel like "wilderness experiences," times of wandering in places unknown, bearing little trace of the sacred. In the wilderness, Christians may lose their orientation. They may become spiritually "narcissistic." They may become fatigued. Yet laity also show a way forward. They point to the possibility of redemption through marriage, theological revelation through parenting, sacramental grace through work.

The debates between lay politicians and the bishops pose enormous theological questions. Both Cuomo and Ferraro claimed that their faith was private. Cuomo distinguished between discernment and doctrine in private life and practical reason in political judgment. I believe that he posited too sharp a dichotomy here. I will argue in the next chapter that faith can inform the exercise of practical reason, and that the integrity of the Christian demands it. More positively, Cuomo argued that his practical judgment must be respected because of his greater political experience. He makes an important argument here for respecting lay competency in practical areas about which church hierarchy has lesser experience. I now will explore these points in more detail.

– Chapter Five –

FORMING THE PEOPLE OF GOD

Theological and Pastoral Considerations

A S ONE LOOKS BACK over this complex story of American Catholic laypersons, it is clear that there are many narratives and
contexts. One cannot draw simple conclusions, nor apply a single
solution to the multiple dilemmas of the lay vocation. I will attempt to clarify, however, some of the theological issues and make
modest recommendations to inform the practice of lay Christians. It
is important first to consider how these stories inform one's understanding of spirituality. This will entail sorting out the different types
of models presented to us in this book and evaluating them. I will
argue that while the contemplative vocation witnesses to the transcendent, this vocation should not be elevated a priori over more
active vocations. I also will identify particular types of lay vocation—politician, prophet, invisible leaven, dialoguer, and domestic
church—and the contours and complexity of each. Second, I will return to the ecclesiological questions that have woven their way into
many of these lay stories. Various understandings of the church can
either inspire or impede the lay vocation. I will argue for the importance of two particular understandings of the church: the church
as the pilgrim People of God and the church as the Mystical Body
of Christ. Finally, I will explore spiritual practice that can better
ground lay work in the world. First, I will show the complexity
of Christian discernment, looking particularly at the relationship
between faith and practical reason. The segregation of faith and
practical reason is one cause of a compartmentalized and privatized
faith. I will argue that a religious perspective can inform the exercise
of practical reason, which should be understood as an important responsibility in a faithful life. At the same time, one must respect the

137

complexity of practical judgments, including the importance of competency and experience. Second, I advocate the Cardijn see-judge-act method as a helpful means of relating faith and practical reason in a prayerful method of discernment and practical theological reflection. Third, I recover the monastic practice of *lectio divina* as a means of lay formation and explore three particular texts that could ground lay vocation and Christian identity. The directions discussed here are applicable across most Christian denominations, and they also may be relevant to other faiths. In addition, each religious community would look to its own traditions for more specific practices and resources to be brought into conversation with contemporary experience.

Contemplation and Christian Hope

The introduction to this book presented a rough outline of how people understood sanctity from the Middle Ages to the twentieth century. With the twentieth century came an opening in Catholic teaching, the possibility of overturning a two-tiered notion of sanctity that for so long undermined lay confidence in the meaning of their lives. This story of lay Catholics shows an ongoing struggle with the two-tiered notion of sanctity. Laity creatively attempted to articulate a spirituality that acknowledged the meaning of daily life in the world. They also searched for that meaning, questioned it themselves, wrestled with a sense of fragmentation, dissipation, and blurred boundaries.

I would argue that we must avoid a two-tiered notion of sanctity while still emphasizing the need for discipline and a hunger for something More. The ordained or religious life is not inherently more holy than the lay vocation. To link sanctity to one or two vocations is false and damaging to the Christian life. There are different states in life, various paths for approaching God. Sanctity is about how one walks on one's path, not the path a priori. The Christian life should be defined more in terms of love, attention, receptivity, fidelity, discernment, and responsibility rather than a priori in terms of a particular path.

Here one can learn from Francis de Sales and John Wesley. One recalls Francis's counsel:

> When he created things God commanded plants to bring forth
> their fruits, each one according to its kind, and in like manner
> he commands Christians, the living plants of his Church, to
> bring forth the fruits of devotion, each according to his po-
> sition and vocation. Devotion must be exercised in different
> ways by the gentleman, the worker, the servant, the prince,
> the widow, the young girl and the married woman.[1]

For Francis, devotion was love aflame, whatever one's particular
path. Wesley too described the spiritual life as a zealous love. This
love demands discipline and responsibility to one's calling, but the
particular calling in and of itself does not constitute perfection.

Of course, it must be noted that the idea of a higher and a lower
path preceded Christianity. Indeed, Plato and Aristotle exalted the
contemplative or philosophical life over the political life. Plato's philosopher is dragged out of the darkness of the cave into the dazzling
light of truth, to "attain what we have called the highest form of
knowledge, and to ascend to the vision of the good."[2] The language
of ascension (also common in classic Christian spiritual writings)
makes clear the hierarchy of the paths, one higher and one lower.
Comparing his life to those of the prisoners in the cave, the philosopher once having contemplated reality would "prefer anything
to a life like theirs."[3] He only reluctantly "descends" to the cave in
service of others, "to take part in the hard work of politics."[4] Like
Plato, Aristotle too exalts theoretical reason. According to Aristotle,
theoretical reason is higher than practical reason, for it contemplates
that which is unchanging and eternal. Practical reason, on the other
hand, deals with the changing realities of temporal, contingent ex-
istence. Aristotle called theoretical wisdom (*sophia*) "science in its
consummation, as it were, the science of the things that are valued
most highly."[5]

The hierarchy of theoretical and practical reason seen in this
Greek thought can easily be translated into a religious hierarchy—
the contemplative monastic life being higher than lay life in the
world. Indeed, medieval synthesizer Thomas Aquinas translated
the Greek hierarchy into his theological system. He too assumed
a "higher" and a "lower" reason, although he saw them as related.
Practical reason helps to create the moral and civic virtue that en-

ables theoretical reason to flourish.[6] Aquinas associated each kind of reason with particular virtues. Wisdom was a virtue of the speculative intellect, for example, while prudence was a virtue of the practical intellect. These natural virtues brought a degree of happiness and they directed us to our supernatural end. Contemplation of God was the highest calling. Yet here I would note a crucial difference between Aquinas and the Greek philosophers. Perfection for Aquinas comes only in the future life, when one sees God in God's essence. Hence, I would read Aquinas as relativizing all human spiritual hierarchies. Perfect happiness consists in nothing less than the vision of God promised in 1 Corinthians 13:12: "For now we see in a mirror, dimly, but then we will see face to face. Now I know only in part; then I will know fully, even as I have been fully known." Aquinas wrote that "man's ultimate felicity consists only in the contemplation of God" and "man's ultimate felicity will lie in the knowledge of God that the human mind has after this life."[7] Thus, reason moves toward an imperfect happiness, but perfection (true contemplation of God) is beyond reason and all human powers.

It is that eschatological hope that must be retained, even as we redefine spirituality in the context of lay worldliness. There are ways of living that are more or less faithful, that give greater or lesser service, that bring one closer or further from glimpsing the divine. Yet ultimately all faithful paths yearn forward. What the traditional two-tiered sanctity did uphold was that sense of transcendence; there was something beyond this world that merited attention. The sacred could be set apart and witnessed to through a separate lifestyle devoted to prayer. Unfortunately, the form of witness got identified with transcendence itself. The contemplative life itself became sanctified above the lay life. I argue that a corrective understanding will emphasize the distinct tasks of different modes of witness, all limited, all good, all pointing beyond themselves.

As Simone Weil so eloquently insisted, to wait on God is our position in this life. Attention is the substance of prayer. Attention and hunger, then, are the marks of a Christian:

> The soul knows for certain only that it is hungry. The important thing is that it announces its hunger by crying. A child does not stop crying if we suggest to it that perhaps there is no

bread.... The danger is not lest the soul should doubt whether there is any bread, but lest, by a lie, it should persuade itself that it is not hungry.[8]

Hunger also brings compassion and an ability to truly love the other. Hence, hunger and hope open into active work of solidarity, love, and justice.

Context and Christian Life

This is the Christian life, but none of it is lived in a vacuum. We are a people in history, influenced by cultural norms, social change, and the circumstances of our own personal biographies. Christianity is an incarnational faith, and so historical particularities take on particular relevance. They are part of the "flesh" of the Body of Christ. This story of Roman Catholic laity and American public life illustrates the importance of context.

American Christians must make sense of secularity, pluralism, and democracy. They must figure out how being Christian makes a difference in public responsibilities. They must decide if their faith will be relegated to a protected space, or whether it bears relevance to economic activity. They also seek meaning in family life, that private sphere that is not so private and that often competes with public duties. They must navigate through American "culture wars" as they determine their "family values." If politics, work, and family cannot be connected to faith, then spirituality becomes quite a narrow slice of life. Yet faith always relativizes every human activity; it bears on but must not be collapsed into our mundane dilemmas. Here is the delicate balance, the spiritual challenge of the laity.

In one sense, laity are called to the same life as any Christian: to live in relationship to a sacred Other, to orient one's life to that presence, to pay attention. They struggle to believe, to trust, to witness, to love. Yet lay Christians also are asked to straddle worlds. They take roles at home, in communities, in the workplace, and in church. They live in many spheres; they bridge secular and sacred. While the church blesses this vocation, it has not adequately explored the complexity of the lay situation nor prepared laypersons for it.

As one examines the cast of characters in this story, it is important to take account of their different social roles and particular historical contexts. They face different pressures and have available different ranges of response. We have looked at people, organizations, and movements. The line between an organization and a movement is difficult to trace in many of these cases. The Christian Family Movement, the United Farm Workers, and Catholic Charismatic Renewal, for example, all were movements that over time developed characteristics of an organization. An organization or movement, of course, faces different challenges than does an individual. It must be maintained amid diverse personalities and changing social contexts. We saw disputes, for example, about race in the Christian Family Movement and about religious identity in the farm workers union. Just as individuals struggle to determine and maintain their religious identity in the changing public space, so too do organizations and movements. But the identity of an organization is different. In some ways, it can be maintained more easily as institutional weight and a tradition can carry it through change. In other ways, identity is more problematic as the context becomes more pluralistic; multiple voices within the organization assert differing identities.

Types of Lay Spirituality

One can identify several different types or models of how to understand the public role of the Christian. Drawing from the contextual examples of this American Catholic story, I will explore the following: the elected politician, the prophet, the invisible leaven, the hospitable dialoguer, and the publicly oriented domestic church.

One type of lay spirituality can be seen in the elected politician. Believing that the ends of American government are compatible with Christian ends, the Christian politician must seek to concretize those ends in particular acts of legislation. Multiple values are at stake: liberty, life, diversity, moral consensus, civil society. This is a complex and often painful position. The model politician, in my view, uses power for good, strives for integrity between personal beliefs and public responsibility, and engages his or her deepest convictions in public reflection and debate. It is true that prudential judgments should not be given ultimacy. Yet this does not mean that faith has no bearing on the exercise of practical reason, as I will discuss below. John F. Kennedy set an unhelpful precedent when he privatized his faith in response to critics. In practice, he was more open to public religious involvement. Yet his precedent continued to influence politicians in the 1980s, including Mario Cuomo and Geraldine Ferraro. Kennedy, Cuomo, and Ferraro were elected officials in a pluralistic democracy. They were charged with protecting and preserving the American political system and representing their constituents. They stood in a particularly complicated position. Recognizing the complexity of their roles, I still would assert, however, that the politician must have integrity. Core "personal" convictions, whatever their source, cannot be divorced from public action without undermining conscience and integrity.

I would prefer a politician who asserted his or her deepest moral convictions in public, allowed them to be critiqued, and refused to seek a position that would compromise those fundamental convictions. Surely, belief about life is such a fundamental position. A politician might have other fundamental convictions that would lead her to continue to work within the system, but then those beliefs also could be asserted publicly. Ferraro, for example, would have done better in her campaign to argue that while her faith convinced her that the fetus is a life worth protecting, her faith also impelled her to seek the protection and nurture of human life through legislation on education, housing, and social services. Or that she valued religious pluralism more than she was convinced of the absoluteness of her position on abortion. She mentioned these beliefs in her autobiography, but she could have made them more public in the campaign rather than asserting that her faith was "very private." Hence, she could have asserted the multiple convictions that convinced her to remain working within the political system. In this way, the politician allows religion in all its complexity to enter the public realm and presents a better model of integrity.

A quite different type of public Christian is the prophet. He or she has more distance from "the system." In the prophetic model, believers take a counter-cultural stand and defend it on the basis of their religious convictions. They call society to repent and turn to a new way of life. Dorothy Day, *Integrity* editors Carol Jackson and Ed Willock, and Cesar Chavez are examples of this type of prophetic spirituality. One sees diversity within this type, of course. For example, Day was far more resistant to the American political system than was Chavez, who actually integrated his prophecy into astute political campaigns. The danger in the prophecy model is that the practical judgments of the prophet can be idolized and absolutized, when in fact they may be misguided.

Cesar Chavez did not face a divide between his faith convictions and his strategic political decisions. In Chavez's eyes, faith pointed him to both the ends and the means. Chavez needed legislative change to allow farm workers representative organization. Despite pluralism in the American public and within his own movement, he publicly integrated faith symbols and practices into the strategic means. He led a pilgrimage to the state capital. He insisted on nonviolence. He fasted. He tried to sustain his movement through living in community. The religious teachings Chavez read as a young man supported his ideals. His appeal to spiritual practices and community further cemented the integration. Certainly one could interject here a more a skeptical interpretation of Chavez's religiosity as a strategic means for drawing support and sympathy. Prophecy can be misused. Yet I think this would be a reductionistic interpretation. One might debate the practical judgments of the prophet, yet it is most probable that people like Chavez and Day had a genuine integrity of faith, private life, and public action. The means Chavez chose allowed him an integrity that Cuomo, for example, could not enjoy. Cuomo simply did not have that seamless blend of personal conviction and political persona. Cuomo's position (and perhaps that of any democratic politician who genuinely values his or her faith) seems more fragmented and agonizing.

Another type of lay spirituality is implicit evangelization. Here believers act to embody the gospel wherever they are, dispersed in multiple public spaces, without necessarily invoking religious language. Here one might recall the image of "leaven." Yeast dissolves in water, becoming invisible as it is kneaded throughout the entire loaf. Yet this unseen leaven causes the whole loaf to rise; laity are mixed invisibly into the world like yeast in bread dough. If the world is the Body of Christ, then in some way Christians as leaven actually reenact the Resurrection, causing Christ to rise. This model is illustrated by less well-known lay writers cited in this book, including the school superintendent Frank Macchiarola and civil attorney Timothy Reuland. We may have fewer public models of this type, because by nature this approach is less explicit and more invisible. This is an important type of spirituality for the majority of Christians, who will be neither politicians nor prophets. Most of us work in complex systems and relationships, hoping to do the decent thing and in small ways embody the gospel. A danger of this model is that invisibility can lead to uncritical assimilation.

One also can identify a type of public Christian life that emphasizes hospitality and reconciliation. Here believers engage a pluralistic public by inviting diverse segments of the society to come together in a calm space for dialogue about difficult social questions. One might see *Commonweal* magazine in this light, at least in its intent to promote dialogue and a public faith. In this type of lay spirituality, Christians acknowledge their limitations in dealing with complex social issues but show social concern and open themselves to listen. The dialogue itself builds a richer civil society. The downside of this type of lay spirituality is that dialogue does not always lead to action, and certain situations of injustice require strong action. It is good to acknowledge the complexity of social problems, but fear of acting may result in greater harm. Christianity needs both dialoguers and prophets.

Another type of lay spirituality is what I will call the publicly oriented domestic church. The Grail and the Christian Family Movement are examples of movements that promoted this spirituality. The many laypersons who quietly found wider meaning in their families are additional illustrations. This type of spirituality focuses on the family as a sphere of meaning and even revelation, yet sees family commitments as a public task and vocation that ripples outward to shape public life. One recalls Barbara and Ralph Whitehead's insistence that parenting is not just a lifestyle choice, but rather a civic calling in service of the public good. Tensions within the Christian Family Movement revealed the difficulties in balancing intense family needs with an "outward" focus. The domestic type of lay vocation holds a danger of privatizing faith. Yet laity also show that family commitments in and of

themselves can be publicly relevant vocations. This type of spirituality has been used to restrict women to the domestic role, but it
need not.

The type of public spirituality to which one gravitates depends on
personal gifts, temperament, opportunity, commitments, and context. It also reflects different visions of the relationship between
sacred and secular. All these types fit within the church, and each
has its particular complexity. They are not mutually exclusive. While
the politician and the prophet may be most difficult to combine, for
example, the hospitable dialoguer and the domestic church can fit
quite well together. In any case, the lay vocation should not be seen
as an individual affair. The calling of each individual is part of a
wider whole, the work of the church in the world.

Ecclesiology

How one understands the church bears greatly on the lay sense of
vocation. I would highlight two images of the church that seem
particularly fruitful. First, the church is the pilgrim People of God.
This image is deeply scriptural, echoing God's special care for the
people of Israel. The people belong to God, this God who wrestles
with them, calls them from scattered places, chastises them, and
shines light on their path. As we read in Isaiah 9:2: "The people
that walked in darkness have seen a great light." The image of the
pilgrim church also is imbedded in Christian tradition and recovered
specifically in the Second Vatican Council texts.[9]

As the pilgrim People of God, the church is on the move, ven-
turing out into all parts of the world. The image also captures the
Christian hope that yearns forward. A pilgrim is a seeker, one who
searches out a place of connection and transcendence, beyond her
ordinary world. She searches out a promised city, as we read in the
Hebrew Scriptures and again in the Letter to the Hebrews: "Therefore, while the promise of entering his rest is still open, let us take
care that none of you should seem to have failed to reach it" (Heb.
4:1). A pilgrimage is actually a dialogue between past and present
in a quest for a future.[10] A pilgrimage site is usually a traditional
sacred site, a place of the past. In this way, the pilgrim is part of a
living tradition, journeying into the past for meaning, bringing the

present back to the past. It is no wonder that pilgrimage held special importance for Cesar Chavez and the farm workers; pilgrimage stirs people to seek what has been promised.

As interpreted by the Second Vatican Council, the "People of God" is an inclusive image that emphasizes the whole community. In my view, while this image is compatible with a hierarchical church, the People of God image deemphasizes the hierarchical structure. All are called. This image counters the still too common tendency to identify the church with its ordained leadership. Rather, laity need the confidence to assert "We are the church." Yet the church also cannot lapse into subjectivity. One should not misinterpret this image to mean that every individual chooses what is church and what is not. (Note that it is "People of God," not "person of God.") Rather, the community as a whole seeks genuinely to orient itself toward God and to witness to the gospel. A People has a fundamental unity even as it holds multiple differences. The People of God ecclesiology also counters a static understanding of the church. The church is not fundamentally a building or an institution, but rather a community of pilgrims in this world.

A second understanding of the church that could be recovered fruitfully is the Mystical Body of Christ ecclesiology. This image—coupled with the liturgical renewal—inspired lay movements in the days before the Second Vatican Council. This ecclesiology has long roots in Scripture and tradition. Patristic writers such as John Chrysostom, for example, embraced this understanding of the reality of the church.

The Mystical Body of Christ ecclesiology emphasizes the incarnate nature of Christ and the church as the sacrament of Christ in the world. As the Second Vatican Council declared, "the Church, in Christ, is in the nature of sacrament—a sign and instrument, that is, of communion with God and of unity among all men."[11] More specifically, the Mystical Body of Christ is a profoundly eucharistic understanding of the church. As Chrysostom preached:

> For as that body is united to Christ, so also are we united to him by this bread.... For what is the bread? The Body of Christ. And what do they become who partake of it? The Body of Christ: not many bodies, but one body. For as the bread

consisting of many grains is made one...so are we conjoined both with each other and with Christ.[12]

Jesuit Walter Burghardt summarized, "The church is the Body of Christ because she lives by the body of Christ."[13] The Mystical Body of Christ image emphasizes the abiding presence of Christ in and through us in the world. Every member of the body receives its life from the head, Christ. Yet so too do the parts of the body bring life—blood, oxygen, energy—to the head. A humbling and incredible mission!

The Mystical Body of Christ image, like the phrase "People of God," emphasizes the spiritual community. The Body is an organic, living unity. Each member is created differently and has a different task. Yet the diversity serves the union. Every member contributes to the life of the Body. Hence, this ecclesiology fits with a living sense of the tradition. The tradition is not static but ongoing. Like the body as it grows and ages, the tradition too can take on different appearances in different seasons of its life. The identity of the person does not fundamentally change even as the body shows changes for new life stages (e.g., puberty, maternity) or shows the weathering effects of life in the world (e.g., stooped shoulders, wrinkles). Our identity, then, is that of the body living throughout history. This understanding of the church reminds us that we are part of something much larger than our own individual life. Stanley Hauerwas wrote:

> Paul did not think that we, as baptized believers, ought to view our bodies as if we were one with one another through Christ, but rather that our bodies are quite literally not our "own" because we have been made (as well as given) a new body by the Spirit. What is crucial, therefore, is not whether the Church is primarily understood as "the body of Christ" or "the people of God," but whether the practices exist through which we learn that our bodies are not "ours."[14]

The Body of Christ also is an image of a church of solidarity. In the body, the pain of one member becomes the pain of all. A broken arm brings a grimace to the face. Pain may make the heart race and the blood flow. Parts of the body compensate for the injured part. Even a stubbed toe causes the hand (and likely the mouth) to react.

In this way, the Mystical Body of Christ ecclesiology sends the laity out to bear the pain in the world. Spirituality is not about retreating, but about solidarity. It is not possible to be Christian and to ignore the pain of another member. To avoid an exclusivist understanding, I would assert that the Mystical Body of Christ is wider than the visible church. Hence, solidarity extends to all. Because suffering is not just about individual relationships, the Christian must enter into the powerful structures that affect the well-being of the whole. This is a public spirituality.

At the same time, the Mystical Body of Christ in its very fleshiness gives dignity to the body and hence to the sphere of family and sexuality. Laity are not "less spiritual" because they spend a great deal of time attending to physical life—giving baths, giving birth, changing diapers, changing bandages, having sex, having dinner. Rather, faith calls us to reverence the body and its life, to see the incarnate Christ there. As one layman wrote: "When my bride and I married, in the days before people began making up their own pallid vows, we promised each other: 'With my body I thee worship.' Jesus put his Last Supper and Crucifixion in that framework, worshiping us with his body."[15] Here the Mystical Body of Christ finds its embodiment in the domestic church.

Church/World, Sacred/Secular

The emphasis on the lay vocation in the secular world is important to recapture the true fullness of the church. The church is the Mystical Body of Christ in the world, the hands and feet and mouth of Christ amid creation. The church stifles its own life when it limits its place to the walls of the building or the workings of the institution. The church is primarily called to witness to the good news of God's overflowing love for creation, to the innate dignity of every person, and the possibility of life with God. That mission cannot be contained to Sunday worship, as important as the liturgy is to feed the Body. Rather, the work of the church is in the workplace, the public square, the family, the neighborhood.

The lay Christian works and moves and relates in that world, and hence it makes sense to speak about the distinctive lay vocation in the temporal world. Ordained ministers are also oriented to the

world, but in and through the sacramental ministry and the care
of the community. This is their primary sphere of action although
this sphere needs to be understood flexibly, depending on particular
contexts and individual gifts. To identify these distinctive ordained
and lay vocations recognizes not only different callings, but also the
limitations of human energy and the need for a division of labor,
though not a segregation of concern.

For too long, the work of the church has been seen in terms of the
internal affairs and worship life of the community. To emphasize the
lay vocation in the world brings a critical corrective. It also recognizes the small, invisible witness of the Christian in the public arena,
civic society, and family. Too many Christians have not understood
themselves as having a vocation; they have not seen their multiple
roles as having religious meaning and dignity.

On the other hand, I would not endorse any notion of lay vocation
that prevented lay involvement in the institutional leadership or internal ministry of the church (or that prevented clergy and religious
from entering traditionally "lay" spheres of action for good reasons).
To do so wrongly uses the notion of lay holiness and creates a false
dichotomy between the church and the world. It deprives the church
of many gifts of the people. (And, certainly, this is not a deprivation
the church can withstand given the shortage of priestly vocations.)
There is much work to be done in and for the Body. Each person
should use her or his distinctive gifts in service of human ends and as
a witness to the sacred. This may mean directing religious education,
working as chancellor for a diocese, serving as pastoral associate,
working in a government office, or creating art. The ministry should
follow from the gifts and human needs. Moreover, the lay voice
must play a role in shaping official church teachings, particularly
regarding social, political, and economic questions. These teachings
are an important part of the church's public presence. Laity should
be able to represent their church community in an official capacity;
public representation need not be linked to sacramental ministry.

Faith and Public Life

Let me be clear. The church's primary mission is to preach the good
news, to nurture human beings in the life of the Spirit, and to witness

to the God who is always More and always Mystery. This primary mission has inevitable social implications. The social mission of the church must not supplant the spiritual mission. Our society blurs the line between spirituality and productivity. Too often we make faith utilitarian, a tool to achieve inner peace, healing, a job, or a social change. These may be good aims, but we lose something essential to faith. The church can overemphasize action and results at the expense of being still, waiting, hoping, even unknowing.

If many members of congregations cannot find a spiritual anchor in their lives, then what do the churches really have to say about social questions that is distinctive—and authentic? Deep religious faith eludes many today, and this, it seems to me, should be the central concern for churches. If the charismatic movement teaches us anything, it is the human hunger for an experience of the Spirit. The church should be a people with a deep hunger for God, a people who pray for the Spirit. That hunger cannot be completely filled by social action, by family, or any other human action or relationship, as good and important as they are. We are a pilgrim people, always seeking and waiting and hoping for that which we have not yet seen. As some laity noted, attention to social issues can diffuse attention to questions of faith that may be even more troubling.

That said, the spiritual and the social missions of the church are intricately interconnected. Both aim for the fullness of the human person. The love of God cannot be known in a vacuum; the incarnate work of human beings acts with grace to make God known in our particular lives. We also learn how to be "spiritual" by— in our very limited ways—seeking to embody holy virtues such as love, justice, mercy, humanity, fidelity, and wisdom. Christian faith is not a private affair; it reaches its fullness in public witness and service. The public mission of the church is complicated, full of gray areas, inadequate information, and unintended consequences. There are dangers to the public vocations. Max Weber went so far as to warn: "He who seeks the salvation of the soul, of his own and of others, should not seek it along the avenue of politics, for the quite different tasks of politics can only be solved by violence. The genius or demon of politics lives in an inner tension with the god of love, as well as with the Christian God as expressed by the church."[16] And yet public responsibility is an essential vocation of the Christian. Politics cannot in and of itself save, but neither can it be abdicated.

It is important to connect faith and public life for several reasons. First, individuals and religious groups experience an enormous sense of fragmentation when faith seems unconnected to the public spheres of life in which we expend so much energy and encounter brokenness and joy. On the one hand, this sense of fragmentation is a natural part of being a finite, limited individual. On the other hand, it is a particularly intense problem of our modern times, one intensified by our multiple roles, by our differing public and private selves, and by an overly private and interior understanding of spirituality, compartmentalized from the rest of life.

The well-being of our society also rests on our ability to find a public dimension of spirituality. Religious groups can add to public discourse distinctive visions of the human person, the common good, the ends of human life, and the transformative power of a Mysterious Other. Society is diminished when these visions cannot make their way into public debate and action. The question, then (as John Courtney Murray showed), is how particular values can enter public life while still upholding the freedoms necessary to a dignified pluralistic society, and indeed necessary to any genuine act of faith.

Individuals and communities may experience a kind of weakening of spiritual intensity as they delve into public action and debates about public issues. Certainly, the language churches use in public debate often shifts; it is less churchy, less pious, less connected perhaps to the core religious vision at the heart of the community. This enables a pluralistic public to hear the church's arguments, but the church itself can experience a distancing from the power of its own message.

The situation is complicated by the diffusion of "spirituality" today. Many people would say that they are spiritual but not religious. There are some good impulses behind such understandings of spirituality. They give value to human experience and expression. They protect the individual seeker from oppressive communities and rote dogma. They preserve the freedom of the search. Yet when one tries to talk about spirituality and public life in the same breath, one may find oneself at a loss. Contemporary understandings of spirituality tend to be highly privatized, the locus being personal, individual, affective, primarily private experience. As Philip Sheldrake writes:

> Some theorists would argue that it is nowadays impossible to describe or defend any overarching framework of explanation or value. In this case the spiritual quest moves away from being an expression of belief. Doctrines appear as eccentric options with no natural spiritual consequences. The result is what might be thought of as a privatization of spirituality and a concentration on interiority that sometimes separates spiritual experience from a social or public vision of ethics.[17]

When I use the word "public" in relation to Christian spirituality, I have in mind two contexts for that word. First is the public nature of the church as a community of believers; the church here is a public that nurtures and guides individual spiritual seekers. Here is a space in which experience can be interpreted in light of the best wisdom of the community, in its Scriptures, traditions, and its own process of discernment. The individual is not left entirely in his or her subjective experience, although this experience is valued as part of the collective journey of the People of God. We do need to strengthen this public church; this does not mean uncritical acceptance. In fact, to bring vigorous critique of the church's injustices and errors, in dialogue with people of all beliefs, affirms the public character of the church.

The second sense of "public" is the church's relation to the wider society of which it is a part. Here, spirituality grounds and propels the community's vision of itself as a hoping, loving, reconciling, witnessing force in the world. The desire for the divine, and any experiences and practices that are part of that desire, help an individual within community to strike a posture in the world. This is a posture of engagement, critical discernment, and humble, careful, hospitable work to address complex social problems.

Practical Reason and Spiritual Discernment

If the religious person is to engage faith with work in the public sphere, then he or she must be guided in discernment. Discernment is, of course, important for all people, ordained or lay. Yet the kinds of decisions that lay people make every day have been neglected in teachings on discernment. Laity must make choices in their private relationships, at work, and in public responsibilities. If they are to be "leaven in the world," then they must daily make practical judgments consistent with this mission. It is important, then, to think through the relationship between faith and practical reason. Too often these are experienced as separate spheres. The practical decisions that people must make at work or in the family often seem irrelevant to religious faith. Thus, many experience a disjuncture between everyday responsibilities and more discrete ecclesial moments of worship or private devotion. Ultimately, I think this produces a compartmentalized faith and an experience of fragmentation. It also diminishes the lay mission in society. If faith has nothing to do with everyday decision-making, then faith will be compartmentalized. Yet one needs to be very careful in how one describes the relationship between faith and practical reason.

Most literature on discernment focuses either on individual choices (e.g., whether to marry or seek ordination) or on decision-making within the church.[18] There are far fewer resources to guide the discernment of laity in positions of public responsibility, such as in government or business. How make choices for a highly pluralistic polity? How weigh imperfect alternatives? Does faith relate to such questions?

Laity may not think about discernment because many of their decisions seem practical and worldly—not the stuff the Spirit usually would swoop down for. Faith relates in a general way to the course of one's life, but its relevance pales as one gets into the nitty-gritty choices of daily life. Those choices people make using their reason, emotions, and intuition. Often they seek the advice of friends, family, work colleagues, talk show hosts, and self-help books. Scripture and tradition offer another model of decision-making: spiritual discernment.

Discernment is the gift of wisdom, the grace to sift out what is of value. Scriptural texts depict discernment within the community of believers (e.g., Acts 15) and as an individual spiritual gift to be used for the good of the community (e.g., 1 Cor.). Discernment means taking on the mind of Christ: "Those who are spiritual discern all things, and they are themselves subject to no one else's scrutiny.... But we have the mind of Christ" (1 Cor. 2:15–16). To take on the mind of Christ is to perceive the will of God: "Do not be conformed to this world, but be transformed by the renewing of your minds, so that you may discern what is the will of God—what is good and acceptable and perfect" (Rom. 12:2). Discernment then is described in the Scriptures as a process of enlightenment and renewal: "as you come to know him, so that, with the eyes of your heart enlightened, you may know what is the hope to which he has called you" (Eph. 1:17–18). It is a way to test: "All must test their own work" (Gal. 6:4). We should "test everything; hold fast to what is good" (1 Thess. 5:21). Discernment, then, presumes moral choice, the capacity to choose the good with the help of grace.

Cuomo: A Case Study in Discernment

The speech made by Governor Mario Cuomo at the University of Notre Dame in 1984 raises this critical question for laity: the relationship between faith and practical reason. Cuomo alleged that his political judgments depended on prudential judgments among less than perfect alternatives. Faith may influence decisions in private life, but the complexity of public policy demanded pragmatic—not religious—judgments. In my view, Cuomo makes a false dichotomy. He rightly notes that pragmatic judgments are imperfect. Yet he too quickly separates practical reasoning from religious conviction. I would assert that religious people can see their practical judgments as part of the life of faith. This stance will not bring moral certainty, but it will offer greater integrity. I will walk through Cuomo's decision, bringing him into dialogue with Aristotle's view of practical reason and with selected church teachings. This exercise should bring greater understanding of the complex vocation of the lay Christian, and some guiding directions.

First, I argue that faith cannot be simply separated from the practical reason demanded in public responsibilities. Here I understand practical reason as related to both ends and means. Practical reason is not simply technical judgment, but rather deliberation about the good life. As Aristotle wrote, the end of practical science is good action (*eupraxia*). Practical wisdom (*phronesis*) is a virtue, a capacity to deliberate well about what will contribute to the good life for the individual and, more importantly, for the community. Indeed, "surely one's own good cannot exist without household management nor without a political system."[19] This is a crucial point for lay people today. So-called "private" life bears on the wider community, and both public and private decisions call for wise deliberation concerning not only means but also good ends. I would argue that because religious beliefs carry visions of the good and notions of the ends we should seek, religion relates to practical judgments.

To understand practical reason as related to both ends and means gives it greater weight. One may distinguish this practical reason from common connotations of "prudence," which imply an ability to safely navigate through situations, preserving the self or an established order. Prudence here means carefulness. John F. Kennedy was prudent when he privatized his faith in response to critics during the presidential campaign. His prudence won him a position of great power, yet also surrendered an important dimension (the public power) of faith. This kind of worldly prudence is not the virtue of which I speak when I discuss practical wisdom. Prudence in this sense is not always a Christian virtue. After all, Christ did overturn much worldly wisdom and relativized our institutions. Thus, Ignatius (who quite affirms the place of reason in the Christian life) can describe the most perfect way of humility as being able to say: "I desire to be regarded as a useless fool for Christ, who before me was regarded as such, rather than as a wise or prudent person in this world."[20] Layman Michael Garvey, discussed earlier, implied that one must be a fool for Christ in marriage. The marriage vow pushes one beyond prudence; it requires faith in the resurrected Christ who is really present in the sacrament of marriage.

Perhaps my understanding of prudence is close to that of Cardinal Suenens. Suenens, one recalls, distinguished between human and supernatural prudence. Supernatural prudence is open to God's wisdom in prayer, even when that wisdom runs counter to ordinary human wisdom. Mindful that faith always requires more than "worldly" or "human" practical wisdom, I still would assert that reason has an important place in a faithful life. Drawing from a fuller understanding of practical reason as related to both ends and means, I would assert that practical wisdom is a virtue that points us to the ultimate Good.

Cuomo served as an elected official, governor of the state of New York. Thus, he represented an institution with certain ends. When Cuomo took his oath of office, he pledged to uphold both the United States Constitution and the Constitution of the state of New York. He swore to "faithfully" discharge the duties of his office. The state Constitution also charged him to "faithfully" execute the laws established by the legislature. (The use of the word "faithful" is interesting here. While not intended in a religious sense, it does refer to integrity and fidelity to that which one has promised. As he debated his stance on abortion legislation, then, fidelity had multiple meanings for Cuomo, being both a religious person and having sworn an oath of office.) Cuomo represented a democratic government that guaranteed, among other things, the free exercise of religion and equal protection under the law.[21] Cuomo, like any elected official, pledged to uphold these ends of government. As a religious person, he has a duty to use his practical reason to assess whether these are good ends, compatible with his faith. Let us assume that he has done so, and that he believes there is nothing in the ends of American government that directly contradicts Christianity. Perhaps he even believes that these political ends preserve values that are dear to Christianity—the dignity of the individual, freedom, and so on.

Cuomo must interpret these general ends in every specific case. This is a hermeneutical task of citizenry. For example, on the abortion issue he must ask: What constitutes a life protected by the Constitution? What are the limits of liberty? Clearly, these are legal questions, but they also are ethical and, I would assert, religious questions. These are ultimate questions about how we as a society define life, what life we protect, and how we understand freedom. To see these questions as purely "technical" legal issues is reductionistic and immoral. To be sure, laity have drawn a distinction between doctrine and practical judgments on other issues, such as church-state relations. One might recall the position of *Commonweal* magazine during the debates about Kennedy: "Senator Kennedy should have made the elementary point that there is no 'Catholic position' on these matters, that they are not doctrinally religious questions at all, merely points of Constitutional interpretation and practical judgment, on which Catholics are perfectly free to disagree and on which they often do disagree."[22] I do not assert that religious teaching can dictate every professional decision, but rather that the laypersons' most informed religious judgment should wrestle with practical questions. Often these questions involve deep issues of meaning and value. This process of practical theological wrestling is essential for an integrated public life of faith. It is also, I would note, more risky for the layperson who does not concur with church authorities. It is easier—perhaps more strategic—to simply say that faith is private.

Cuomo says that he concurs with the Catholic teaching on abortion. He asserts that the fetus is a "life," or at least "the full potential of human life is indisputably there. That . . . by itself should demand respect, caution, indeed—reverence."[23] Cuomo sees this as a moral and religious judgment, which he separates from political judgment. Of course, many have accused Cuomo of simple political maneuvering here. This could be seen simply as a pragmatic move akin to how Kennedy responded to critics. Yet I think it worthwhile to seriously analyze his arguments, to take them at face value.

I infer from his speech two reasons for the distinction between religious and political judgment. The first is that he values another end higher than the protection of this life: the preservation of a pluralistic democracy. He is, after all, pledged to uphold the Constitutions of the United States and of New York State. Yet I would question this rationale. First, if Cuomo is convinced that the fetus is a "life" worthy of reverence, why would he want to uphold a system that did not protect that life? Second, this rationale seems dubious given Cuomo's strong stand against the death penalty. Cuomo consistently vetoed legislation that would have introduced the death penalty. He told a group of district attorneys, "You don't have to abandon your position on the death penalty, [but] you won't get death as long as I'm governor."[24] Why would life in this case be worth defending, despite the will of a democratic legislature, but not worth protecting in the case of abortion? The second reason Cuomo offers seems more to the point. This rationale focuses on means. For Cuomo asserts that while he agrees with the church's moral end, he cannot find an acceptable and achievable political means to realize that end. Cuomo in fact more emphasizes the problem of the means. In doing so, he reduces his sphere of intellectual responsibility (and the exercise of practical reason), in my view.

As he notes in his speech, the problem comes with specific legislative decisions. Cuomo asserts that part of his job is to protect freedom of belief. He does not state that the public sphere should be devoid of morality, but that public morality "depends on a consensus view of right and wrong."[25] Here I would note an interesting contrast between Cuomo and Aristotle. Aristotle sees law as a way to develop moral virtue, not just a reflection of moral consensus. Moral virtues develop through habit. We become just, for example, by acting justly. This is one reason why law is important in Aristotle's thought: "Lawgivers make the citizens good by inculcating (good) habits in them, and this is the aim of every lawgiver; if he does not succeed in doing that, his legislation is a failure."[26] Cuomo is more hesitant to use law as a means of moral formation. Perhaps he rightly fears the totalitarian abuses of an Aristotelian position. And, of course, the modern democracy is a different context than the Greek *polis*. In any case, Cuomo tells the bishops that their job (not his) is to teach and persuade the public of the rightness of their moral position. Religiously based values do not have an a priori place in public policy; the pluralistic public must endorse values. Given that Catholic teaching on abortion has not been accepted by a consensus of the American public, the lay politician must determine the realistic options for making this moral ideal a civil law.

This is a choice among imperfect and often unknown alternatives: "so the Catholic trying to make moral and prudent judgments in the political realm must discern which, if any, of the actions one could take would be best."[27] Aristotle too noted the messy nature of practical reason. The knowledge proper to practical reason is prima facie—probable but not certain, admitting of exceptions. As practical science concerns variable human action, one cannot expect it to be completely precise. Catholic teachings concur on this point. In his 1962 encyclical on Christianity and social progress, Pope John XXIII wrote: "When it comes to reducing these teachings to action, it sometimes happens that even sincere Catholic men have differing views. When this occurs they should take care to have and to show mutual esteem and regard, and to explore the extent to which they can work in cooperation among themselves."[28] The American bishops also note in *Economic Justice for All* that prudential judgments do not have the same certainty or moral authority as theoretical statements of moral principles, for prudential judgments depend on the accuracy of empirical data.[29]

Recognizing that his practical judgments cannot be precise, Cuomo discerns that a constitutional amendment prohibiting abortion is not the best approach. First, it would be extremely difficult to pass such an amendment. Even if passed, it would be ineffective and ultimately undermining to law itself (like Prohibition). Cuomo implies that he, not the bishops, is competent to make that decision, as he has the experience of a politician. This, it seems to me, is a valid argument. Here Cuomo could appeal to Aristotle, who also asserted the importance of experience in practical wisdom. Because universals arise out of particulars in practical matters, argued Aristotle, the person of practical wisdom must have knowledge of both. If the practically wise thinker must have knowledge of particulars, then he (e.g., a legislator) must have experience.[30] Theoretical wisdom, on the other hand, does not depend on experience. Pope John XXIII had made a similar point: "No one can insinuate himself into public life unless he be scientifically competent, technically capable, and skilled in the practice of his own profession."[31]

Cuomo argues in effect that laity should have autonomy in their own spheres because they have the experience and the competency to make decisions there. The bishops, on the other hand, have the competency to teach. Yet Cuomo confuses the issue, for he also asserts that as a layperson he deserves to be heard on theological issues and in church settings. One recalls his statement, "We lay people have a right to be heard." Yet isn't this "trespassing" onto the traditional competency of the magisterium? At the same time, Cuomo seems to assert his lay status as a mitigating factor in case of error: "If you do something that's in accord with a well-formed, sincerely formed belief, without being a theologian, it seems to me any God of good judgment would understand that."[32] This position is shaky. Can the layperson claim the right to make public theological judgments, but not claim responsibility for them? Of course, any theologian must ultimately lay her or his best attempts at the feet of God. Cuomo's comments, however, indicate a real problem as the roles of laity and clergy shift without clear definition of roles. I would argue that theology should not be the exclusive province of the magisterium. Yet one sees here an extraordinarily large can of worms. If the layperson can be trained to teach theology, should not clergy be able to train in political affairs? How is a "well-formed" belief formed? At the very least, one can assert the need for better lay theological education and further reflection about lay and clerical roles.

Cuomo appeals to practical reason in making his political judgments, yet he reduces practical reason to deliberation about means. In my view, practical judgments concern not only questions about means but also often deep questions about the ends of human life. Cuomo separates his political decisions from the more religiously informed discernment that happens in his private life. Many laypersons find themselves in similar positions. Day-to-day decisions in secular spheres appear quite removed from spirituality. The danger here is that faith gets more and more separated from the rest of life, which in turn becomes more and more secularized. Cuomo's approach to his faith is a better model for laypersons than was the approach taken by Kennedy. Cuomo took his faith seriously, publicly wrestled with its meaning for his public responsibilities, and affirmed the importance of competency and experience in making prudential judgments. Yet on the abortion question Cuomo drew a dangerous dichotomy between private belief and public responsibility. While he was right that faith cannot unequivocally dictate practical decisions in particular situations, faith can be part of the process of making practical judgments. I look now to Ignatius of Loyola and to the see-judge-act method to explore this more integrated relationship.

Practical Reason and Faith

Spiritual discernment is not a process in which one suspends reason. Rather, faith must be understood as engaging and directing practical reason. Scripture describes discernment as a gift of the Holy Spirit. Still, the Spirit can work through nature, through reason. Luke Timothy Johnson writes: "We would not go far wrong, then, if we were to regard discernment as similar to the virtue of prudence (*phronesis*), which the New Testament, like the entire milieu of Hellenistic moral teaching, regards as the capacity to make proper practical decision."[33]

Of course, the relationship between reason and faith is a contested issue in the history of Christianity. Calvin, for example, had a much less optimistic view of reason than did Aquinas. Calvin asserted that while God had planted in human beings an awareness of divinity, sin has weakened and corrupted our understanding. In the elect, the Spirit can guide practical reason toward the good. Yet the human condition should make us extremely cautious about our ability to use our faculties well.[34] One also could turn (as Calvin did) to 1 Corinthians, which speaks of the foolishness of human wisdom. Indeed, this is a hard text: "Has not God made foolish the wisdom of the world? For since, in the wisdom of God, the world did not know God through wisdom, God decided, through the foolishness of our proclamation, to save those who believe" (1 Cor. 1:20–21). Should this overturn our trust in human reason? Certainly, such texts imply a radical overturning of the taken-for-granted views of the world; in the face of the crucifixion and resurrection, reason and all human strength pales. Yet I would assert that reason still plays a role in the Christian life. One cannot rely solely on reason, but it can be integrated in a prayerful process of discernment, as Ignatius of Loyola asserted.

Let us consider, however, before moving to Ignatius, another important caution. This comes from Martin Luther. Luther sharply distinguished between the heavenly kingdom and the worldly kingdom. Law governs the kingdom of the world, while the gospel of Christ rules the spiritual kingdom. Each has a different purpose, and though they are not opposed, they must not be confused. Secular duties are necessary to maintain order in the world and to care for the neighbor, but they do not produce piety. Luther wrote:

> For this reason these two kingdoms must be sharply distinguished, and both be permitted to remain; the one to produce piety, the other to bring about external peace and prevent evil deeds; neither is sufficient in the world without the other. For no one can become pious before God by means of the secular government, without Christ's spiritual rule.... Without the Holy Spirit in the heart no one becomes really pious, he may do as fine works as he will.[35]

Moreover, one learns little about professional competence from the gospel. One does not learn the particulars of how to do work well from religion. H. Richard Niebuhr described Luther's position in this way:

> As there is no way of deriving knowledge from the gospel about what to do as physician, builder, carpenter, or statesman, so there is no way of gaining the right spirit of service, of confidence and hopefulness, of humility and readiness to accept correction, from any amount of technical or cultural knowledge. No increase of scientific and technical knowledge can renew the spirit within us; but the right spirit will impel us to seek knowledge and skill in our special vocations in the world in order that we may render service. It is important for Luther that these things be kept distinct despite their interrelations, for to confuse them leads to the corruption of both.[36]

My understanding of practical reason takes into account this Lutheran caution, in that religious doctrine cannot dictate practical judgments in the world—whether family, work, or politics. Here experience and competency are key. Yet I would not draw as sharp a distinction as does Luther between the two kingdoms. Rather, I see "worldly" responsibility in more of a continuum with faith. Secular work does not earn salvation, but it is part of the calling of the faithful person. I would emphasize Luther's point that faith can impel one to seek the information and skills to make wise practical decisions. Indeed, I would say that practical reasoning is part of the faithful life. Moreover, I would say that these practical vocations shape us; they form us in ways that either foster or impede rightful relationship to the sacred. Particularly given the loss of a sense of public vocation, it is important to reconsider the connection between practical judgments and the life of faith.

Ignatius of Loyola and Discernment

In the *Spiritual Exercises,* Ignatius of Loyola (1491–1556) details a process of discernment that uses practical reason. He shows that a rational calculation of pros and cons can be part of religious discernment. In fact, he uses this process as he deliberates about whether the new Society of Jesus should require poverty or accept a fixed income.[37] What is important to see is that reason here considers both ends and means. Everything is to serve our ultimate end, the praise and service of God and the salvation of our souls. (Note the Jesuit standard of judgment: all for the greater glory of God.)

Practical reason directs the will to serve the human being's ultimate end, and it discerns how to love and serve God in the particularities of a specific moment and context. Because the will can impede movement toward the ultimate end, Ignatius counsels people to rid themselves of self-will and cultivate detachment or indifference. In this way, they will be free to love God wholly and to love created things rightly, insofar as they move one toward one's final end in God.

The Exercises were given to a wide range of people, including many laypersons. They are structured into four weeks. During the second week Ignatius introduces discernment for an election of a state in life. One should note here Ignatius clearly places discernment within the orthodox boundaries of the church. One can discern only about lawful choices (for example, a priest cannot discern about whether to marry). One chooses between good alternatives, not between good and bad. (This raises the question of how to discern in a situation when one cannot know whether an option is good; how discern among quite gray alternatives, whose consequences cannot be known with any certainty?)

In the *Spiritual Exercises,* there are three times in which one can properly make a major decision. In the first time, God leads one so strongly to the choice that it seems automatic. In the second time, one discerns the movement of consolation and desolation in the soul. Ignatius believed that these movements were produced by external sources. The good spirit brings consolation, which entails a sense of tranquility and closeness to God. In consolation, the soul is "inflamed with love" for God, and hence can love all created things properly. The bad spirit, on the other hand, produces desolation, which brings temptation, anxiety, and despair. One should never make a decision in a time of desolation, for then the bad spirit may guide the will. In the third time for discernment, one does not detect such movements within one's soul and must rely on other means. In this situation Ignatius proposes as one means of discernment a kind of rational calculation, a list of pros and cons.

In this third method of discernment, then, Ignatius identifies practical reason as an important tool in the practice of discernment. I will examine this method in more detail. In order to make a good election, one must begin in indifference, not more emotionally disposed to take one option over the other. One should be in the middle, "like the pointer of a balance." In this way, one will be free of disordered affections and open to the movement of God. Ignatius notes that often people seek to bend God to their disordered affections. They make an end of the means and a means of the end. Rather: "I should beg God our Lord to be pleased to move my will and to put into my mind what I ought to do in regard to the matter proposed, so that it will be more to his praise and glory. I should beg to accomplish this by reasoning well and faithfully with my intellect, and by choosing in conformity with his most holy will and good pleasure."[38] The intellect weighs the advantages and disadvantages of each option, considering the end for which the person is created. Thus, practical reason here is engaged in a process of spiritual discernment that considers not only means but also ultimate ends. Ignatius continues:

> I should consider and reason out how many advantages or benefits accrue to myself from having the office or benefice proposed, all of them solely for the praise of God our Lord and the salvation of my soul; and on the contrary I should similarly consider the disadvantages and dangers in having it.... After I have considered and thought out every aspect of the proposed matter, I should see to which side reason inclines. It is in this way that I ought to come to a decision about the matter proposed, namely, in accordance with the preponderating motion of reason.[39]

As a gift of God, reason can point us to the will of God, our ultimate end. Yet this is not a reason detached from spiritual practices. Rather, the exercise of reason here *is* a spiritual practice. Furthermore, the decision reached by reason then must be brought before God in prayer for confirmation: "When that election or decision has been made, the person who has made it ought with great diligence to go to prayer before God our Lord, to offer him that election, and to beg his Divine Majesty to receive and confirm it, provided it is conducive to his greater service and praise."[40]

In my view, Ignatius rightly gives practical reason a place in faithful decision-making. To be clear, one must acknowledge that this argument can be misused to give divine ratification to eminently subjective decisions. This must be guarded against. The point is not to give religious endorsement to every practical judgment, but rather to encourage religious people to engage their faith in the practical choices that comprise so much of their lives and their public and private responsibilities. In fact, reason here serves as a corrective to emotionalism or subjective claims to the Holy Spirit. Reason cannot verify religion. Yet reason allows for public debate—and thus brings religion responsibly into the pluralistic public arena.

Cardijn Method: See-Judge-Act

Ignatius offers one method of exercising practical reason in a discernment process. The Cardijn see-judge-act method, so influential on lay movements in the twentieth century, offers another vision of spiritual formation that integrates discernment with practical theological reflection and action. Unfortunately, membership in lay movements such as the Young Christian Workers and Christian Family Movement today is quite low. However, the method still is used by such groups and also appears as a framework of thinking in diverse religious sources. For example, the Southern African Alliance of Reformed Churches structured its 1995 statement on the poor according to the see-judge-act method.[41] I also see parallels in Don Browning's practical theological method, which moves in a cyclical fashion from descriptive theology (seeing) to historical theology to systematic theology (judging) to strategic practical theology (acting).[42]

The see-judge-act method is an important resource for forming publicly engaged believers. The situation, the gospel, tradition, and reason all play a role in this process. The process integrates empirical description, theological evaluation, practical judgment, and action—all done within a community. This is an excellent model of spiritual formation and practical theology. It resists unreflective action that too easily assumes a theological rationale or misses the reality of the situation. The method also resists quietism, an otherworldly spirituality, or a compartmentalized faith that does not engage the concrete human situation. Moreover, as a process it can be used in any religious tradition, incorporating the normative sources of that tradition.

The first step is to gather the facts about a situation and context. This is an active process that acknowledges the importance of context and description in theological evaluation. Yet it need not be seen as a strictly secular moment, to be done by the local sociologist. Rather, it is integral to Christian faith, to the call to pay attention, as Simone Weil put it. To truly see requires that one suspend self-perspective enough to look at an other. It means observing that which may pass us by, blinded by our interests and social location.

To illustrate with a concrete example from this study, one may look again at Cuomo's dilemma. Had Cuomo thought through his dilemma about abortion legislation using the Cardijn method, he would have in this first step fully assessed the situation. Ideally, he would have worked through the process in a small group of believers. He would have gathered data to respond to these kinds of questions: What legal alternatives could be identified on the abortion question? What were the likely consequences of each alternative? What was public opinion on abortion? How many abortions were performed in New York State?

The second step is to judge the facts that have been observed in light of the gospel and its interpretation in the tradition. This step involves a theological conversation between the situation and the core values of the faith, leading to a normative judgment. Here Cuomo would need to enter into the moral and religious dimensions of his dilemma. If indeed he judged that his faith tradition gave fetal life dignity, then he must bring that judgment into play. He also would consider how the gospel and tradition speak about, for example, conscience, women, the role of law, and pluralism. He then would make normative judgments about his responsibilities and the ends for which he must strive. He would weigh the potential harm and good of each legislative alternative in light of his normative judgments about the highest good.

The next step would be to act. In practice, lay movements such as Young Christian Workers or the Christian Family Movement used the Cardijn method around much less complex issues. Often the process resulted in a small, manageable action, such as painting a playground or befriending co-workers. To relate the process to policy decisions is the most difficult test case. Cuomo, for example, perhaps still would have no unambiguous course of action. Part of the difficulty stems from inadequate knowledge about policy consequences—what harm to life would result from restrictions on abortion, for example? Faith may not unequivocally dictate one course or another. Yet this process gives the believer a framework that allows faith to wrestle seriously with practical situations. What is certain is that Cuomo would not simply call his faith "private." Again, to relate practical reason and faith does not give moral certainty, but the process of theological and spiritual wrestling does ground integrity.

Lectio Divina: Assimilating the Word

This discussion of discernment shows the possibility of integrating reason in a prayerful process of making practical judgments. Another spiritual practice that also develops the habit of integrating intellect, prayer, and contemplation is *lectio divina*. This could be a very fruitful means of forming lay Christians, drawing deeply from the wisdom of the monastic tradition yet nurturing the lay vocation. *Lectio divina* (literally "divine reading") is an ancient monastic practice of praying with the Scriptures. St. Benedict placed great importance on this reading in his guide to monastic communities. The sixth-century Rule of St. Benedict stipulates: "Therefore, the brothers should have specified periods for manual labor as well as for prayerful reading."[43] The reading was a spiritual discipline essential to the daily rhythm and the formation process.

A Carthusian monk named Guigo II systematized the practice in the twelfth century. He identified four steps: reading (*lectio*), meditation (*meditatio*), prayer (*oratio*), and contemplation (*contemplatio*). Reading takes the Scriptures onto the lips; meditation brings it to the mind; prayer carries it to the heart; and contemplation delights in it. As Guigo II wrote in *The Ladder of Monks*: "Reading, as it were, puts food whole into the mouth, meditation chews it and breaks it up, prayer extracts its flavor, contemplation is the sweetness itself which gladdens and refreshes."[44] This is a way of sinking into the Scriptures, making them part of one's life. *Lectio divina* can be done individually or in a group. It is a practice that develops the habit of integrating intellect, senses, emotion, and prayer.

Lectio divina could be a very fruitful means of lay spiritual formation. I propose here three texts that would be particularly rich for laity: John 15:1–17; 1 Corinthians 12:4–31, 13; and 1 Peter 1:15–16, 2:4–5, 9–10. Each text carries ecclesiological implications; indeed, meditative reading of these texts would help to form laity to be church in the world. Considering how important liturgy was in forming the laypersons discussed here, it is important to see the interrelationships between the practice of *lectio divina,* the liturgy, and these particular texts. *Lectio divina* can be done not only individually but also communally, flowing from the Word preached in the assembly. The Eucharist was particularly important to lay Catholics, patterning them into a sacramental vision of the world. This sacramental understanding opened up meaning for many. *Lectio divina* actually provides a eucharistic way of assimilating the Scriptures—one chews on the texts, which transform. The texts I discuss are rich, and meant to be digested slowly. In *lectio,* one would take just one verse, or phrase, or even one word at a time, savoring it. I envision the practice of *lectio divina* as a focal space for prayerfully considering the difficult questions raised by laity.

John 15:1–17

This passage emphasizes the disciples' rootedness in Christ, the vine, the source of life. The vine image appears in numerous Hebrew Bible texts, where the vine is identified with the people of Israel. In Isaiah, Yahweh is the diligent keeper of the "pleasant vineyard," anticipating that: "In days to come, Jacob shall take root, Israel shall blossom and put forth shoots, and fill the whole world with fruit" (Isa. 27:2–6). Now, in this Johannine text, Jesus himself is the "true vine," the source of life. The disciples are the branches, drinking of this life.

The text emphasizes that the disciples are to bear fruit; this is no quietist mysticism. Discipleship entails bearing fruit, which gives glory to God: "My Father is glorified by this, that you bear much fruit and become my disciples" (John 15:8). Indeed, Jesus sends his friends forth; he commissions them to go out and bear fruit (John 15:16). Yet all human fruit grows out of life with Christ. This passage could help to sustain laity who must bear fruit, often in places that seem far from Christ. The branch has its roots in the vine, but grows outward from that place. Thus, disciples bear fruit in many spaces but always keep their identity in their roots. We have seen how fragile religious identity can be as laity immerse themselves in complex public issues, or in the mundane details of family life. Coming back again and again to this text, to this reminder of the life source, offers a practice of remembrance, nurturance, and reorientation. Christians are a chosen people, organically connected to Christ, with a vocation to grow outward and bear fruit.

One sees too in John 15:9–12 the absolute centrality of love. The love of the Creator flows out in the love of Christ. This is the ultimate love, expressed in Jesus' deed of laying down his life. The disciples are intimately drawn into divine love; Jesus calls them "friends." He calls them to "abide in my love" by keeping God's commandments. Indeed, the ultimate commandment is this: "Love one another as I have loved you" (John 15:12). This gospel then unites the mystical and the ascetic paths. The deepest intimacy with God comes from the path of love, including, one might say, the concrete acts of love that are part of the ascetic way.

Finally, this gospel offers an ecclesiological vision. Christ is the vine and the disciples are those who grow from this life and bear fruit in many places, doing the work of love. The branches may grow in many different directions. There is much work to be done. Yet the common vine gives all life—and ultimately, "complete joy." This is a joyful church that lives with discipline. Branches that bear no fruit, God prunes away. God prunes every branch to make it bear more. But this is all for the glory of God and our own joyful life. Christians are a people of growth, rooted in Christ, pruned by the Creator, nurtured by the common life.

Of course, to meditate on this text (John 15:1–17) also means grappling with the difficult verses that follow. The latter part of this fifteenth chapter of John depicts the world as alien and hostile territory. To be a disciple means to withdraw from this world and to bear its hatred, in contrast to the love flowing from Christ: "If the world hates you, be aware that it hated me before it hated you. If you belonged to the world, the world would love you as its own. Because you do not belong to the world, but I have chosen you out of the world—therefore the world hates you" (John 15:18–19). Such a depiction of the world poses great problems for laity, commissioned in church tradition to bring the faith into the world. In light of the preceding text, this passage should not be seen as a sectarian call to withdrawal. Rather, it braces Christian disciples for the cost of faithfulness in the world. Many laypersons spoke of this cost. To be rooted in Christ's love in a community of disciples sustains them as they go forth to bear lasting fruit. The gospel emphasizes that prayer too sustains those who are commissioned: "The Father will give you whatever you ask him in my name" (John 15:16).

1 Corinthians 12:4–31, 13

Paul's First Letter to the Corinthians offers another metaphor of Christian common life. The church is the Body of Christ in the world. The body is made up of many parts, yet it has a fundamental, organic unity. The body *is* Christ. The text states: "For just as the body is one and has many members, and all the members of the body, though many, are one body, so it is with Christ" (1 Cor. 12:12). Then, Paul specifically identifies the church with the body that is Christ: "Now you are the body of Christ and individually members of it. And God has appointed in the church first apostles, second prophets, third teachers" (1 Cor. 12:27–28). Later Pauline letters portray Christ as the "head" of the body that is the church (e.g., Col. 1:18).

The Spirit binds the body together: "For in the one Spirit we were all baptized into one body—Jews or Greeks, slaves or free—and we were all made to drink of one Spirit" (1 Cor. 12:13). The story of American Catholics has showed that pluralism challenges laity in the world, particularly in the public sphere. This text presents an ecclesiology that may help Christians make sense of pluralism, although of course the contemporary context differs from that of Paul. The text offers a vision of unity-in-diversity. Moreover, the image of the body was common in the ancient world, and this image had been applied to the body politic, as seen in the Roman appeal for unity after the secession of the plebeians in 494 B.C.E.[45] This ecclesiology has the potential, then, to shed light on the political vocation of the Body of Christ.

Moreover, the text emphasizes the many different gifts of the Spirit: "Now there are varieties of gifts but the same Spirit; and there are varieties of services, but the same Lord; and there are varieties of activities, but it is the same God who activates all of them in everyone" (1 Cor. 12:4–6). Each member of the body is important to the whole, although each has different work. All are interdependent; in some sense the life of Christ in our world depends on each member. Gifts of the Spirit are to be used for the common good, in service of God. This affirms the distinct work of the laity, who go out into multiple spheres and use their gifts in service of God. Not all are called to be preachers or prophets. The task is to discern one's own gifts; to develop relevant knowledge and skills to exercise those gifts; to keep the heart focused on the work of God; and to retain concern for the whole Body of Christ. This is both an awesome affirmation of the diversity of lay vocations and a humbling reminder that one's individual work is but a small part of the whole. Sinking into this text forms an ecclesial identity even as it empowers laity to go outward and bear fruit.

Moreover, Paul goes on to assert that the highest gift of all is love (*agape*). All other gifts are impermanent. The gift of prophecy will end. The gift of knowledge will end. Here again, we are re-minded of the incompleteness of our work in the world. This is not to say that we should not use those fleeting gifts; we must. Yet al-ways we work in humility and in anticipation of the fullness of the kingdom. All our service is relativized by the eschatological hope that infuses Paul's letter. This sustains laity as they confront the im-perfect structures of government and work, as they face imperfect choices, as they seek fidelity in fragile relationships. Yet we are re-assured: "Love never ends" (1 Cor. 13:8). Indeed, "faith, hope, and love abide, these three; and the greatest of these is love" (1 Cor. 13:13). Mystical vision is not the height of the spiritual life; love is. The grace-filled love given us by God defines the Christian life. Indeed, love secures "for the exercise of all other gifts the pursuit of their proper ends, the love of God and the building up of the Church."[46]

1 Peter 1:15–16; 2:4–5, 9–10

Like Paul's First Letter to the Corinthians, the First Letter of Peter must be understood within its eschatological anticipation. God has given us "a new birth into a living hope" (1 Pet. 1:3). Christians look forward in faith to a salvation still to be revealed. In this life we are called to holiness: "Be holy yourselves in all your conduct, for it is written, 'You shall be holy, for I am holy' " (1 Pet. 1:15–16). Through the practice of *lectio divina,* laity could focus on this call to holiness in a faith that always anticipates the More. The text echoes Leviticus 11:44–45. The People of Israel have been made holy, or sanctified, through Yahweh's own holiness. To be holy here is to be set apart, kept undefiled. The People share in God's own holiness.

The author of 1 Peter applies this sanctity to the church, the new "People of God." Just as Yahweh brought the Israelites out of Egypt to be their God, so too God called the People of God out of the darkness into God's marvelous light. This vision of the church (so influential in the ecclesiology of the Second Vatican Council) embraces all in the call to sanctity. The people are a "chosen race, a royal priesthood, a holy nation" (1 Pet. 2:9–10). Again, to be God's People means to be set aside as an obedient nation, as we read in Exodus 19:5–6: "If you obey my voice and keep my covenant, you shall be my treasured possession out of all the peoples.... You shall be for me a priestly kingdom and a holy nation." Priesthood is linked with being the People of God. Priests offer sacrifices to God; in 1 Peter we see that these sacrifices are to be spiritual, not physical: "to be a holy priesthood, to offer spiritual sacrifices acceptable to God through Jesus Christ" (1 Pet. 2:5). This is the Pauline vision of sacrifice, as expressed in Romans 12:1: "Present your bodies as a living sacrifice, holy and acceptable to God, which is your spiritual worship."[47]

The whole People of God, then, are called to offer living sacrifice to God with their whole selves, in all that they do. Luther relied on this text from 1 Peter as he asserted the priesthood of all believers. Catholic texts also have endorsed the image of laity as priests. Pope John Paul II, for example, referred to the "priestly, prophetic, and kingly" mission of the laity (*Christifideles Laici*). One recalls that layman Thomas McCabe saw marriage as a kind of priesthood. Laity are called to be priests in the world, offering sacrifices in the work of their hands. As one meditates on this text, one could chew on its meaning in light of the questions raised by American Catholics. Is there a distinction between the lay priesthood and the ordained priesthood? What does it mean for an elected politician to have a priestly mission, or for a priest to have a political mission?

The church builds itself around Christ, the "living stone." One can hear the clear call of this text, echoing the intimacy of the vine image in John: "Come to him, a living stone, though rejected by mortals yet chosen and precious in God's sight, and like living stones, let yourselves be built into a spiritual house, to be a holy priesthood" (1 Pet. 2:4–5). To be built into a spiritual house means to become alive with Christ's own life. The church is the house-hold—or the temple—of God. Christ is its cornerstone, the rock of life.

Sustaining the Tension

Developments within the church as well as the particular pressures of public life in the United States raise significant questions. Laity in twentieth-century America have been engaged in a struggle to define their place, their meaning, indeed, even their vocations. Out of this struggle I would assert the dignity and the complexity of the lay task. The lay life of faith is not inferior to the ordained or religious vo-cation, nor to a contemplative path. It is, rather, an important way of living toward God in the world. This way involves difficult prac-tical judgments, fragile relationships, competing commitments, and inadequacy to the task. Yet the necessary complexity tumbles into unnecessary confusion when combined with inadequate theology, ecclesiology, and spirituality. This study makes clear that imbedded in many practical dilemmas are fundamental questions about how God relates to us, how to define the church, how to discern the Spirit. Laity themselves inevitably engage such questions. Whether they are well prepared to do so, or whether church leaders real-ize the theological stakes, is another matter. Continued theological reflection on these questions is critical.

Despite the ambiguities of operating in secular structures and en-gaging deep-seated social problems, the lay vocation must remain public. Faith is not meant to be privatized; to do so lets go of God's creation and our responsibility. At the same time, a public faith needs nurture. Laity need guidance, opportunities for theological reflection, community, and intentional spiritual practices to pattern them into a public vocation and sustain them amid its tensions. This is the continuing work of the whole People of God.

NOTES

Introduction

1. See, for example, José Casanova, *Public Religions in the Modern World* (Chicago: University of Chicago Press, 1994); James Davidson Hunter, *Culture Wars: The Struggle to Define America* (New York: Basic Books, 1991); Stephen L. Carter, *The Culture of Disbelief: How American Law and Politics Trivialize Religious Devotion* (New York: Basic Books, 1993); and Don Browning et al., eds., *From Culture Wars to Common Ground: Religion and the American Family Debate* (Louisville: Westminster John Knox Press, 1997).

2. See, for example, Jean Bethke Elshtain, *Public Man, Private Woman: Women in Social and Political Thought* (Princeton, N.J.: Princeton University Press, 1981), and Pope John Paul II, "The Role of the Christian Family in the Modern World" (*Familiaris Consortio*) (Boston: St. Paul Books & Media, 1982).

3. Robert Bellah et al., *Habits of the Heart: Individualism and Commitment in American Life* (New York: Harper & Row, 1985), 56.

4. Ibid., 66.

5. Peter Berger and Richard John Neuhaus, *To Empower People: The Role of Mediating Structures in Public Policy* (Washington, D.C.: American Enterprise Institute for Public Policy Research, 1977).

6. Martin E. Marty, "Public and Private: Congregation as Meeting Place," in *American Congregations,* vol. 2, ed. James P. Wind and James W. Lewis (Chicago: University of Chicago Press, 1994), 133–66.

7. Bernard McGinn, "The Letter and the Spirit: Spirituality as an Academic Discipline," *Christian Spirituality Bulletin* 1, no. 2 (Fall 1993): 5. See also Philip Sheldrake, *Spirituality and History: Questions of Interpretation and Method* (New York: Crossroad, 1992).

8. Hans Urs Von Balthasar, "The Word Made Flesh," in *Explorations in Theology 1* (San Francisco: Ignatius, 1989), 222.

9. Rita M. Gross, *Buddhism after Patriarchy: A Feminist History, Analysis, and Reconstruction of Buddhism* (Albany: State University of New York Press, 1993), 228–31.

10. "Doctrine on the Sacrament of Marriage," in *Dogmatic Canons and Decrees* (Rockford, Ill.: Tan Books, 1977), 164.

11. Leonard Doohan, "Laity," in *The HarperCollins Encyclopedia of Catholicism,* ed. Richard P. McBrien (New York: HarperCollins, 1995), 747.

12. Carolyn Bynum, *Jesus as Mother* (Berkeley: University of California Press, 1982), 5.

13. Jacques Fontaine, "The Practice of Christian Life: The Birth of the Laity," in *Christian Spirituality,* vol. 1: *Origins to the Twelfth Century,* ed. Bernard McGinn et al. (New York: Crossroad, 1985, 1992), 453–91.

14. For an accessible introduction to Beguine spirituality, see Saskia Murk-Jansen, *Brides in the Desert* (Maryknoll, N.Y.: Orbis Books, 1998).

15. André Vauchez, *The Laity in the Middle Ages* (Notre Dame, Ind.: University of Notre Dame Press, 1993), 72.

16. Vida Scudder, ed., *Saint Catherine of Siena as Seen in Her Letters* (New York: E. P. Dutton, 1927), 173–74.

17. See Karen Scott's essay, "Catherine of Siena and Lay Sanctity in Fourteenth-Century Italy," in *Lay Sanctity, Medieval and Modern,* ed. Ann W. Astell (Notre Dame, Ind.: University of Notre Dame Press, 2000), 77–90.

18. Martin Luther, "The Pagan Servitude of the Church," in *Martin Luther: Selections from His Writings,* ed. John Dillenberger (Garden City, N.Y.: Anchor Books, 1961), 345.

19. Martin Luther, "An Appeal to the Ruling Class of German Nationality as to the Amelioration of the State of Christendom," in ibid., 407.

20. Max Weber, *The Protestant Ethic and the Spirit of Capitalism* (New York: Charles Scribner's Sons, 1958), 36.

21. For a more developed analysis, see John Witte Jr., *From Sacrament to Contract: Marriage, Religion, and Law in the Western Tradition* (Louisville: Westminster John Knox Press, 1997).

22. John Wesley, "Christian Perfection," in *John Wesley's Sermons: An Anthology,* ed. Albert C. Outler and Richard P. Heitzenrater (Nashville: Abingdon Press, 1991), 73.

23. Ibid., 73–74.

24. John Wesley, "The More Excellent Way," in *John Wesley's Sermons: An Anthology,* 513.

25. Ibid., 515.

26. Francis de Sales, *Introduction to the Devout Life* (New York: Image Books, 1989), 33.

27. Ibid., 40, 41, 43.

28. Ibid., 43.

29. Ibid.

30. Letter dated October 14, 1604, in *Francis de Sales, Jane de Chantal: Letters of Spiritual Direction,* ed. Wendy M. Wright and Joseph F. Power, trans. Marie Thibert Peronne, V.H.M. (New York: Paulist Press, 1988), 134. See also pp. 138–39 on detachment, prayer, and care of neighbor.

31. Jane de Chantal to André Frémyot (June 1, 1626), in *Francis de Sales, Jane de Chantal: Letters of Spiritual Direction,* 205.

32. Jay Dolan, *The American Catholic Experience: A History from Colonial Times to the Present* (Notre Dame, Ind.: University of Notre Dame Press, 1992), 188–89.

33. R. Scott Appleby, "Present to the People of God: The Transformation of the Roman Catholic Parish Priesthood," in *Transforming Parish Ministry: The Changing Roles of Catholic Clergy, Laity, and Women Religious,* ed. Jay Dolan et al. (New York: Crossroad, 1989), 12.

34. "Decree on the Apostolate of the Laity" (*Apostolicam Actuositatem*), no. 2, in *Documents of Vatican II,* ed. Austin P. Flannery (Grand Rapids, Mich.: Eerdmans, 1975), 768.

35. "Dogmatic Constitution on the Church" (*Lumen Gentium*), no. 31, in *Documents of Vatican II,* 388.

36. See Madonna Kolbenschlag, H.M., ed., *Between God and Caesar: Priests, Sisters and Political Office in the United States* (New York: Paulist Press, 1985).

1. Seizing the Lay Vocation

1. The description of Ryan comes from Francis L. Broderick's biography, *Right Reverend New Dealer: John A. Ryan* (New York: Macmillan, 1963).

2. Pius XI, "On the Reconstruction of the Social Order" (*Quadragesimo Anno*), no. 130, in *The Papal Encyclicals 1903–1939*, ed. Claudia Carlen (Wilmington, N.C.: McGrath, 1981), 436.

3. See "The Revival of Christian Economics," *Commonweal* 14 (May 6, 1931): 2.

4. Pius XI, *On Christian Marriage* (*Casti Connubi*), no. 23, in *The Papal Encyclicals 1903–1939*, ed. Claudia Carlin (Raleigh, N.C.: Purian Press, 1990), 395.

5. Andrew Greeley, cited in Colleen McDannell, "Catholic Domesticity, 1860–1960," in *American Catholic Women*, ed. Karen Kennelly, C.S.J. (New York: Macmillan, 1989), 73–74.

6. Debra Campbell, "The Heyday of Catholic Action and the Lay Apostolate, 1929–1959," in *Transforming Parish Ministry: The Changing Roles of Catholic Clergy, Laity, and Women Religious,* ed. Jay Dolan et al. (New York: Crossroad, 1989), 248, 250.

7. Rev. Joseph P. Fitzpatrick, S.J., "Dorothy Dohen: A Lay Apostle, Reflection of an Era," *Commonweal* 111 (June 1, 1984): 325.

8. Virgil Michel, cited in Jay Dolan, *The American Catholic Experience: A History from Colonial Times to the Present* (Notre Dame, Ind.: University of Notre Dame Press, 1992), 408.

9. Pope Pius XII, *On the Mystical Body of Christ and Our Union in It with Christ* (*Mystici Corporis*) (Boston: St. Paul Books & Media, n.d.), 14.

10. Campbell, "The Heyday of Catholic Action," 252.

11. Mary Irene Zotti, *A Time of Awakening: The Young Christian Worker Story in the United States, 1938 to 1970* (Chicago: Loyola University Press, 1991), 45.

12. Ibid., 95.

13. An anonymous former San Francisco YCW member, cited in ibid., 122.

14. Agatha Ross Fierro, letter to the editor, *Commonweal* 107 (February 29, 1980): 98.

15. "An Introduction," *Commonweal* 1 (November 12, 1924): 1.

16. Rodger Van Allen, *The Commonweal and American Catholicism: The Magazine, the Movement, the Meaning* (Philadelphia: Fortress Press, 1974), 1. Note that the magazine was entitled *The Commonweal* from 1924 to 1965, at which time the name changed to *Commonweal*. For the sake of clarity, I refer to it as *Commonweal* throughout this book.

17. "An Explosion of Truth," *Commonweal* 13 (December 24, 1930): 197.

18. Abigail McCarthy, "An Era of Emergence," *Commonweal* 111 (July 13, 1984): 390.

19. "Nineteen Thirty-Three," *Commonweal* 17 (January 4, 1933): 253.

20. McCarthy, "An Era of Emergence," 391.

21. Dolan, *The American Catholic Experience,* 411.

22. Robert Ellsberg, ed., *Dorothy Day: Selected Writings* (Maryknoll, N.Y.: Orbis Books, 1992), 339.

23. Dorothy Day, *The Long Loneliness* (New York: Harper & Brothers, 1952), 286.

24. John C. Cort, "My Life at the Catholic Worker," *Commonweal* 107 (June 20, 1980): 365.

25. Ellsberg, *Dorothy Day: Selected Writings,* 241.

26. Ibid., 262.

27. Ibid., 266.

28. Mel Piehl, *Breaking Bread: The Catholic Worker and the Origin of Catholic Radicalism in America* (Philadelphia: Temple University Press, 1982). In particular, see chapter 7.

29. Day, *The Long Loneliness,* 134.

30. Ibid., 140.

31. Ibid., 135.

32. Ibid., 136–37, 140.

33. Ibid., 136.

34. Dorothy Day, "All Is Grace," unpublished manuscript, 67, cited in James T. Fisher, *The Catholic Counterculture in America, 1930–1962* (Chapel Hill: University of North Carolina Press, 1989), 59.

35. Day, *The Long Loneliness,* 149.

36. Ellsberg, *Dorothy Day: Selected Writings,* 183.

37. Ibid., 237.

38. June O'Connor, *The Moral Vision of Dorothy Day: A Feminist Perspective* (New York: Crossroad, 1991), 31.

39. Ibid.

40. Day, *The Long Loneliness,* 236.

41. Ibid.

42. Debra Campbell, "*Both Sides Now:* Another Look at the Grail in the Postwar Era," *U.S. Historian* 11, no. 4 (Fall 1993): 16.

43. Dolan, *The American Catholic Experience,* 414–15.

44. Campbell, "The Heyday of Catholic Action," 242.

45. See Fisher, *The Catholic Counterculture in America,* 95. Fisher also noted the Brooklyn origins of many Grail women.

46. Quotations by Kalven and Hellriegel are cited in Campbell, "The Heyday of Catholic Action," 242, 243.

47. Jacques van Ginneken, S.J., cited in Dolan, *The American Catholic Experience,* 414.

48. Quotations are from Janet Kalven, cited in Alden V. Brown, *The Grail Movement and American Catholicism, 1940–1975* (Notre Dame, Ind.: University of Notre Dame Press, 1989), 54, 55.

49. Lydwine van Kersbergen, "Toward a Christian Concept of Woman," *Catholic World* 182, no. 1 (October 1955): 11.

50. Speech by Janet Kalven, cited in Campbell, "The Heyday of Catholic Action," 242.

51. *Grailville* newsletters; see, for example, *Grailville* (January 2000): 8.

52. Joseph Cardijn, cited in Meinrad Scherer-Edmunds, "See-Judge-Act: How

Young Christian Workers Renened the Church," *Salt of the Earth* 16, no. 2 (March–April 1996): 19–20.

53. Joseph Cardijn, "The World Today and the Apostolate of the Laity," in *Challenge to Action: Addresses of Monsignor Joseph Cardijn,* ed. Eugene Langdale (Chicago: Fides, 1955), 26.

54. An anonymous former Cleveland YCW member, cited in Zotti, *A Time of Awakening,* 68.

55. Regina Weissert, telephone interview with author, March 12, 2001.

56. *Social Harmony: 1956–57 Inquiry Program* (Chicago: Christian Family Movement, 1956), 3, cited in Jeffrey M. Burns, *Disturbing the Peace: A History of the Christian Family Movement, 1949–1974* (Notre Dame, Ind.: University of Notre Dame Press, 1999), 124.

57. Rita Kuhn Strubbe, "To Grow in Christ through Action," *Apostolate* 4, no. 2 (1957): 20, cited in Jeffrey M. Burns, *American Catholics and the Family Crisis, 1930–1962* (New York: Garland, 1988), 301.

58. Cited in Burns, *Disturbing the Peace,* 104.

59. See John Kotre, *Simple Gifts: The Lives of Pat and Patty Crowley* (Kansas City, Mo.: Andrews and McMeel, 1979), 152.

60. "Editorial," *Integrity* 1, no. 6 (March 1947): 2.

61. Carol Jackson to Thomas Reese, December 3, 1946, cited in Fisher, *The Catholic Counterculture in America,* 107. Fisher also details biographical information about Jackson and Willock in his helpful chapter "The Limits of Personalism: *Integrity* and the Marycrest Community, 1946–1956."

62. "Editorial," *Integrity* 1, no. 1 (October 1946): 1, 4.

63. Peter Michaels (Carol Jackson), "The Frustration of the Incarnation," *Integrity* 1, no. 1 (October 1946): 13.

64. "Editorial," *Integrity* 1, no. 1 (October 1946): 2–3.

65. Neil MacCarthy, "Among So Many," *Integrity* 1, no. 8 (May 1947): 8.

66. "Editorial," *Integrity* 1, no. 8 (May 1947): 3.

67. Ed Willock, "Marriage for Keeps," *Integrity* 5, no. 1 (1950): 17.

68. "Editorial," *Integrity* 1, no. 8 (May 1947): 1.

69. Fisher, *The Catholic Counterculture in America,* 123, 125.

70. Ed Willock, "The Family Has Lost Its Head," *Integrity* 1, no. 8 (May 1947): 42.

71. Elaine Malley, "Springboards for Sanctity," *Integrity* 3, no. 11 (August 1949): 15.

72. Elizabeth M. Sheehan, "The Spirituality of Married Life," *Integrity* 3, no. 2 (November 1948): 26.

73. James Hitchcock, "Catholic Activist Conservatism in the United States," in *Fundamentalism Observed,* ed. Martin E. Marty and R. Scott Appleby (Chicago: University of Chicago Press, 1991), 119.

74. Salvador Canals, *Institutos seculares y estado de perfección,* 2d ed. (Madrid: Rialp, 1961), 85, cited in Joan Estruch, *Saints and Schemers: Opus Dei and Its Paradoxes* (New York: Oxford University Press, 1995), 253–54.

75. Canals, *Institutos seculares,* cited in Estruch, *Saints and Schemers,* 254.

76. Josemaría Escrivá, *The Way* (Manila: Sinag-tala, 1991), 328–29.

77. Ibid., 21, 152.

78. Estruch, *Saints and Schemers,* 241. Estruch offers a Weberian analysis of Opus Dei.

79. Escrivá, *The Way,* 114, 273–74.

80. Escrivá, "That All May Be Saved," in *Friends of God: Homilies by Josemaría Escrivá* (Princeton, N.J.: Scepter, 1981), 416.

81. Escrivá, *The Way,* 35, 335, 337.

82. Ibid., 9, 8, 71.

83. Ibid., 342, 2, 308.

2. The Call of the Public Sphere

1. "City of Man and God," *Time* (December 12, 1960): 64.

2. Fletcher Knebel, "Democratic Forecast: A Catholic in 1960," *Look* (March 3, 1959): 17.

3. John F. Kennedy, speech to the Greater Houston Ministerial Association, Houston, Texas, September 12, 1960, in *"Let the Word Go Forth": The Speeches, Statements, and Writings of John F. Kennedy 1947 to 1963* (New York: Laurel, 1988), 130–36.

4. John F. Kennedy, speech to the American Society of Newspaper Editors, Washington, D.C., April 21, 1960, in *"Let the Word Go Forth,"* 127.

5. Gary Wills, *Bare Ruined Choirs* (Garden City, N.Y.: Doubleday, 1972), 88.

6. "The Commonweal Approach: An Editorial," *Commonweal* 71 (October 30, 1959): 115.

7. "A Catholic for President?" *Commonweal* 69 (March 6, 1959): 588. Note, however, that former *Commonweal* editor John Cogley contributed to Kennedy's Houston speech. Cogley argued that Kennedy saw no necessary conflict between his conscience—or the conscience of any American Catholic—and the Constitution of the United States. See John Cogley, "A Catholic for President–1," *Commonweal* 69 (March 20, 1959): 649.

8. Cited in "Senator Kennedy and His Critics," *Commonweal* 69 (March 20, 1959): 645.

9. "Catholics and the Presidency," *Ave Maria* 89 (March 7, 1959): 18.

10. "Statement of 166 Catholic Laymen on Religious Freedom in a Presidential Campaign," October 5, 1960, in *Catholic Mind* 59 (March–April 1961): 179–80, reprinted in *Public Voices: Catholics in the American Context,* ed. Steven M. Avella and Elizabeth McKeown (Maryknoll, N.Y.: Orbis Books, 1999), 364–65.

11. "Another Era Underway in the American Venture," *Christianity Today* (November 21, 1960): 21.

12. "Pre-Election Review of the 'Religious Issue,'" *Christianity Today* (October 24, 1960): 25.

13. "Another Era Underway in the American Venture," 21.

14. "Pastoral Constitution on the Church in the Modern World" (*Gaudium et Spes*), no. 76, in *Documents of Vatican II,* ed. Austin P. Flannery (Grand Rapids, Mich.: Eerdmans, 1975), 984.

15. John Courtney Murray, "The Declaration on Religious Freedom," in *Bridging the Sacred and the Secular: Selected Writings of John Courtney Murray,*

ed. J. Leon Hooper, S.J. (Washington, D.C.: Georgetown University Press, 1994), 194.

16. "Declaration on Religious Freedom," no. 4, in *Documents of Vatican II,* ed. Flannery, 803.

17. Murray, "Towards a Theology for the Layman: The Problem of Its Finality," *Theological Studies 5,* no. 1 (March 1944): 68–69.

18. Ibid., 73.

19. See Harvey Cox, *The Secular City* (New York: Macmillan, 1965), 62–70.

20. Ibid., 3.

21. "Fortieth Anniversary Symposium," *Commonweal* 81 (November 20, 1964): 279.

22. James Hitchcock, "Catholic Activist Conservatism in the United States," in *Fundamentalism Observed,* ed. Martin E. Marty and R. Scott Appleby (Chicago: University of Chicago Press, 1991), 115.

23. "Fortieth Anniversary Symposium," 268.

24. Thomas Merton, "Is the World a Problem?" *Commonweal* 84 (June 3, 1966): 307.

25. Ibid., 309.

26. "Pastoral Constitution on the Church in the Modern World" (*Gaudium et Spes*), no. 4, 905.

27. Ibid., no. 11, 912.

28. "Dogmatic Constitution on the Church" (*Lumen Gentium*), no. 12, 364.

29. Ibid., no. 40, 397.

30. "Decree on the Apostolate of Lay People" (*Apostolicam Actuositatem*), no. 2, in *Documents of Vatican II,* 768.

31. "The Constitution on the Sacred Liturgy" (*Sacrosanctum Concilium*), no. 14, in *Documents of Vatican II,* 8.

32. "Dogmatic Constitution on the Church" (*Lumen Gentium*), no. 34, 391.

33. John XXIII, *Peace on Earth* (*Pacem in Terris*), no. 41, in *The Papal Encyclicals 1958–1981,* 111.

34. Ibid., no. 148, 123.

35. Ibid., no. 36, 111.

36. John XXIII, *On Christianity and Social Progress* (*Mater et Magistra*), no. 256, in *The Papal Encyclicals 1958–1981,* 86.

37. Cox, *The Secular City,* 183, 191.

38. Max Weber, *The Protestant Ethic and the Spirit of Capitalism* (New York: Charles Scribner's Sons, 1958), 181.

39. Philip Scharper, "The Teaching of Religion," *Commonweal* 70 (April 3, 1959): 16–21.

40. John Cogley, "Wanted, Theologians," *Commonweal* 70 (May 22, 1959): 204.

41. Robert Barrat, "Passing of the Worker-Priests," *Commonweal* 71 (October 23, 1959): 102–4.

42. Rev. James V. Schall, "Christmas and the World," *Commonweal* 79 (December 27, 1963): 391.

43. Sidney Lens, "A Shorter Work Week?" *Commonweal* 72 (April 29, 1960): 122.

44. John Cort, "The Feeling of Failure," *Commonweal* 74 (September 8, 1961): 495.

45. Pierre Teilhard de Chardin, *The Divine Milieu* (New York: Harper Torchbooks, 1960), 62.

46. George Lawler, "Chardin and Human Knowledge," *Commonweal* 68 (April 11, 1958): 44; Joseph Cypriano, "Christian Worship and the Historical Dimension," *Commonweal* 76 (August 24, 1962): 466.

47. Teilhard de Chardin, *The Divine Milieu*, 65.

48. John Cogley, "The Layman Rediscovered," *Commonweal* 79 (November 22, 1963): 255.

49. Teilhard de Chardin, *The Divine Milieu*, 65–66.

50. A study of migrant workers in 161 (arch)dioceses across the United States, conducted in 1974 by the United States Catholic Conference Secretariat for the Spanish Speaking, found that 71 percent of migrant workers were Catholic. The great majority of migrants were Mexican-American, while 15 percent were black and 8 percent were Puerto Rican. See *Origins 4*, no. 20 (March 27, 1975): 640.

51. Pat Hoffman, "The More Trouble We Get, the More Religion We Get: Interview with Cesar Chavez," *Sojourners* 21 (October 1977): 21–26.

52. Ibid.

53. Spencer Bennett, "Civil Religion in a New Context: The Mexican-American Faith of César Chávez," in *Religion and Political Power,* ed. Gustavo Benavides and M. W. Daly (Albany: State University of New York Press, 1989), 159.

54. Susan Ferriss and Ricardo Sandoval, *The Fight in the Fields: Cesar Chavez and the Farmworkers Movement* (San Diego: Harcourt Brace, 1997), 128.

55. Bennett, "Civil Religion," 161.

56. Jacques Levy, *Cesar Chavez: Autobiography of La Causa* (New York: W. W. Norton, 1975), 272.

57. Ferriss and Sandoval, *The Fight in the Fields,* 143.

58. Levy, *Cesar Chavez,* 277, 276.

59. Ferriss and Sandoval, *The Fight in the Fields,* 143.

60. Robert Ellsberg, ed., *Dorothy Day: Selected Writings* (Maryknoll, N.Y.: Orbis Books, 1992), 255, 257.

61. "Feedback," *U.S. Catholic 35*, no. 3 (March 1970): 15–16.

62. *Origins 4*, no. 24 (December 5, 1974): 371.

63. Archbishop Giovanni Benelli, cited in "Cesar Chavez: Far from Defeated," *Christian Century* (November 13, 1974): 1069.

64. *Origins 5*, no. 4 (June 19, 1975): 49, 51.

65. United Methodist Annual Conference, "Special Needs of Farm Workers" (1976), reprinted in *The Book of Resolutions of the United Methodist Church 1988* (Nashville: United Methodist Publishing House, 1988), 377–79.

66. Daniel Callahan, "The Secular City," *Commonweal* 82 (September 17, 1965): 660.

67. I rely on Rodger Van Allen's account of Callahan's educational history in *The Commonweal and American Catholicism* (Philadelphia: Fortress Press, 1974), 173–74.

68. Daniel Callahan, "Commonweal's Future: How Should the Magazine See Itself and Its Future Role? Former Editors Reply," *Commonweal* 91 (Novem-

ber 14, 1969): 222. On the editors' debate, see also Van Allen, *The Commonweal and American Catholicism,* 177.

69. Quotations are taken from the current web site of the Hastings Center (www.thehastingscenter.org).

70. John G. Deedy Jr., "The Catholic Press," *Commonweal* 81 (February 19, 1965): 667.

71. John XXIII, *Pacem in Terris,* nos. 44, 111–12.

72. John T. McGreevy, *Parish Boundaries: The Catholic Encounters with Race in the Twentieth-Century Urban North* (Chicago: University of Chicago Press, 1996), 149.

73. Quoted in James F. Findlay, "Religion and Politics in the Sixties: The Churches and the Civil Rights Act of 1964," *Journal of American History* 77, no. 1 (June 1990): 79.

74. Administrative Board, National Catholic Welfare Conference, "Discrimination and Christian Conference" (November 14, 1958), in *Public Voices,* 255.

75. National Conference of Catholic Bishops, "Statement on National Race Crisis" (April 25, 1968), in *Public Voices,* 260.

76. McGreevy, *Parish Boundaries,* 172.

77. Cited in Samuel Southard, "The Southern 'Establishment,'" *Christian Century* (December 30, 1964): 1619.

78. Jeffrey M. Burns, *Disturbing the Peace: A History of the Christian Family Movement, 1949–1974* (Notre Dame, Ind.: University of Notre Dame Press, 1999), 93, 161.

79. Kay Atchison, telephone interview with author, March 12, 2001.

80. "National Convention Focuses on Parish," *ACT* (October 1963): 20.

81. "Civil Rights Bill," *ACT* (April 1964): 16.

82. *Encounter in Politics and Race: 1964–1965 C.F.M. Inquiry Program* (Chicago: Christian Family Movement, 1964), 6.

83. See Burns's chapter "CFM and Race" in *Disturbing the Peace,* 119–43.

84. Regina Weissert, telephone interview with author, March 12, 2001.

85. Patty Crowley, interview with author, Chicago, March 12, 2001. Reprinted with permission.

86. Cited in Burns, *Disturbing the Peace,* 151.

87. Regina Weissert, telephone interview with author, March 12, 2001.

3. Turning Inward

1. Carlo Weber, "The Time of the Fugitive," *Commonweal* 90 (April 18, 1969): 140.

2. Peter Steinfels, "The New Interiorism," *Commonweal* 98 (April 27, 1973): 176.

3. Peter J. Henriot, "An Integral Faith for Today," *Commonweal* 101 (November 15, 1974): 147, 149.

4. Henri Nouwen, "Generation without Fathers," *Commonweal* 92 (June 12, 1970): 291.

5. Raymond A. Schroth, review of *Church Politics,* by Keith R. Bridston, *Commonweal* 92 (April 24, 1970): 150.

6. Joseph Fichter, "The Trend to Spiritual Narcissism," *Commonweal* 105 (March 17, 1978): 172.

7. Margaret Rowe, "Down from the Mountain," *Commonweal* 95 (February 25, 1972): 492.

8. John C. Meagher, "Creating a Christian Identity," *Commonweal* 95 (February 11, 1972): 440, 443, 444.

9. James V. Schall, "The University, the Monastery, and the City," *Commonweal* 96 (April 7, 1972): 107–10.

10. Cited in Christopher Vecsey, "Black Catholics," *Commonweal* 104 (May 27, 1977): 334.

11. Ibid., 332–36.

12. Patty Mansfield, speech at the 1992 National Catholic Charismatic Renewal Conference, Pittsburgh (June 5, 1992). Reprinted with the permission of Chariscenter.

13. See, for example, "Charisma on the Rise," *Time* (June 14, 1968): 64.

14. Jay Dolan, *The American Catholic Experience: A History from Colonial Times to the Present* (Notre Dame, Ind.: University of Notre Dame Press, 1992), 432.

15. Kilian McDonnell, "The Holy Spirit and Christian Initiation," in *The Holy Spirit and Power: The Catholic Charismatic Renewal,* ed. Kilian McDonnell (Garden City, N.Y.: Doubleday, 1975), 58.

16. Ralph Keifer, letter to the editor, *Commonweal* 103 (July 1, 1976): 447.

17. Kevin Ranaghan and Dorothy Ranaghan, *Catholic Pentecostals* (New York: Paulist, 1969), 189, cited in Meredith B. McGuire, *Pentecostal Catholics: Power, Charisma, and Order in a Religious Movement* (Philadelphia: Temple University Press, 1982), 3.

18. Danièle Hervieu-Lèger, " 'What Scripture Tells Me': Spontaneity and Regulation within the Catholic Charismatic Renewal," in *Lived Religion in America: Toward a History of Practice,* ed. David D. Hall (Princeton, N.J.: Princeton University Press, 1997), 22–40.

19. Ralph Martin, *Unless the Lord Build the House* (Notre Dame, Ind.: Ave Maria Press, 1971), 13.

20. Ibid., 26–27.

21. Léon Joseph Cardinal Suenens, *A New Pentecost?* (New York: Seabury Press, 1975), 89, 92.

22. Robert J. Armbruster, "The Gathering of the Charismatics," *Commonweal* 96 (June 29, 1972): 348.

23. Brian Wicker, "Charismatics in Britain," *Commonweal* 103 (June 18, 1976): 401.

24. Archbishop Alfonso López Trujillo, "Renewal in the Spirit," in *Presence, Power, Praise: Documents on the Charismatic Renewal,* ed. Kilian McDonnell (Collegeville, Minn.: Liturgical Press, 1980), 2:363.

25. William J. Whalen, "Catholic Pentecostals," *U.S. Catholic* 35, no. 10 (November 1970): 11.

26. Edward J. Mulroy, comment in "Feedback," *U.S. Catholic* 38, no. 12 (December 1973): 17.

27. Léon Cardinal Suenens and Dom Helder Camara, "Charismatic Renewal and Social Action: A Dialogue—Malines Document III" (1979), in *Presence, Power, Praise,* ed. McDonnell (Collegeville, Minn.: Liturgical Press, 1980), 3:316.

28. "Guidelines: The United Methodist Church and the Charismatic Move-

ment," United Methodist Church, U.S.A. (1976), in *Presence, Power, Praise,* 2:270–91.

29. Cindy Conniff, "Fourth Annual International Presbyterian Conference on the Holy Spirit," *New Covenant 5*, no. 1 (July 1975): 34.

30. Ibid.

31. Cited in Rick Casey, "Charismatics: Beyond Catholicism?" *U.S. Catholic* 41, no. 11 (November 1976): 23.

32. "Responsible Parenthood, Majority Report of the Birth Control Commission," in Robert McClory, *Turning Point* (New York: Crossroad, 1995), 176–79.

33. McClory, *Turning Point,* 105.

34. Paul VI, *On the Regulation of Birth (Humanae Vitae),* no. 28, in *The Papal Encyclicals 1958–1981,* ed. Claudia Carlin (Raleigh, N.C.: Purian Press, 1990), 231.

35. Ibid., no. 29, 231.

36. The Gallup poll is cited in John A. O'Brien, " 'Humanae Vitae': Reactions and Consequences," *Christian Century* (February 26, 1969): 289.

37. "A Protestant Affirmation on the Control of Human Reproduction," *Christianity Today* (November 8, 1968): 18–19.

38. "The Birth Control Encyclical," *Commonweal* 88 (August 9, 1968): 515.

39. "A Critical Juncture," *Commonweal* 82 (April 16, 1965): 100.

40. Cited in John A. O'Brien, " 'The Vatican Speaks Out,' " *Christian Century* (December 10, 1969): 1582.

41. Mr. and Mrs. David Dresser, letter to the editor, *Commonweal* 79 (March 20, 1964): 753.

42. Michael Novak, "Marriage: The Lay Voice," *Commonweal* 79 (February 14, 1964): 590.

43. Daniel I. O'Neill, letter to the editor, *Commonweal* 88 (September 27, 1968): 645.

44. Daniel Maguire, "Holy Spirit and Church Authority," *Commonweal* 89 (November 8, 1968): 218.

45. Clement Frank, letter to the editor, *Commonweal* 88 (September 27, 1968): 645.

46. Mrs. John Hurlbut, letter to the editor, *Commonweal* 89 (October 11, 1968): 70–71.

47. Mary Joyce, letter to the editor, *Commonweal* 89 (October 25, 1968): 134.

48. "Fortieth Anniversary Symposium," 275.

49. Mrs. Ruth B. Moynihan, letter to the editor, *Commonweal* 89 (December 13, 1968): 387.

50. Almon G. Farnsworth, letter to the editor, *Commonweal* 88 (September 6, 1968): 606.

51. William J. Nagle, "Failures—Lay and Clerical," *Commonweal* 76 (July 27, 1962): 424.

52. "Pastoral Constitution on the Church in the Modern World" (*Gaudium et Spes*), nos. 48, 47, in *Documents of Vatican II,* ed. Austin P. Flannery (Grand Rapids, Mich.: Eerdmans, 1975), 950, 949.

53. "Dogmatic Constitution on the Church" (*Lumen Gentium*), no. 11, in *Documents of Vatican II*, 362.

54. "Decree on the Apostolate of Lay People" (*Apostolicam Actuositatem*), no. 4, in *Documents of Vatican II*, 770.

55. Novak, "Marriage: The Lay Voice," 587–90.

56. Michael Novak, "On Celibacy and Marriage," *Commonweal* 98 (July 27, 1973): 398, 415.

57. John Garvey, "A Married Layman on Celibacy," *Commonweal* 106 (October 26, 1979): 586.

58. Adrian Hastings, "I Am Free as a Priest to Marry," *Commonweal* 105 (October 13, 1978): 657–58.

59. Donald Goergen disputes this understanding of celibacy in *The Sexual Celibate*, reviewed by John N. Kotre, *Commonweal* 102 (December 19, 1975): 632–34.

60. Rosemary Radford Ruether, "The Ethic of Celibacy," *Commonweal* 97 (February 2, 1973): 394.

61. Gerhart B. Lander, letter to the editor, *Commonweal* 98 (March 16, 1973): 27.

62. Suzanne Polen, letter to the editor, *Commonweal* 98 (March 16, 1973): 47.

63. Mary Jo Weaver, "Single Blessedness?" *Commonweal* 106 (October 26, 1979): 589, 591. See too Edward Wakin, "The Single Catholic, Marriage Is Not a Commandment," *U.S. Catholic* 41, no. 10 (October 1976): 6.

64. Eugene Fontinell, "Marriage, Morality, and the Church," *Commonweal* 97 (November 10, 1972): 127. Note too a later article by Rev. Eugene Hillman, "Reconsidering Polygamy: Is Our Theology of Marriage Catholic or Ethnocentric?" *Commonweal* 102 (November 21, 1975): 560–62.

65. See, for example, Lawrence G. Wrenn, ed., *Divorce and Remarriage in the Catholic Church* (Garden City, N.Y.: Doubleday, 1973). See also Peter J. Riga, "Divorce and Remarriage in the Catholic Church," *U.S. Catholic* 38, no. 3 (March 1973): 18–20; Kenneth Guentert, "A Tough-and-Tender Solution for Divorced Catholics," *U.S. Catholic* 41, no. 12 (December 1976): 12–13, and Stephen J. Kelleher, "The Laity, Divorce and Remarriage," *Commonweal* 102 (November 7, 1975): 521–24.

66. Dolan, *The American Catholic Experience*, 436.

67. Michael True, "Divorce and Remarriage, 1—A Meeting of Divorced Catholics," *Commonweal* 101 (November 22, 1974): 185–86.

68. "Feedback," *U.S. Catholic* 41, no. 12 (December 1976): 13–14.

69. Bruce Flautt, comment in "Feedback," *U.S. Catholic* 41, no. 12 (December 1976): 14.

70. Michael Zeik, "Twilight of the Gonads," *Commonweal* 97 (November 10, 1972): 135.

71. Name Withheld, comment in "Feedback," *U.S. Catholic* 41, no. 12 (December 1976): 14.

72. Betsy Darken, letter to the editor, *Commonweal* 104 (September 30, 1977): 611.

73. Francis X. Murphy, "Christianity, Marriage and Sex," *Commonweal* 105 (June 16, 1978): 384.

74. McCarthy, "The Displaced Homemaker," *Commonweal* 103 (January 16, 1976): 38, 63.

4. The Politicians and the Bishops

1. Sandra H. Johnson, "I Wondered If I Would Pass the Test," *Commonweal* 116 (April 7, 1989): 208.

2. Russell Shaw, "The Christian in the World: Sanctifying Everyday Work" (New Rochelle, N.Y.: Scepter Booklets, 1991), 8–9.

3. Georgia M. Keightley, letter to the editor, *Commonweal* 110 (April 22, 1983): 253.

4. Mary Durkin, "From the Council to the Synod," *Commonweal* 112 (October 18, 1985): 561.

5. William A. Schmitt, letter to the editor, *Commonweal* 116 (October 6, 1989): 541–42.

6. Ruan Seeley, "Opus Dei: To Live a Holy Life in the Whole of Life," *Catholic Moment* (September 16, 1998), reprinted on www.opusdei.org/media/itm990329.html.

7. "Feedback," *U. S. Catholic* 50, no. 6 (June 1985): 15.

8. Daniel Mulhollan, in "Prayer: When? How? Why?" *Commonweal* 116 (February 10, 1989): 74.

9. Barbara Grizzuti Harrison, in "Prayer: When? How? Why?" *Commonweal* 116 (February 10, 1989): 74.

10. Marian Burkhart, in "Prayer: When? How? Why?" *Commonweal* 116 (February 10, 1989): 74.

11. Frank Macchiarola, in "Prayer: When? How? Why?" *Commonweal* 116 (February 10, 1989): 77.

12. John R. Willingham, comment in "Feedback," *U.S. Catholic* 50, no. 6 (June 1985): 16.

13. John Garvey, "Spirituality Made Simple," *Commonweal* 117 (October 26, 1990): 602.

14. John Garvey, "Prayer, Politics, and Doubt," *Commonweal* 113 (February 28, 1986): 103.

15. John Kotre, "Psychotherapy and Spirituality" (review of *The Christian Neurosis,* by Pierre Solignac, *The Christian Psychology,* by John M. McDonagh, *The Observing Self,* by Arthur J. Deikman, and *Care of Mind/Care of Spirit,* by Gerald C. May), *Commonweal* 109 (November 5, 1982): 594.

16. Meredith B. McGuire, *Pentecostal Catholics: Power, Charisma, and Order in a Religious Movement* (Philadelphia: Temple University Press, 1982), 213.

17. Pope John Paul II, "Seek to Be Active in the Life of Your Local Church," Address to Catholic Charismatics, November 9, 1996. Reprinted at the Catholic Charismatic Center on the World Wide Web (www.garg.com/ccc).

18. Dolores Leckey, "Mixed and Ambiguous," *Commonweal* 107 (February 1, 1980): 50.

19. Statement by Robert F. Drinan, S.J., May 5, 1980, reprinted in *Between God and Caesar: Priests, Sisters and Political Office in the United States,* ed. Madonna Kolbenschlag, H.M. (New York: Paulist Press, 1985), 314–15.

20. See statement by Agnes Mary Mansour, May 11, 1983, reprinted in *Between God and Caesar,* 316–18.

21. See Paul Taylor, "Falwell Hits Mondale on Religion; Democrat's Actions Called 'Hypocrisy,' " *Washington Post* (September 10, 1984): A6.

22. R. W. Apple Jr., "The Question of Mario Cuomo," *New York Times* (September 14, 1986): section 6, p. 44.

23. Charles Krauthamme, "Cuomo Won't Take the Easy Route," *Washington Post* (August 15, 1986): A17.

24. Kenneth A. Briggs, "Cuomo vs. Bishops," *New York Times* (September 14, 1984): A22.

25. Mario Cuomo, "Religious Belief and Public Morality: A Catholic Governor's Perspective," address at the University of Notre Dame, September 13, 1984, reprinted in *Public Voices: Catholics in the American Context,* ed. Steven M. Avella and Elizabeth McKeown (Maryknoll, N.Y.: Orbis Books, 1999), 371–75.

26. "Cuomo's Defense of Politicians' Rights," *Christian Science Monitor* (September 17, 1984): 21.

27. Cited in Paul Taylor, "Morality, Policy Held Inseparable: Catholic Bishops Reject Stance of Ferraro, Cuomo," *Washington Post* (August 10, 1984): A1.

28. Cited in Mary Connelly and Carlyle C. Douglas, "Cuomo Clashes with Archdiocese," *New York Times* (September 7, 1986): section 4, p. 7.

29. Jane Perlez, "Ferraro Says Religion Won't Influence Policy," *New York Times* (September 13, 1984): B16.

30. "Archbishop Contends Abortion Is Key Issue," *New York Times* (June 25, 1984): D13.

31. Geraldine A. Ferraro with Linda Bird Francke, *Ferraro: My Story* (New York: Bantam Books, 1985), 221.

32. Ibid., 230. See also 228, 213.

33. "Excerpts from Interview with Ferraro on Campaign Plane," *New York Times* (August 14, 1984): A21.

34. Ferraro with Francke, *Ferraro: My Story,* 215, 227.

35. Ibid., 211.

36. Henry J. Hyde, "Keeping God in the Closet," *Catholicism in Crisis* (December 1984): 36.

37. Bernard Weinraud, "Mondale Defends Himself on Religion Issue in South," *New York Times* (September 14, 1984): A18.

38. William M. Sullivan and Richard Madsen, "The Bishops and Their Critics," *Commonweal* 115 (February 26, 1988): 117.

39. See, for example, Sullivan and Madsen, "The Bishops and Their Critics" (review of Walter Block, *The U.S. Bishops and Their Critics; The Deeper Meaning of Economic Life,* ed. R. Bruce Douglass; *The Catholic Challenge to the American Economy,* ed. Thomas M. Gannon; *The Pastoral on the Economy,* ed. John Langan; and *God, Goods, and the Common Good,* ed. Charles P. Lutz), 117–20.

40. See discussion in T. R. Martin and Gene R. Laczniak, "Executives' Scoreboard," *Commonweal* 115 (June 3, 1988): 336–38.

41. "The Search for a Just Economy," *Commonweal* 113 (December 5, 1986): 644.

42. National Conference of Catholic Bishops, *Economic Justice for All: Pas-*

toral Letter on Catholic Social Teaching and the U.S. Economy (Washington, D.C.: National Conference of Catholic Bishops, 1986), 68 (chap. 3, par. 134).

43. Ibid., vii (Intro, par. 7).

44. Ibid., xiv–xv (Intro, par. 25).

45. Ibid., xv (Intro, par. 25).

46. McCarthy, "Cuomo and the Lay Voice," *Commonweal* 111 (October 19, 1984): 550.

47. David J. O'Brien, "Join It, Work It, Fight It," *Commonweal* 116 (November 17, 1989): 629–30.

48. John Garvey, "A Dangerous Equation," *Commonweal* 113 (November 21, 1986): 615.

49. Frank Macchiarola, "Prayer and the Pursuit of Public Virtue," *Commonweal* 114 (August 14, 1987): 441.

50. "Feedback," *U.S. Catholic* 60, no. 4 (April 1995): 22–25.

51. Fr. Richard Siefer, comment in "Feedback," *U.S. Catholic* 60, no. 4 (April 1995): 25.

52. See Abigail McCarthy, "As the Synod Nears—II," *Commonweal* 113 (September 12, 1986): 455.

53. Ibid., 456.

54. John Paul II, "The Lay Members of Christ's Faithful People" (*Christifideles Laici*), nos. 40, 42 (Boston: St. Paul Books & Media, 1988), 101, 105, 107.

55. Ibid., nos. 41, 16, 42, pp. 103, 104, 38, 105.

56. Ibid., nos. 23, 22, pp. 56, 53.

57. "Lecturing (Sigh!) the Laity," *Commonweal* 116 (March 10, 1989): 132.

58. Ibid., 133.

59. Dolores R. Leckey, letter to the editor, *Commonweal* 116 (May 5, 1989): 258.

60. Thomas C. Fox, "Made in Detroit," *Commonweal* 103 (November 19, 1976): 746.

61. *New York Times* (February 28, 1990): B4.

62. Ibid.

63. See the Call to Action website: www.cta-usa.org.

64. Stephen Buttry, "Catholics in Conflict: Shepherds Guide Rebellious Flock," *Omaha World Herald* (May 14, 1996): 1.

65. "Some Catholics in Nebraska Face Excommunication Order," *New York Times* (May 17, 1996): A23.

66. "A Chicago Declaration of Christian Concern," December 1977, cited in *Commonweal* 105 (February 17, 1978): 110.

67. "Only the Beginning," *Commonweal* 106 (April 13, 1979): 198.

68. "A Chicago Declaration of Christian Concern," 109.

69. Ed Marciniak, "Salvation: The Thirst for Justice," review of S. Haughey, ed., *The Faith That Does Justice,* and Brian Wren, *Education for Justice, Commonweal* 105 (December 22, 1978): 823.

70. John A. Coleman, "The Worldly Calling," *Commonweal* 105 (February 17, 1978): 116.

71. John Cort, "Labor on the March," *Commonweal* 108 (October 9, 1981): 551.

72. Philip J. Murnion, "The Laity and the Shape of Things to Come," *Commonweal* 119 (September 11, 1992): 27–28.

73. David J. O'Brien, "The Summons to Responsibility," *Commonweal* 113 (June 6, 1986): 333.

74. David R. Carlin Jr., "Vocations to the Laity," *Commonweal* 113 (October 10, 1986): 520.

75. Ibid., 521.

76. Robert Dylak, letter to the editor, *Commonweal* 114 (February 13, 1987): 92.

77. Claudia Fletcher, letter to the editor, *Commonweal* 110 (November 18, 1983): 610.

78. Edward K. Braxton, "Authentically Black, Truly Catholic," *Commonweal* 112 (February 8, 1985): 76–77.

79. Phillip Bess, comment in "Work of Human Hands: Fifteen People Talk about Faith on the Job," *U.S. Catholic* 57, no. 9 (September 1992): 9.

80. Paul Wilkes, "An Honest Day's Work," *Commonweal* 117 (May 18, 1990): 318.

81. Timothy J. Reuland, "God Is My Client," *Commonweal* 116 (October 6, 1989): 528.

82. Frank McConnell, "The Vanishing Family," *Commonweal* 110 (February 11, 1983): 86.

83. David J. O'Brien, "Sex (How about Love?) on Catholic Campuses," *Commonweal* 116 (March 24, 1989): 171.

84. Christopher Lasch, *Haven in a Heartless World: The Family Besieged* (New York: Basic Books, 1977).

85. "The Family Way," *Commonweal* 114 (February 13, 1987): 69.

86. "Feedback," *U.S. Catholic* 60, no. 7 (July 1995): 22–23.

87. Liz Leibold McCloskey, "Turning Wine into Vinegar: Pre-Cana Needs Work," *Commonweal* 120 (November 5, 1993): 7–8. For another article on the two-career marriage, see Dolores Curran, "How to Find Time for Faith in a Two-Career Marriage," *U.S. Catholic* 54, no. 10 (October 1989): 19–24.

88. "Feedback," *U.S. Catholic* 47, no. 6 (June 1982): 13–14.

89. "Feedback," *U.S. Catholic* 50, no. 7 (July 1985): 17–18.

90. See, for example, Bruce Fowler, comment in "Feedback," *U.S. Catholic* 57, no. 8 (August 1992): 17, and Mary T. Kalnin, comment in "Feedback," *U.S. Catholic* 57, no. 8 (August 1992): 17.

91. Margaret O'Brien Steinfels, "Rights 'R Us," *Commonweal* 119 (May 8, 1992): 4.

92. John Garvey, "A Role of One's Own," *Commonweal* 119 (March 26, 1993): 8–9.

93. Barbara and Ralph Whitehead, "The High Costs of Parenthood," *Commonweal* 117 (September 14, 1990): 505.

94. Jo McGowan, "Marriage versus Just Living Together," *Commonweal* 108 (March 13, 1981): 145.

95. Paul Vallely, "Tony, the Sin Doctor," *The Independent* (London) (October 27, 1998): Features, 8.

96. John Garvey, "Fidelity and Faultlines," *Commonweal* 114 (March 27, 1987): 169.

97. Michael Garvey, "The Scary Fidelity of Jesus," *Commonweal* 116 (March 24, 1989): 173–74.

98. Thomas A. McCabe, "A Married Priest," *Commonweal* 118 (July 12, 1991): 435.

99. Reuland, "God Is My Client," 528.

100. Ibid.

101. Mary D. Murray, letter to the editor, *Commonweal* 1980 (March 28, 1980): 191. See also Dolores Leckey, "Mixed and Ambiguous," *Commonweal* 107 (February 1, 1980): 50; John Garvey, "Family Photographs," *Commonweal* 114 (April 22, 1988): 233–34; and James P. Emswiler, "Is the Holy Family Really Holier-Than-Thou?" *U.S. Catholic* 46, no. 12 (December 1981): 8–12.

102. Ruth Ames Gelber, letter to the editor, *Commonweal* 114 (November 20, 1987): 642.

103. Mary Studer Shea, letter to the editor, *Commonweal* 111 (April 6, 1984): 194.

104. Jo McGowan, "Two Is Not Enough," *Commonweal* 117 (May 4, 1990): 282.

105. Jane Lewis Engelke, "Return from the Wilderness," *Commonweal* 117 (October 26, 1990): 610–12.

106. See discussion in McCarthy, "Hitting Home," *Commonweal* 118 (October 11, 1991): 566–67.

107. John Garvey, "An Eye on the Sparrow," *Commonweal* 119 (January 31, 1992): 7.

108. McGowan, "Two Is Not Enough," 281.

109. Liz Leibold McCloskey, "Plush Lawns," *Commonweal* 120 (April 23, 1993): 9.

110. Interview with Kathleen O'Connell Chesto, "Faith Is Best Served Family Style," *U.S. Catholic* 60, no. 6 (June 1995): 6–12.

111. Kathy Coffey, "Eight Ways Your Kids Give You the Gift of Faith," *U.S. Catholic* 60, no. 8 (August 1995): 9.

112. Ibid., 10–11.

113. Reuland, "God Is My Client," 529.

114. Alex García-Rivera, "Homemade Faith," *U.S. Catholic* 59, no. 11 (November 1994): 50.

5. Forming the People of God

1. Francis de Sales, *Introduction to the Devout Life* (New York: Image Books, 1989), 43.

2. Plato, *The Republic* (London: Penguin Books, 1987), 323.

3. Ibid., 319.

4. Ibid., 324.

5. Aristotle, *Nichomachean Ethics* (New York: Macmillan, 1962), 156.

6. Thomas Aquinas, *Summa Contra Gentiles, Book Three: Providence, Part I* (Garden City, N.Y.: Doubleday, 1956), 12.

7. Aquinas, *Summa Contra Gentiles,* 125, 167.

8. Simone Weil, *Waiting for God* (New York: Putnam, 1951), 210.

9. See the discussion of the "Pilgrim Church" in the Second Vatican Council statement "Dogmatic Constitution on the Church," in *Documents of Vatican II,*

ed. Austin P. Flannery (Grand Rapids, Mich.: Eerdmans, 1975), nos. 48–51, 407–13.

10. For a related essay, see Paul Post, "The Modern Pilgrim: A Christian Ritual between Tradition and Post-Modernity," in *Pilgrimage,* Concilium 1996/4, ed. Virgil Elizondo and Sean Freyne (Maryknoll, N.Y.: Orbis Books, 1996), 1–9.

11. "Dogmatic Constitution on the Church," no. 1, p. 350.

12. John Chrysostom, "Homily 24," in John Chrysostom, *Homilies on the Epistles of Paul to the Corinthians* (Grand Rapids, Mich.: Eerdmans, 1956), 140.

13. Walter J. Burghardt, S.J., "The Body of Christ: Patristic Insights," in *The Church as the Body of Christ,* ed. Robert S. Pelton (Notre Dame, Ind.: University of Notre Dame Press, 1963), 91.

14. Stanley Hauerwas, "What Could It Mean for the Church to Be Christ's Body?" *Scottish Journal of Theology* 48, no. 1 (1995): 9.

15. Julian Pleasants, letter to the editor, *Commonweal* 117 (October 26, 1990): 594.

16. Max Weber, "Politics as a Vocation," in *Max Weber on the Methodology of the Social Sciences,* ed. A. Shils and Henry Finch (Glencoe, Ill.: Free Press, 1949), 126.

17. Philip Sheldrake, "The Crisis of Modernity," *Christian Spirituality Bulletin* 4, no. 1 (Summer 1996): 6.

18. Most contemporary literature focuses on individual discernment. For examples of the sparse literature on communal discernment, see Danny E. Morris and Charles M. Olsen, *Discerning God's Will Together: A Spiritual Practice for the Church* (Bethesda, Md.: Alban Publications, 1997), and Luke Timothy Johnson, *Scripture and Discernment: Decision Making in the Church* (Nashville: Abingdon Press, 1996).

19. Aristotle, *Nichomachean Ethics,* 159.

20. Ignatius of Loyola, *The Spiritual Exercises,* in *Spiritual Exercises and Selected Works,* ed. George E. Ganss, S.J. (New York: Paulist Press, 1991), 160.

21. On the governor's oath of office, see New York State Constitution, Article XIII, Section 1, and for discussion of the governor's responsibility to "faithfully" execute the laws, see Article I, particularly Section 3 (free exercise of religion) and Section 11 (equal protection).

22. "A Catholic for President?" *Commonweal* 69 (March 6, 1959): 588.

23. Mario Cuomo, "Religious Belief and Public Morality: A Catholic Governor's Perspective," address at University of Notre Dame, September 13, 1984, reprinted in *Public Voices: Catholics in the American Context,* ed. Steven M. Avella and Elizabeth McKeown (Maryknoll, N.Y.: Orbis Books, 1999), 371–75.

24. Edward Gargan, "Governor Revives Proposal to Deny Paroles for Killers," *New York Times* (January 25, 1985): B2.

25. Cuomo, "Religious Belief and Public Morality," 372.

26. Aristotle, *Nichomachean Ethics,* 34.

27. Cuomo, "Religious Belief and Public Morality," 374.

28. Pope John XXIII, *On Christianity and Social Progress (Mater et Magistra),* no. 238, in *The Papal Encyclicals 1958–1981,* ed. Claudia Carlin (Raleigh, N.C.: Purian Press, 1990), 84.

29. National Conference of Catholic Bishops, *Economic Justice for All: Pas-*

toral Letter on Catholic Social Teaching and the U.S. Economy (Washington, D.C.: National Conference of Catholic Bishops, 1986), 68.

30. See Aristotle, *Nichomachean Ethics,* 160.

31. John XXIII, *Peace on Earth (Pacem in Terris),* no. 148, in *The Papal Encyclicals 1958–1981,* 123.

32. Sam Howe Verhovek, "Cuomo's Abortion View Fails to Silence Critics," *New York Times* (February 12, 1990): B3.

33. Johnson, *Scripture and Discernment,* 109–10.

34. See John Calvin, *Institutes of the Christian Religion* (Philadelphia: Westminster Press, 1960), particularly Book 1, chapter 3.

35. Martin Luther, "Secular Authority: To What Extent It Should Be Obeyed," in *Martin Luther: Selections from His Writings,* ed. John Dillenberger (Garden City, N.Y.: Anchor Books, 1961), 371.

36. H. Richard Niebuhr, *Christ and Culture* (New York: Harper & Row, 1951), 176.

37. Ignatius of Loyola, "The Deliberation on Poverty," in Ignatius of Loyola, *Spiritual Exercises and Selected Works,* 225–28.

38. Ignatius, *The Spiritual Exercises,* 163–64.

39. Ibid., 164.

40. Ibid.

41. Discussed in Dirkie Smit, "On Learning to See?: A Reformed Perspective on the Church and the Poor," address to the International Academy of Practical Theology, University of Stellenbosch, South Africa, April 7, 2001. Smit makes insightful comments about seeing as attention.

42. Don S. Browning, *A Fundamental Practical Theology: Descriptive and Strategic Proposals* (Minneapolis: Fortress Press, 1991).

43. Timothy Fry, O.S.B., ed., *The Rule of St. Benedict in English* (Collegeville, Minn.: Liturgical Press, 1982), 69.

44. Guigo II, *The Ladder of Monks* (Kalamazoo, Mich.: Cistercian Publications, 1979), 69.

45. See James Moffatt, *The First Letter of Paul to the Corinthians* (New York: Harper and Brothers, 1930), 183.

46. W. G. H. Simon, *The First Epistle to the Corinthians* (London: SCM Press, 1959), 131.

47. See C. E. B. Cranfield, *I and II Peter and Jude: Introduction and Commentary* (London: SCM Press, 1960), 67.

SELECTED BIBLIOGRAPHY

This bibliography provides references to selected books and articles cited in the text. Because complete bibliographical data is provided in the end notes, most magazine articles and interviews have not been included here. The author has selected texts that provide helpful historical or theological background. She also has included a selection of articles by well-known contributors to or editors of magazines. Articles from secular newspapers and magazines also have been included in order to indicate the larger context of this story.

Administrative Board, National Catholic Welfare Conference. "Discrimination and Christian Conference" (November 14, 1958). Pp. 254–55 in *Public Voices: Catholics in the American Context*. Ed. Steven M. Avella and Elizabeth McKeown. Maryknoll, N.Y.: Orbis Books, 1999.

Aristotle. *Nichomachean Ethics*. New York: Macmillan, 1962.

Bellah, Robert, et al. *Habits of the Heart: Individualism and Commitment in American Life*. New York: Harper & Row, 1985.

Bennett, Spencer. "Civil Religion in a New Context: The Mexican-American Faith of César Chávez." Pp. 151–66 in *Religion and Political Power*. Ed. Gustavo Benavides and M. W. Daly. Albany: State University of New York Press, 1989.

Berger, Peter, and Richard John Neuhaus. *To Empower People: The Role of Mediating Structures in Public Policy*. Washington, D.C.: American Enterprise Institute for Public Policy Research, 1977.

Bredeck, Martin J. *Imperfect Apostles: The Commonweal and the American Catholic Laity, 1924–1976*. New York: Garland Press, 1988.

Briggs, Kenneth A. "Cuomo vs. Bishops." *New York Times* (September 14, 1984): A22.

Brown, Alden V. *The Grail Movement and American Catholicism, 1940–1975*. Notre Dame, Ind.: University of Notre Dame Press, 1989.

Browning, Don S. *A Fundamental Practical Theology: Descriptive and Strategic Proposals*. Minneapolis: Fortress Press, 1991.

Browning, Don, et al., eds. *From Culture Wars to Common Ground: Religion and the American Family Debate*. Louisville: Westminster John Knox Press, 1997.

Burghardt, Walter J., S.J. "The Body of Christ: Patristic Insights." Pp. 69–101 in *The Church as the Body of Christ*. Ed. Robert S. Pelton. Notre Dame, Ind.: University of Notre Dame Press, 1963.

Burns, Jeffrey M. *American Catholics and the Family Crisis, 1930–1962*. New York: Garland Publishing Inc., 1988.

196

————. *Disturbing the Peace: A History of the Christian Family Movement, 1949–1974*. Notre Dame, Ind.: University of Notre Dame Press, 1999.

Bynum, Carolyn. *Jesus as Mother*. Berkeley: University of California Press, 1982.

Callahan, Daniel. "The Secular City." *Commonweal* 82 (September 17, 1965): 658–62.

Callahan, Daniel, et al. "Commonweal's Future: How Should the Magazine See Itself and Its Future Role? Former Editors Reply." *Commonweal* 91 (November 14, 1969): 222, 224–29.

Calvin, John. *Institutes of the Christian Religion*. Philadelphia: Westminster Press, 1960.

Campbell, Debra. "The Heyday of Catholic Action and the Lay Apostolate, 1929–1959." Pp. 222–52 in *Transforming Parish Ministry: The Changing Roles of Catholic Clergy, Laity, and Women Religious*. Ed. Jay Dolan et al. New York: Crossroad, 1989.

————. "*Both Sides Now*: Another Look at the Grail in the Postwar Era." *U.S. Historian* 11, no. 4 (Fall 1993): 13–27.

Cardijn, Joseph. *Challenge to Action: Addresses of Monsignor Joseph Cardijn*. Ed. Eugene Langdale. Chicago: Fides, 1955.

Carlin, David R., Jr. "Vocations to the Laity." *Commonweal* 113 (October 10, 1986): 520–21.

Carter, Stephen L. *The Culture of Disbelief: How American Law and Politics Trivialize Religious Devotion*. New York: Basic Books, 1993.

"Charisma on the Rise." *Time* (June 14, 1968): 64.

Christian Family Movement. *Encounter in Politics and Race: 1964–1965 C.F.M. Inquiry Program*. Chicago: Christian Family Movement, 1964.

"City of Man and God." *Time* (December 12, 1960): 64–70.

Cogley, John. "Wanted, Theologians." *Commonweal* 70 (May 22, 1959): 204.

————. "The Layman Rediscovered." *Commonweal* 79 (November 22, 1963): 253–55.

Coleman, John A. "The Worldly Calling." *Commonweal* 105 (February 17, 1978): 115–16.

Connelly, Mary, and Carlyle C. Douglas, "Cuomo Clashes with Archdiocese." *New York Times* (September 7, 1986): section 4, p. 7.

"The Constitution on the Sacred Liturgy" (*Sacrosanctum Concilium*). Pp. 1–282 in *Documents of Vatican II: Constitutions, Decrees, Declarations*. Ed. Austin Flannery, O.P. Northport, N.Y.: Costello, 1996.

Cort, John. "The Feeling of Failure." *Commonweal* 74 (September 8, 1961): 494–95.

————. "My Life at the Catholic Worker." *Commonweal* 107 (June 20, 1980): 361–67.

————. "Labor on the March." *Commonweal* 108 (October 9, 1981): 550–51.

Cox, Harvey. *The Secular City*. New York: Macmillan, 1965.

Cranfield, C. E. B. *I and II Peter and Jude: Introduction and Commentary*. London: SCM Press, 1960.

Cuomo, Mario. "Religious Belief and Public Morality: A Catholic Governor's Perspective." Address at the University of Notre Dame, September 13, 1984. Reprinted in *Public Voices: Catholics in the American Context*. Ed. Steven M.

Avella and Elizabeth McKeown, 371–75. Maryknoll, N.Y.: Orbis Books, 1999.

Curran, Dolores. "How to Find Time for Faith in a Two-Career Marriage." *U.S. Catholic* 54, no. 10 (October 1989): 19–24.

Day, Dorothy. *The Long Loneliness*. New York: Harper & Brothers, 1952.

De Chantal, Jane, and Francis de Sales. "Jane de Chantal to André Frémyot (June 1, 1626)." Pp. 200–207 in *Francis de Sales, Jane de Chantal: Letters of Spiritual Direction*. Ed. Wendy M. Wright and Joseph F. Power. Trans. Marie Thibert Peronne, V.H.M. New York: Paulist Press, 1988.

"Decree on the Apostolate of Lay People" (*Apostolicam Actuositatem*). Pp. 766–98 in *Vatican Council II: Constitutions, Decrees, Declarations*. Ed. Austin Flannery, O.P. Northport, N.Y.: Costello, 1984.

Deedy, John G., Jr., "The Catholic Press." *Commonweal* 81 (February 19, 1965): 666–67.

De Sales, Francis. *Introduction to the Devout Life*. New York: Image Books, 1989.

"Doctrine on the Sacrament of Marriage." P. 164 in *Dogmatic Canons and Decrees*. Rockford, Ill.: Tan Books, 1977.

Dolan, Jay P. *The American Catholic Experience: A History from Colonial Times to the Present*. Notre Dame, Ind.: University of Notre Dame Press, 1992.

Doohan, Leonard. "Laity." Pp. 746–47 in *The HarperCollins Encyclopedia of Catholicism*. Ed. Richard P. McBrien. New York: HarperCollins, 1995.

Ellsberg, Robert, ed., *Dorothy Day: Selected Writings*. Maryknoll, N.Y.: Orbis Books, 1992.

Elshtain, Jean Bethke. *Public Man, Private Woman: Women in Social and Political Thought*. Princeton, N.J.: Princeton University Press, 1981.

Emswiler, James P. "Is the Holy Family Really Holier-Than-Thou?" *U.S. Catholic* 46, no. 12 (December 1981): 8–12.

Engelke, Jane Lewis. "Return from the Wilderness." *Commonweal* 117 (October 26, 1990): 610–12.

Escrivá, Josemaría. *Friends of God: Homilies by Josemaría Escrivá*. Princeton, N.J.: Scepter, 1981.

———. *The Way*. Manila: Sinag-Tala, 1991.

Estruch, Joan. *Saints and Schemers: Opus Dei and Its Paradoxes*. New York: Oxford University Press, 1995.

"Excerpts from Interview with Ferraro on Campaign Plane." *New York Times* (August 14, 1984): A21.

Ferraro, Geraldine A., with Linda Bird Francke. *Ferraro: My Story*. New York: Bantam Books, 1985.

Ferriss, Susan, and Ricardo Sandoval. *The Fight in the Fields: Cesar Chavez and the Farmworkers Movement*. San Diego: Harcourt Brace, 1997.

Findlay, James F. "Religion and Politics in the Sixties: The Churches and the Civil Rights Act of 1964." *Journal of American History* 77, no. 1 (June 1990): 66–92.

Fisher, James T. *The Catholic Counterculture in America, 1933–1962*. Chapel Hill: University of North Carolina Press, 1989.

Fontaine, Jacques. "The Practice of Christian Life: The Birth of the Laity." Pp. 453–91 in *Christian Spirituality,* vol. 1: *Origins to the Twelfth Century.* Ed. Bernard McGinn et al. New York: Crossroad, 1985, 1992.

Garvey, John. "A Married Layman on Celibacy." *Commonweal* 106 (October 26, 1979): 585–88.

———. "Prayer, Politics, and Doubt." *Commonweal* 113 (February 28, 1986): 102–3.

———. "A Dangerous Equation," *Commonweal* 113 (November 21, 1986): 614–15.

———. "Fidelity and Faultlines." *Commonweal* 114 (March 27, 1987): 168–69.

———. "Family Photographs." *Commonweal* 114 (April 22, 1988): 233–34.

———. "Spirituality Made Simple." *Commonweal* 117 (October 26, 1990): 601–2.

———. "An Eye on the Sparrow." *Commonweal* 119 (January 31, 1992): 7–8.

———. "A Role of One's Own." *Commonweal* 120 (March 26, 1993): 8–9.

Garvey, Michael. "The Scary Fidelity of Jesus." *Commonweal* 116 (March 24, 1989): 173–74.

Gross, Rita M. *Buddhism after Patriarchy: A Feminist History, Analysis, and Reconstruction of Buddhism.* Albany: State University of New York Press, 1993.

"Guidelines: The United Methodist Church and the Charismatic Movement." United Methodist Church, U.S.A. (1976). Pp. 270–90 in *Presence, Power, Praise: Documents of the Charismatic Renewal,* vol. 3. Ed. Kilian McDonnell. Collegeville, Minn.: Liturgical Press, 1980.

Guigo II, *The Ladder of Monks.* Kalamazoo, Mich.: Cistercian Publications, 1979.

Hauerwas, Stanley. "What Could It Mean for the Church to Be Christ's Body?" *Scottish Journal of Theology* 48, no. 1 (1995): 1–21.

Hervieu-Lèger, Danièle. " 'What Scripture Tells Me': Spontaneity and Regulation within the Catholic Charismatic Renewal." Pp. 22–40 in *Lived Religion in America.* Ed. David D. Hall. Princeton, N.J.: Princeton University Press, 1997, 22–40.

Hitchcock, James. "Catholic Activist Conservatism in the United States." Pp. 101–41 in *Fundamentalism Observed.* Ed. Martin E. Marty and R. Scott Appleby. Chicago: University of Chicago Press, 1991.

Hoffman, Pat. "The More Trouble We Get, the More Religion We Get: Interview with Cesar Chavez." *Sojourners* 21 (October 1977): 21–26.

Hunter, James Davidson. *Culture Wars: The Struggle to Define America.* New York: Basic Books, 1991.

Hyde, Henry J. "Keeping God in the Closet." *Catholicism in Crisis* (December 1984): 32–40.

Ignatius of Loyola. *Spiritual Exercises and Selected Works.* Ed. George Ganss, S.J. Mahwah, N.J.: Paulist Press, 1991.

John Chrysostom. "Homily 24." In *Chrysostom: Homilies on the Epistle of Paul to the Corinthians.* Grand Rapids, Mich.: Eerdmans, 1956.

John XXIII. *On Christianity and Social Progress (Mater et Magistra).* Pp. 59–90 in *The Papal Encyclicals 1958–1981.* Ed. Claudia Carlin. Raleigh, N.C.: Purian Press, 1990.

———. *Peace on Earth (Pacem in Terris).* Pp. 107–29 in *The Papal Encyclicals 1958–1981.* Ed. Claudia Carlin. Raleigh, N.C.: Purian Press, 1990.

John Paul II. "The Role of the Christian Family in the Modern World" (*Familiaris Consortio*). Boston: St. Paul Books & Media, 1982.

———. "The Lay Members of Christ's Faithful People" (*Christifideles Laici*). Boston: St. Paul Books & Media, 1988.

———. "Seek to Be Active in the Life of Your Local Church." Address to Catholic Charismatics, November 9, 1996.

Johnson, Luke Timothy. *Scripture and Discernment: Decision Making in the Church.* Nashville: Abingdon Press, 1996.

Kennedy, John F. *"Let the Word Go Forth": The Speeches, Statements, and Writings of John F. Kennedy 1947 to 1963.* New York: Laurel, 1988.

Knebel, Fletcher. "Democratic Forecast: A Catholic in 1960." *Look* (March 3, 1959): 13–17.

Kolbenschlag, Madonna, H.M., ed. *Between God and Caesar: Priests, Sisters and Political Office in the United States.* New York: Paulist Press, 1985.

Lasch, Christopher. *Haven in a Heartless World: The Family Besieged.* New York: Basic Books, 1977.

Leckey, Dolores. "Mixed and Ambiguous." *Commonweal* 107 (February 1, 1980): 50

Levy, Jacques. *Cesar Chavez: Autobiography of La Causa.* New York: W. W. Norton, 1975.

López Trujillo, Archbishop Alfonso. "Renewal in the Spirit." Pp. 358–64 in *Presence, Power, Praise: Documents in the Charismatic Renewal.* Vol. 3. Ed. Kilian McDonnell. Collegeville, Minn.: Liturgical Press, 1980.

Luther, Martin. "An Appeal to the Ruling Class of German Nationality as to the Amelioration of the State of Christendom." Pp. 403–85 in *Martin Luther: Selections from his Writings.* Ed. John Dillenberger. Garden City, N.Y.: Anchor Books, 1961.

———. "The Pagan Servitude of the Church." Pp. 249–359 in *Martin Luther: Selections from His Writings.* Ed. John Dillenberger. Garden City, N.Y.: Anchor Books, 1961.

Macchiarola, Frank. "Prayer and the Pursuit of Public Virtue." *Commonweal* 114 (August 14, 1987): 440–42.

Macchiarola, Frank, et al. "Prayer: When? How? Why?" *Commonweal* 116 (February 10, 1989): 73–78.

Mansfield, Patty. Speech at the 1992 National Catholic Charismatic Renewal Conference, Pittsburgh (June 5, 1992).

Martin, Ralph. *Unless the Lord Build the House.* Notre Dame, Ind.: Ave Maria Press, 1971.

Marty, Martin E. "Public and Private: Congregation as Meeting Place." Pp. 133–68 in *American Congregations.* Vol. 2. Ed. James P. Wind and James W. Lewis. Chicago: University of Chicago Press, 1994.

McCarthy, Abigail. "The Displaced Homemaker." *Commonweal* 103 (January 16, 1976): 38, 63.

———. "An Era of Emergence." *Commonweal* 111 (July 13, 1984): 390–91.

———. "Cuomo and the Lay Voice." *Commonweal* 111 (October 19, 1984): 550–51.

———. "As the Synod Nears—II." *Commonweal* 113 (September 12, 1986): 455–56.

———. "Hitting Home." *Commonweal* 118 (October 11, 1991): 566–67.

McClory, Robert. *Turning Point.* New York: Crossroad, 1995.

McDannell, Colleen. "Catholic Domesticity, 1860–1960." Pp. 48–80 in *American Catholic Women: A Historical Exploration.* Ed. Karen Kennelly, C.S.J. New York: Macmillan, 1989.

McDonnell, Kilian. "The Holy Spirit and Christian Initiation." Pp. 57–90 in *The Holy Spirit and Power: The Catholic Charismatic Renewal.* Ed. Kilian McDonnell. Garden City, N.Y.: Doubleday, 1975.

McGinn, Bernard. "The Letter and the Spirit: Spirituality as an Academic Discipline." *Christian Spirituality Bulletin* 1, no. 2 (Fall 1993): 1, 3–9.

McGowan, Jo. "Marriage versus Just Living Together." *Commonweal* 108 (March 13, 1981): 142–45.

———. "Two Is Not Enough." *Commonweal* 117 (May 4, 1990): 281–83.

McGreevy, John T. *Parish Boundaries: The Catholic Encounters with Race in the Twentieth-Century Urban North.* Chicago: University of Chicago Press, 1996.

McGuire, Meredith B. *Pentecostal Catholics: Power, Charisma and Order in a Religious Movement.* Philadelphia: Temple University Press, 1982.

Merton, Thomas. "Is the World a Problem?" *Commonweal* 84 (June 3, 1966): 305–9.

Michaels, Peter (Carol Jackson). "The Frustration of the Incarnation." *Integrity* 1, no. 1 (October 1946): 13.

Moffatt, James. *The First Letter of Paul to the Corinthians.* New York: Harper and Brothers, 1930.

Morris, Danny E., and Charles M. Olsen, *Discerning God's Will Together: A Spiritual Practice for the Church.* Bethesda, Md.: Alban Publications, 1997.

Murk-Jansen, Saskia. *Brides in the Desert: The Spirituality of the Beguines.* Maryknoll, N.Y.: Orbis Books, 1998.

Murnion, Philip J. "The Laity and the Shape of Things to Come." *Commonweal* 119 (September 11, 1992): 23–29.

Murray, John Courtney. "Towards a Theology for the Layman: The Problem of Its Finality." *Theological Studies* 5, no. 1 (March 1944): 43–75.

———. "The Declaration on Religious Freedom." Pp. 187–99 in *Bridging the Sacred and the Secular: Selected Writings of John Courtney Murray.* Ed. J. Leon Hooper, S.J. Washington, D.C.: Georgetown University Press, 1994.

National Conference of Catholic Bishops. "Statement on National Race Crisis" (April 25, 1968). Pp. 259–60 in *Public Voices: Catholics in the American Context.* Ed. Steven M. Avella and Elizabeth McKeown. Maryknoll, N.Y.: Orbis Books, 1999.

———. *Economic Justice for All: Pastoral Letter on Catholic Social Teaching and the U.S. Economy.* Washington, D.C.: National Conference of Catholic Bishops, 1986.

Niebuhr, H. Richard. *Christ and Culture.* New York: Harper & Row, 1951.

"Nineteen Thirty-Three." *Commonweal* 17 (January 4, 1933): 253.

Nouwen, Henri. "Generation without Fathers." *Commonweal* 92 (June 12, 1970): 287–94.

Novak, Michael. "Marriage: The Lay Voice." *Commonweal* 79 (February 14, 1964): 587–90.

———. "On Celibacy and Marriage." *Commonweal* 98 (July 27, 1973): 398, 415.

O'Brien, David J. "The Summons to Responsibility." *Commonweal* 113 (June 6, 1986): 332–37.

———. *Public Catholicism.* New York: Macmillan, 1989.

———. "Sex (How about Love?) on Catholic Campuses." *Commonweal* 116 (March 24, 1989): 169–71.

———. "Join It, Work It, Fight It." *Commonweal* 116 (November 17, 1989): 624–34.

O'Brien, John A. " 'Humanae Vitae': Reactions and Consequences." *Christian Century* (February 26, 1969): 288–89.

———. " 'The Vatican Speaks Out.' " *Christian Century* (December 10, 1969): 1580–82.

O'Connor, June. *The Moral Vision of Dorothy Day: A Feminist Perspective.* New York: Crossroad, 1991.

"Pastoral Constitution on the Church in the Modern World" (*Gaudium et Spes*). Pp. 903–1001 in *Vatican Council II: Constitutions, Decrees, Declarations.* Ed. Austin Flannery, O.P. Northport, N.Y.: Costello, 1996.

Paul VI. *Humanae Vitae.* Pp. 223–38 in *The Papal Encyclicals 1958–1981.* Ed. Claudia Carlin. Raleigh, N.C.: Pierian Press, 1990.

Piehl, Mel. *Breaking Bread: The Catholic Worker and the Origin of Catholic Radicalism in America.* Philadelphia: Temple University Press, 1982.

Pius XI. *On Christian Marriage (Casti Connubi).* Pp. 391–414 in *The Papal Encyclicals 1903–1939.* Ed. Claudia Carlin. Raleigh, N.C.: Purian Press, 1990.

———. *Quadragesimo Anno.* Pp. 415–43 in *The Papal Encyclicals 1903–1939.* Ed. Claudia Carlin. Raleigh, N.C.: Purian Press, 1990.

Pius XII. *Mystici Corporis (On the Mystical Body of Christ and Our Union in It with Christ).* Boston: St. Paul Books & Media, n.d.

Plato. *The Republic.* London: Penguin Books, 1987.

Post, Paul. "The Modern Pilgrim: A Christian Ritual between Tradition and Post-Modernity." Pp. 1–9 in *Pilgrimage.* Concilium 1996/4. Ed. Virgil Elizondo and Sean Freyne. Maryknoll, N.Y.: Orbis Books, 1996.

Ranaghan, Kevin, and Dorothy Ranaghan. *Catholic Pentecostals.* New York: Paulist, 1969.

"Responsible Parenthood, Majority Report of the Birth Control Commission." Pp. 176–79 in Robert McClory, *Turning Point.* New York: Crossroad, 1995.

Ruether, Rosemary Radford. "The Ethic of Celibacy." *Commonweal* 97 (February 2, 1973): 390–94.

Scharper, Philip. "The Teaching of Religion." *Commonweal* 70 (April 3, 1959): 16–21.

Scherer-Edmunds, Meinrad. "See-Judge-Act: How Young Christian Workers Renewed the Church." *Salt of the Earth* 16, no. 2 (March–April 1996): 19–20.

Scott, Karen. "Catherine of Siena and Lay Sanctity in Fourteenth-Century Italy." Pp. 77–90 in *Lay Sanctity, Medieval and Modern: A Search for Models*. Ed. Ann W. Astell. Notre Dame, Ind.: University of Notre Dame Press, 2000.

Scudder, Vida, ed. *Saint Catherine of Siena as Seen in Her Letters*. New York: E. P. Dutton, 1927.

Shaw, Russell. "The Christian in the World: Sanctifying Everyday Work." New Rochelle, N.Y.: Scepter Booklets, 1991.

Sheehan, Elizabeth M. "The Spirituality of Married Life." *Integrity* 3, no. 2 (November 1948): 26.

Sheldrake, Philip. "The Crisis of Modernity." *Christianity Spirituality Bulletin* 4, no. 1 (Summer 1996).

Simon, W. G. H. *The First Epistle to the Corinthians*. London: SCM Press, 1959.

"Some Catholics in Nebraska Face Excommunication Order." *New York Times* (May 17, 1996): A23.

"Statement of 166 Catholic Laymen on Religious Freedom in a Presidential Campaign," October 5, 1960. In *Catholic Mind* 59 (March–April 1961): 179–80. Reprinted in *Public Voices: Catholics in the American Context*. Ed. Steven M. Avella and Elizabeth McKeown. Maryknoll, N.Y.: Orbis Books, 1999, 364–65.

Steinfels, Margaret O'Brien. "Rights 'R Us." *Commonweal* 119 (May 8, 1992): 4–5.

Steinfels, Peter. "The New Interiorism." *Commonweal* 98 (April 27, 1973): 176.

Suenens, Léon Joseph Cardinal. *A New Pentecost?* New York: Seabury Press, 1975.

Suenens, Léon Cardinal, and Dom Helder Camara. "Charismatic Renewal and Social Action: A Dialogue—Malines Document III." Pp. 291–357 in *Presence, Power, Praise: Documents in the Charismatic Renewal*. Vol. 3. Ed. Kilian McDonnell. Collegeville, Minn.: Liturgical Press, 1980.

Taylor, Paul. "Morality, Policy Held Inseparable: Catholic Bishops Reject Stance of Ferraro, Cuomo." *Washington Post* (August 10, 1984): A1.

———. "Falwell Hits Mondale on Religion; Democrat's Actions Called 'Hypocrisy.'" *Washington Post* (September 10, 1984): A6.

Teilhard de Chardin, Pierre. *The Divine Milieu*. New York: Harper Torchbooks, 1960.

Thomas Aquinas. *Summa Contra Gentiles, Book Three: Providence, Part I*. Garden City, N.Y.: Doubleday, 1956.

United Methodist Annual Conference. "Special Needs of Farm Workers" (1976). Reprinted on pp. 377–79 in *The Book of Resolutions of the United Methodist Church 1988*. Nashville: United Methodist Publishing House, 1988.

Van Allen, Rodger. *The Commonweal and American Catholicism: The Magazine, the Movement, the Meaning*. Philadelphia: Fortress Press, 1974.

Van Kersbergen, Lydwine. "Toward a Christian Concept of Woman." *Catholic World* 182, no. 1 (October 1955): 11.

Vauchez, André. *The Laity in the Middle Ages*. Notre Dame, Ind.: University of Notre Dame Press, 1993.

Von Balthasar, Hans Urs. *Explorations in Theology* 1. San Francisco: Ignatius, 1989.

Weaver, Mary Jo. "Single Blessedness?" *Commonweal* 106 (October 26, 1979): 589, 591.

Weber, Max. *The Protestant Ethic and the Spirit of Capitalism.* New York: Charles Scribner's Sons, 1958.

———. "Politics as a Vocation." Pp. 77–128 in *Max Weber on the Methodology of the Social Science.* Ed. A. Shils and Henry Finch. Glencoe, Ill.: Free Press, 1949.

Weil, Simone. *Waiting for God.* New York: Putnam, 1951.

Weinraud, Bernard. "Mondale Defends Himself on Religion Issue in South." *New York Times* (September 14, 1984): A18.

Wesley, John. "Christian Perfection." P. 73 in *John Wesley's Sermons: An Anthology.* Ed. Albert C. Outler and Richard P. Heitzenrater. Nashville: Abingdon Press, 1991.

———. "The More Excellent Way." Pp. 512–21 in *John Wesley's Sermons: An Anthology.* Ed. Albert C. Outler and Richard P. Heitzenrater. Nashville: Abingdon Press, 1991.

Willock, Ed. "The Family Has Lost Its Head." *Integrity* 1, no. 8 (May 1947): 38–42.

———. "Marriage for Keeps." *Integrity* 5, no. 1 (1950): 17.

Wills, Gary. *Bare Ruined Choirs.* Garden City, N.Y.: Doubleday, 1972.

Zotti, Mary Irene. *A Time of Awakening: The Young Christian Worker Story in the United States, 1938 to 1970.* Chicago: Loyola University Press, 1991.

INDEX